TIME, CULTURE AND IDENTITY

MATERIAL CULTURES

Interdisciplinary studies in the material construction of social worlds

Series Editors
Daniel Miller, Dept of Anthropology, University College London
Michael Rowlands, Dept of Anthropology, University College London
Christopher Tilley, Institute of Archaeology, University College London
Annette Weiner, Dept of Anthropology, New York University

TIME, CULTURE AND IDENTITY

——•◆•——

An interpretive archaeology

Julian Thomas

ROUTLEDGE

London and New York

First published 1996
by Routledge
11 New Fetter Lane, London EC4P 4EE

Simultaneously published in the USA and Canada
by Routledge
29 West 35th Street, New York, NY 10001

© 1996 Julian Thomas

Typeset in Stempel Garamond by
Florencetype, Stoodleigh, Devon

Printed and bound in Great Britain by
Redwood Books, Trowbridge, Wiltshire

British Library Cataloguing in Publication Data
A catalogue record for this book is available from the British Library

Library of Congress Cataloguing in Publication Data
A catalogue record for this book has been requested

ISBN 0–415–11861–1

CONTENTS

——— •❖• ———

LIST OF ILLUSTRATIONS

——— •◆• ———

ACKNOWLEDGEMENTS

——— •◆• ———

I should like to thank a number of people who have read parts of this book while it was in the process of being written. They include Richard Bradley, Mark Edmonds, Siân Jones, Ingereth MacFarlane, Sue Pitt, Colin Richards, Chris Tilley, Mike Shanks, Stephen Shennan and Alasdair Whittle. None of them should be held responsible for what remains, and without their help it would have been much the poorer. While the text was coming together, many other people have helped me greatly, by commenting on some of the ideas when I presented them as seminars and conference papers, by sitting and talking, and in sundry other ways. I am sure that I have forgotten many of them, but the following certainly deserve many thanks: Mary Baker, John Barrett, Barbara Bender, Tim Champion, Bob Eaglestone, Clive Gamble, J.D. Hill, Matt Leivers, Yvonne Marshall, Danny Miller, Mike Pearson, Rick Peterson, Keith Ray, Maggie Ronayne, Mike Rowlands, Peter Ucko and David Walford.

Much of Chapter Seven relies on material studied in Dorchester Museum, and I should like to thank the staff for access to the collections. Other unpublished material was kindly made available by Ros Cleal and Frances Healey. Gavin Lucas allowed me to read parts of his unpublished Ph.D. thesis, which helped greatly in clarifying the discussion of context in Chapter Six.

The drawings were all executed by Rick Peterson, except for the computer-generated diagrams, which were created by the author.

A NOTE ON CONVENTIONS

Throughout this book, 'Being' with a capital 'B' is taken to refer to the category of Being in general, while 'being' with a small 'b' refers to a particular being or creature.

In the case of dates, 'bc' indicates an uncalibrated radiocarbon date, and BC a date in calendar years. Throughout, the Stuiver calibration curve is employed (Stuiver and Becker 1993; Stuiver and Pearson 1993).

INTRODUCTION

———— •◆• ————

ABOUT THIS BOOK

This volume probably requires a certain amount of explanation. Some books are written as a means of imparting a body of information which already exists in a fairly coherent form before the writing begins. In other cases, the writing itself forms the means by which ideas and evidence are brought together and synthesised. In this way of working, the author is writing as a means of collecting their thoughts on a particular issue. This book is certainly of the latter kind. When I was in the final stages of writing *Rethinking the Neolithic* (Thomas 1991a), one particularly perceptive reader suggested that what I was doing with that book was establishing a personal agenda for future work. What he had in mind, I think, was that I should follow up the rather broad-brush approach of *Rethinking the Neolithic* with a series of more detailed studies, concentrating on artefacts, funerary practice and so on. It is certainly the case that I no longer feel a need to attempt to rewrite a whole period of prehistory, and am happier undertaking a project which is much more focused. None the less, in this book I have followed a rather more perverse strategy than that of concentrating on a particular set of material. While *Rethinking the Neolithic* outlined a general approach to prehistory, by the time that it was published I found myself painfully aware of a number of problems which it had not addressed. These were both theoretical and empirical questions, several of which seemed to me to be linked to each other. My feeling was that I would be unable to find adequate answers to some of the problems which I recognised in British prehistory until I had addressed certain theoretical issues, and vice versa. As Gilles Deleuze once wrote, 'practice is a set of relays from one theoretical point to another, and theory is a relay from one practice to another' (Deleuze in Foucault 1977, 206).

This is not intended as either a book about archaeological theory or a book about British prehistory. Although this volume is separated into two parts, one of which is overtly theoretical while the other is composed of a series of case-studies, these two sections were not written separately. There is no sense in which I formulated a set of theoretical principles and then proceeded to 'apply' them to the material. In practice, I moved back and forth between theoretical problems which were suggested to me by the evidence, and empirical problems which were set up by theoretical arguments. As the project proceeded it became clear to me that the issues of temporality, material culture and human identity were central to what I was attempting to achieve. Thinking about each of these concepts seemed unavoidably to lead back into a consideration of each of the others. It seems to me that this nexus of questions has been axial to the history of archaeological thought, and yet that more often than not the concepts of time, culture and identity have been taken for granted. Moreover, it may be that the ways in which they have been conceptualised within archaeology are lodged within broader formations of modern western thought. By concentrating on these problems directly, it appeared to me that I might be able to clarify some of the areas of prehistory which I had found intractable (What was the role of material things in the Mesolithic/Neolithic transition? Were the complex artefacts of the later Neolithic constitutive of identities rather then a reflection of prestige? How were architecture, movement and depositional practice linked in the use of later Neolithic monuments?).

Two factors were to condition the way in which this project developed. The first was the continuing debate within archaeology concerning the nature of material culture: as record, as semiotic system, as text, as evidence (Patrik 1985; Barrett 1988a; Tilley 1989). The second was my introduction to the thought of Martin Heidegger. Over the period between 1988 and 1990, while working at St David's University College, Lampeter, I was lucky enough to be able to sit in on David Walford's seminars on *Being and Time*. Before this, I was aware of the influence which Heidegger had exerted on a number of thinkers whose work I had found useful (Derrida, Foucault, Ricoeur, Gadamer, Bourdieu, Giddens, and the list goes on), and it seemed logical to want to follow certain ideas back to their 'origin'. My initial reaction to Heidegger's work was one of slight disappointment: much of what I read seemed rather distant from my immediate concerns. However, after a while I began to feel that this body of thinking might profoundly challenge the way in which I thought about archaeology. As I progressed, the first part of this book became more and more an exercise in working out what a 'Heideggerian archaeology' might look like, and I found myself increasingly willing to follow Heidegger's ideas through to their conclusions, rather than simply lifting the odd concept or turn of phrase. This, in itself, raises certain problems.

USING HEIDEGGER

If Heidegger believed that his philosophy could provide spiritual direction for National Socialism, does this mean that his philosophy is essentially fascist?

(Zimmerman 1990, 35)

Over the past decade or more, many of the more interesting developments within the discipline have stemmed from the consideration of the archaeological implications of the ideas of philosophers and social and cultural theorists (e.g. Tilley 1990). While this practice has frequently been derided as an attempt to increase one's academic capital by discovering a new and more difficult continental thinker (Bintliff 1991a), the growing body of archaeological analysis which draws on these ideas suggest that this is not entirely the case. None the less, it is clearly not adequate to simply pick up theories from other disciplines and apply them unquestioningly. Ideas are transformed by the context within which they are deployed (Thomas 1995), and it is essential that archaeologists should *work with* the concepts which they routinely employ. Yet, over and above this, making use of Heidegger's work in particular introduces much more serious issues. Although I am convinced that this material is of critical importance for the development of archaeology, recent revelations concerning Heidegger's political activities (e.g. Farias 1989; Pöggeler 1993; Wolin 1990) must render its use problematic. There is by now little doubt that Heidegger was a card-carrying member of the Nazi party from the time of his election to the rectorship of Freiburg University in 1933 until 1945. It is also beyond question that in the postwar period he went out of his way to obscure the extent of his complicity with the Nazi regime (e.g. Heidegger 1993a), and that he repeatedly failed to properly acknowledge or atone for his guilt in this respect (Habermas 1993). To be sure, there are defences which can be raised on his behalf. It seems probable that Heidegger's philosophical version of National Socialism came into conflict with party ideology very quickly, and that he did realise he had made a terrible mistake in choosing his allies. And of course, it is easy with hindsight for us to recognise the utter evil of fascism in a way which might not have been immediately apparent in the early 1930s. And it is possible that, as he claimed, Heidegger's reluctance to disavow his political past in 1945 arose from his disgust with those former Nazis who made elaborate shows of repentance as a means of securing positions in the postwar regime.

However, these are excuses. Introducing the ideas of such a person into archaeology involves a responsibility, and this simply cannot imply one's becoming an apologist for someone who may or may not have been a convinced Nazi. It is by far the most prudent course to assume the worst, and then to ask whether Heidegger's philosophy bears with it the irreducible burden of fascism. This, it would seem, is not a straightforward question. As Bourdieu (1990a) has argued, Heidegger's ideas cannot be reduced to a political ideology, yet it is not possible to consider his philosophy in abstraction from the social and political context in which they were written. There seem to be three possible answers to dealing with Heidegger. The first is that taken by many philosophers: the ideas are the ideas, the man was the man, and what should concern one is the validity or usefulness of the ideas. For the reasons cited by Bourdieu, I do not consider this argument to be acceptable. While some of Heidegger's thought certainly has no political content, one must be aware that some aspects of his philosophy could be given a particular slant and fitted into the Nazi programme, as is evident in the 1933 rectoral address (Heidegger 1993b). Secondly, one could take the view that some Marxists have taken, that Heidegger's thought is so tarnished by its association with Nazism that one simply cannot entertain any element of it. Using this philosophy will unavoidably lead one into fascist modes of thought. On reflection, I do not find this argument any more satisfactory than the first. What it seems to suggest is that ideas can be intrinsically 'true' or 'false', 'correct' or 'wrong'. This would seem to me to be a dangerous essentialism, in which the worth of a philosophy can be established independently of its context. It smacks of the distinction between ideology and science, in which corrupt ideas can be separated from pure and wholly good ways of thinking (Foucault 1980, 84). This itself can be used as a means of establishing hegemony, since it enables one to declare certain knowledges illegitimate without having to seriously engage with them (Smart 1986, 161). In the case of Marxism itself, it is evident that the ideas themselves cannot be evaluated in isolation from the contexts in which they have been deployed. Marxism has simultaneously been the inspiration for numerous liberation struggles and the instrument of state repression in the former Soviet Union. It is meaningless to argue as to which of these manifestations represents the 'true' essence of Marxism.

The third possible attitude to Heidegger's philosophy lies, then, in recognising that no set of ideas is likely to be either so wholly correct as to be above suspicion or so wholly corrupt as to be dismissed out of hand. Instead, all sets of ideas deserve to be regarded with equal suspicion. Marxism was not so perfect as to prevent the Gulag from being constructed. Heidegger was not so perfect a philosopher as to prevent his complicity with Nazism and, by implication, the Holocaust. There are insights to be found in both of these systems of thought, but in both cases history makes us aware that anything which we take from them must be treated with the utmost scepticism. The most powerful ideas may also be the most dangerous, and the most susceptible to abuse, even by their own authors. Foucault (1984a, 245) once argued that nothing in life should be seen as absolutely liberating. In contrast to a utopian belief that certain ideas could lead to an end of history in which all social conflicts had been dissolved, Foucault asserted that liberation was a practice, a struggle that can never come to an end. Accordingly, ideas must be assessed in terms of usefulness, and of their likely effects and consequences. Ideas can help us to understand the world, but we must also be aware of their ethical implications. By ethics, in this case, I do not mean an abstract value accorded to conceptual schemes, but the practical ways in which they encourage us to think about and act in relation to other people. If I am advocating some use of Heidegger's philosophy as a means of investigating past societies, then this must be in the context of a critical engagement with and evaluation of that philosophy. At every step of the way, these ideas must be questioned and their implications considered. As Habermas (1993, 197) wrote, our task may be one of 'thinking with Heidegger against Heidegger'. Following Derrida (1989) I will suggest that the major problem with Heidegger's thought is his failure to follow his arguments to their radical conclusion and finally overcome metaphysics by obliterating all essences and presences. It is a nostalgic yearning for some transcendental wholeness which betrays Heidegger to totalitarianism.

In order to make use of Heidegger's ideas at all, it is absolutely necessary to understand which aspects of the philosophy allowed it to find an affinity with National Socialism, and to consider how the remainder might be put to work. I should make it quite clear at the outset that I do not believe that any discourse can be rendered apolitical, and it is not my objective to construct a politically neutral version of Heidegger. Rather, I suggest that while the authoritarian tone of Heidegger's more millenarian ideas found an easy alliance with Nazism, his arguments against positivism, naturalism, Cartesianism and essentialism have far more affinity with aspects of contemporary left thought, such as feminism, 'deep' ecology and radical democracy. These considerations can be drawn out by dwelling for a while on the nature of Heidegger's political engagement in the 1930s. Although Heidegger had considered himself largely apolitical during the 1920s, in the period after the writing of *Being and Time* his concern shifted from the *nature* of Being, as having been covered up by western thought, to the *history* of Being. In particular, he was interested in the changing place of human beings in relation to the world within which they found themselves enmeshed. Several different influences on his thought at this time can be discerned. First, following Kierkegaard, Heidegger was concerned with the emergence of nihilism, in the sense of a meaningless, drained, directionless condition of humanity (Dreyfus 1993, 291). Second, he drew increasingly on German Romanticism, and in particular the poetry of Hölderlin, which represented a critique of the atomised, scientistic thinking of the Enlightenment. Finally, he had developed an interest in the work of a number of contemporary reactionary political thinkers, such as Spengler and, particularly, Ernst Jünger (Zimmerman 1990, 34). Jünger's critique of the modern era was based upon the premise that in nations which were increasingly concerned with material production, human beings were gradually becoming reduced to the status of workers, representing no more than cogs in a gigantic technological apparatus. While Heidegger rejected the notion that one might return to any bucolic idyll, he none the less held that Jünger's 'era of total mobilisation' must be overcome by the foundation of a new way of Being on earth.

Heidegger's perception of Germany's position in the early 1930s was of a people afflicted by a series of 'deadly symptoms' of decline: positivism, scientific reductionism, industrialism, American democracy, communism (Zimmerman 1990, xviii). Germany was at 'the sharpest squeeze of the pincers' between America and the USSR (Habermas 1993, 193). To the west was the rampant egocentrism and all-consuming industrial capitalism of America, to the east the anonymous workerism of the Soviet Union. Throughout Heidegger's later philosophy, the history of Being is presented as connected with a history of technology in which the relationship between people and the material world declines away from the 'golden age' of the Greeks. If for the Greeks *techne* represented an attuned and craftsmanlike attitude to materiality which covered both art and technology, the modern era had seen the development of industrial production and eventually cybernetic control (Dreyfus 1992, 175; Heidegger 1993c). In such a world, technology had seemingly solved all problems, systems theory had replaced philosophy, and the planet was conceived as no more than a vast storehouse of resources to be freely exploited by humankind (Heidegger 1977a, 14; Dreyfus 1993, 305). Society was dominated by an instrumental logic, in which all things might be assessed in terms of their function, and people sank into a listless, aimless nihilism of sensory gratification and spiritual homelessness. In separating themselves from a condition of *dwelling* on the earth, and instead continually *challenging* the earth to produce ever more resources to be consumed, human beings had rendered themselves strangers in their own home. It need hardly be added that while all of this was to lead Heidegger in a disastrous direction, some elements of the argument connect with contemporary radical thought, and the themes of alienation and estrangement have some resonance with Marx (Ollman 1971).

Placed in this world-historical predicament, Heidegger considered that the Germans might prove uniquely capable of developing a 'third way' beyond capitalism and communism. Since the Germans had a particular cultural heritage which derived ultimately from Greece and expressed itself in Romanticism, it might be possible for them to take up the destiny which historical contingency had imposed upon them. Their particular historical experience was such that they might achieve a rethinking of the western tradition (Heidegger 1993a, 113), a goal which could not be attained through the importation of an external framework, such as Zen Buddhism. What this would require would be a drawing together of the national, ethnic community of Germans, submitting resolutely to a higher power, thereby achieving renewal through the renunciation of egotism. Heidegger's hope in 1933 was that National Socialism would provide Germany with a new myth within which the national community would cohere, gaining a sense of purpose and resisting the complacent nihilism of the age (Dreyfus 1993, 314). Heidegger's belief that a work of art founds and enables human dwelling on earth finds an echo in the 'aestheticisation of the political' of

Nazism (Lacoue-Labarthe 1990, 61). Yet while Heidegger saw art as revealing and opening up the world, Nazi aesthetics were monolithic and transcendental, geared to the foundation and expression of the 'thousand-year Reich'. That Heidegger could mistake the aestheticisation of the state for the healing power of the artwork may suggest that he was simply desperate to find an optimistic trend in world history, but he was evidently foolish enough to believe that the actual course which the party took was one which diverged from 'the inner truth and greatness of that movement' (Heidegger 1959, 199). For while Heidegger approved of the *Fürer* principle, submission to the leader as the embodiment of the nation, he saw the racism and anti-Semitism of the Nazis as a form of scientific naturalism, another abomination of Enlightenment science (Zimmerman 1990, 4; Heidegger 1993d, 86). By the end of 1933, Heidegger had evidently lost faith in the possibility of spiritual renewal through Nazism, and had resigned from the Freiburg rectorship. On his own account, his course of lectures on Nietzsche in the mid-1930s was conceived as 'a confrontation with National Socialism' (Heidegger 1993a, 101). This is almost certainly a generous self-estimate. It is more likely that, although disillusioned and compromised, Heidegger was simply not brave enough to criticise the murderous regime with which he had sided.

What all of this suggests is that while Heidegger had to tailor his philosophy in order to suit it to the demands of National Socialism, totalitarianism is at least an implicit danger within his thought. However, as Lacoue-Labarthe (1990) points out, most of the details of Heidegger's complicity were well known long before the publication of Victor Farias' *Heidegger and Nazism* (1990). The question thus immediately arises as to why so much interest was generated by the 'Heidegger affair' in France and America in the late 1980s and early 1990s (Spanos 1993). In the case of Luc Ferry and Alain Renaut, whose *Heidegger and Modernity* (1990) draws upon Farias' work, Spanos (1993, 183) suggests that the attack on Heidegger serves as a means of de-legitimising those whose ideas ultimately derive from Heidegger. Ferry and Renaut advocate a return to humanism, and thus represent Heidegger, Nietzsche, Marx and Freud (and by implication their post-structuralist heirs, Derrida, Foucault, Bourdieu and Lacan) as writers who would deny human agency. It might be more accurate to suggest that these thinkers *problematise* agency, rather than taking the human subject for granted. Heidegger's critique of humanism points out that it is always a metaphysics. Humanism holds that certain transcendental and ahistorical characteristics of humanity can be defined (Heidegger 1993e, 225). Thus human beings are fundamentally the same in all epochs of history. Humanism looks for a metaphysical essence for 'Man' (*sic*), without first asking the question of Being which underlies the existence of humanity (ibid., 247). How is it, after all, that we come to ask such questions about the kind of being that we are? In America, Spanos goes on to suggest, the same set of accusations are used as a means of attacking the scourge of the literary establishment, deconstructive criticism. Thus in both cases the Heidegger issue is used as a means of discrediting the left by association with the excesses of the right.

This book is in no sense to be seen as an apology for the particular actions or views of Martin Heidegger. Heidegger was a great philosopher, whose thought (I believe) can be of critical importance to the archaeological project of understanding social life in the past. But he was also fallible, and as a result became implicated in some of the most monstrous crimes which human beings have ever committed. Let us be in no doubt: no excuse for the Holocaust and its perpetrators can ever be tolerated. What this means is that if we are to read Heidegger and use his ideas, we must do so critically, and with the utmost vigilance. In a sense, this kind of scepticism is no more than we should afford to any set of writings. Any philosophy might potentially be turned to barbaric ends. The difference is that in Heidegger's case *it was*.

PART ONE
A PHENOMENOLOGICAL
ARCHAEOLOGY?

CHAPTER ONE

AFTER DESCARTES: ARCHAEOLOGY, CULTURE AND NATURE

———— •◆• ————

NATURE, CULTURE, MIND AND BODY

From its earliest origins, the discipline of archaeology has been concerned with time, culture and identity. Material culture has been used as evidence for the existence of persons and ethnic and racial groups at some time in the past, and in order to document processes of social and cultural change across time. In this chapter, I will suggest that one of the major constraints upon archaeological inference has been the implicit acceptance of a Cartesian view of the world. By this I mean a set of philosophical ideas which became coherent in early modernity, and which are most clearly articulated in the work of René Descartes. The principal elements of this perspective are the categorical distinctions which are drawn between mind and body, and culture and nature. Both of these antinomies, I will suggest, are of relatively recent origin, and in their more developed forms are peculiarities of a western, metaphysical habit of thought. Both serve to limit our appreciation of materiality, and to impose a modernist understanding on the past. Moreover, the two are closely linked in the conception of human beings as 'rational animals': 'natural' creatures to which something else has been added. Even in the critical discourse of gender studies, human beings are frequently portrayed as consisting of a stable, biologically given material form (a sexed body) onto which a cultural identification (a gender) is grafted (Butler 1993, 4). Yet such a division appears to surrender a status of undisputed truth to biological science, as if the 'facts' of bodily sex were simply eternal and had not been produced by the operation of a scientific discourse within a given set of historical conditions (Butler 1990, 7). There is no way that we can gain access to the biological constitution of creatures which evades language and history. In this particular case another binary pair is evident: the body is solid, material, exists prior to language and is the prerogative of the natural sciences, whereas culture is immaterial, secondary and metaphysical (ibid., 28). Archaeology, since it concerns itself with *material* culture, has long been bedevilled by this opposition between the mental and the material. Where precisely does material culture fit in this scheme of things? There appears to be a constant unease over the status of archaeology's object, presented as a choice between 'materialist' and 'idealist' interpretations. One of the intentions of this book is to demonstrate that this assessment of the discipline's potential is not merely unnecessarily pessimistic, but actually incoherent.

We could argue that while archaeology is burdened by a particular mode of thinking which is characteristic of the modern era, the irony is that it was itself made possible by the emergence of modernity. With the parallel development of commodified, linear work-time and the nation-state, the establishment of the antiquity of particular population groups came to be of greater interest (Trigger 1989). However, rather than attempt to point to a particular stage in human history at which the world 'became modern', it might be more profitable to consider modernity as an attitude, a particular way of getting on with the world (Foucault 1984a, 39). This way of dealing with existence can be seen to have gained coherence over a very long period of time. As Foucault argues (1970), the pattern of thought which we associate with the Enlightenment was the product of the operation of a series of developing discourses whose functioning brought a number of the givens of our contemporary world into being. Perhaps a cardinal element in modern thinking was the separation of the messy and richly networked character of existence into a definable set of elements (Latour 1993, 7). The understanding is that these elements represent real units of analysis which have been found by science, rather than objects which have been produced by discourse. In the construction of discursive objects, further analytical fields were generated, amongst them archaeology. With its practice of uncovering the hidden past, stripping away layers of detritus in order to disclose older and more profound realities, archaeology provides the perfect paradigm for modern thought. Structural linguistics, in its search for the deep generators of language, or Freudian psycho-analysis, identifying the sedimented strata of the personality: both had recourse to the metaphor of archaeology in establishing the separation between surface and depth. Yet if these depths were not found but created, we could suggest that discourse itself was operative in a generalised process of alienation, involving not simply the separation of the worker from her product, but of humanity from the earth.

Recent ethnographic writings have stressed the way in which non-western (that is, 'non-modern') modes of thought emphasise the *relational* character of existence (Strathern 1988). Yet where an analytical separation can be made between the things of the world, many of the relationships in which we first find ourselves are severed, or at least covered over. People can appear to be self-sufficient and internally motivated units, and their 'environment' can be reduced to a series of boxes in a flow-chart. As separate entities, things or units can be valorised against each other. One entity can be held to be more solid than another, or to underlie another, or to give rise to another, or to be more fundamental than another. This is the principle which gives us the logic of economic base and cultural superstructure, unconscious and conscious self, essence and substance. Under this analytic, it can equally be argued that biology provides a more solid basis for the ideological or that deep structures underlie and determine material production. Whether one chooses to be a 'materialist' or an 'idealist' is almost inconsequential: in either case one *thing* is being posited as primordial in relation to another. One *thing* is a given, whose emergence is beyond analysis or question, and another is derived from it. This way of thinking can be described as a metaphysics of substance or presence, since it presents particular objects as being so fundamental that they evade analysis.

Another consequence of this valorisation of analytical objects in relation to each other is that they can be held to be active or passive, dominant or dominated. In the opposition between culture and nature with which we are particularly concerned here, the things of nature come to be seen as a passive store of goods, dominated and exploited by humanity (Heidegger 1977a, 14; Haar 1993, 18). In the modern world, the domination of nature is presented as the price which must be paid for the emancipation of humanity. Ultimately, it is suggested that human beings will not have to work: they will have created a technological utopia in which the more efficient exploitation of resources has freed them from worldly concerns. Curiously, this utopia still shows little sign of emerging. Bruno Latour has recently pointed out that this conceptual 'purification', by which the human is rigidly divided from the non-human, has actually been elaborated over a period in which more and more complex hybrid processes have developed, in which it is impossible to separate out the technological, the social, the political and the material (Latour 1993, 10). Looked at from a 'non-modern' or non-western frame these processes of 'translation' might be thought of as forging and revealing unexpected relationships, and bringing new aspects of the networked character of our world into unconcealment (Heidegger 1977a, 11).

If we were to argue that the Enlightenment represented a conjuncture at which the distinctive elements of modern thought began to crystallise, it is significant that it was at this time that the meanings of 'culture' and 'nature' began to change. As Ludmilla Jordanova (1989, 37) has argued, 'culture' had hitherto referred to the nurture and cultivation of living things, whereas it now took on a more abstract connotation, concerned with the development of human society. We should remember that this was also a period in which statecraft, as the management of large human collectivities in mathematical terms (and the very notion of 'the society' as a unit of analysis), emerged (Foucault 1984b). As culture came to be associated with the cognitive aspects of human progress, nature was increasingly opposed to it as representing the substantial. As Jordanova (1989, 25) suggests, both culture and nature were considered to represent aspects of the environment which surrounded the individual human organism: one concerned with tradition and governance, the other with biology and geography. However, if nature and culture were to be found surrounding human beings, they also both contributed to the 'dual constitution' of humanity. For Descartes, human beings were composed of both physical matter, characterised by its spatial extension, and an incorporate matter, characterised by thought. The proof of the existence of the latter lay in the manifestation of thought itself. Consequently, human beings are both of the world and otherworldly, physical and metaphysical.

One repercussion of the separation of culture and nature was a gradual division of intellectual labour, eventually formalised in Dilthey's distinction between the natural and the human sciences. Yet even before this, a difference of emphasis is clear between those who chose to prioritise the encounter with the physical, and those who preferred the abstract logic of mathematics. The former would include the empirical natural science which derives from Bacon and Boyle, and the latter the rationalism of Hobbes and Descartes. As Latour (1993, 27) suggests, each of these is grounded upon a particular kind of bracketing or closure. Experimental science prides itself on empirical observation of the things of the world, yet abstracts itself from the 'cultural' part of its environment, such that power and politics are considered to be irrelevant. Mathematics and statistics are the ground for sciences of social order, yet base themselves on a logic which is entirely abstracted, and held to be prior to any worldly experience. Mathematics is timeless, universal, and a ground for all other forms of knowledge. Such an appeal to a 'pure' knowledge is, of course, a metaphysics (Heidegger 1993c, 299): but perhaps no more so than the metaphysics of substance found in natural science. Experimental science can only legitimately talk about experienced material things, yet its every attempt to do so depends upon a logical order existing within the universe which can be addressed only indirectly (Heidegger 1993f, 96).

In a certain way, rationalism and empiricism, and natural and human science, are the antagonistic yet complementary parts of a greater whole, which Latour calls the 'Constitution of Modernity' (1993, 32). This division of knowledge holds nature and culture apart from each other by main-taining a gulf between the modes of investigation which address either. Empirical science is left in its laboratory, untroubled by the possibility that it constructs rather than discovers its empirical facts, while culture is studied as if it were an attribute of the internal lives of sovereign individuals. While one discourse may attempt to invade the conceptual space of the other on occasion – as with the positivist naturalism that asserts that human beings are 'just like other kinds of animals' – this constitution is a form of collusion. For both the emerging natural sciences of biology, chemistry and physics, and the human sciences of economics and linguistics accepted that their objects of enquiry were pre-given and substantial (Foucault 1972).

Moreover, both saw nature as passive, and dominated either by science or culture. The immersion of the modern world-view in the contingent politics of a particular historical era is made graphically clear by the explicit gendering of this relationship. Nature was a female realm, 'unveiling herself before science', the passive object of the male gaze (Jordanova 1989, 87; Rose 1993, 67).

> Nature was taken to be that realm upon which mankind acts, not just to intervene in or manipulate directly, but also to understand or render intelligible, where 'nature' includes people and the societies they construct.
>
> (Jordanova 1989, 41)

A close link thus came to be perceived between humanity's scientific understanding of the natural world, and social developments which were based upon the domination of nature. Hence, 'culture' as the means by which people were able to control and exploit their environment was increasingly conceived as a realm of ideas. This realm included the 'high culture' of literature, music and the visual arts, since these represented instances of human mental life transcending the animal. By producing culture, it was possible for Man to stand outside of nature (Strathern 1980, 177). Such a position of exteriority then provides the necessary vantage from which to carry out operations upon the passive body of nature. None the less, the rupture is never complete, and nature remains a fundamental substratum upon which the layers of culture and society are built up (Heidegger 1962, 131). This way of thinking would seem to lie behind the model of infrastructure and superstructure, including those versions in which juridical and political superstructures are presented as 'semi-autonomous' of the economic base (Althusser 1969).

Modern thought proceeds by establishing entities, and placing them in opposition with each other. By professing to investigate the relationships between objects, it succeeds in naturalising them as given and beyond question (Strathern 1988, 69). Through the seventeenth and eighteenth centuries, structured oppositions came to dominate western thought: town and country, public and private, objectivity and subjectivity (Jordanova 1989, 21; Haraway 1991, 8). Increasingly, these opposed pairs came to be overlaid in order to form a grid of classification and specification, which could be manipulated in a relatively flexible manner (Strathern 1980, 177). Of course, these binary pairs are not balanced. As Judith Butler indicates, each is composed of a presence and its Other. Classically, the gender order of the modern west is composed of man and not-man, beings distinguished by the presence or absence of a penis (Butler 1990, 12). The overlaying and recombination of opposed pairs in western thought draws upon their unequal character: thus in Freudian psychoanalysis the natural, inner self and its urges have to be dominated and domesticated by the conscious mind

(Haraway 1991, 9). Interestingly, Gillian Rose has recently suggested that gender represents the paradigm of structured inequality which underscores the relative valorisation of other opposed pairs (Rose 1993, 74). Gender presents the metaphor for thinking through the relationship between mind and body, objectivity and subjectivity, culture and nature. In a sense, gender became the master discourse of the Enlightenment. It may have been the development of a nexus of linguistic connections linking women with the emotional, the subjective and the bodily which was responsible for an increased clarity in the definition of gender roles in the eighteenth century (Jordanova 1989, 20).

HUMANS AND ANIMALS

As we have seen, Enlightenment thought struggles to cope with the complexity of human existence by setting up the notion of the 'rational animal'. The depiction of humanity as having a 'dual nature' is an attempt to encompass the way in which we are ourselves living entities, and yet we are also the means by which other beings register meaningfully (Heidegger 1993c, 234). In Descartes' philosophy, substances become accessible through their attributes. In the manner that we have already discussed, these attributes are categories which are presumed to have a reality which extends beyond language and classification: they are real. To give an example, matter has the principal attribute of spatial extension. On this basis, addressing the problem of humanity, knowledge and culture begins by asking what are the main attributes of a human being. Descartes' method here was to begin by defining the attributes of other creatures, and then to consider what differentiated human beings from these. Human beings are thus considered as a subset of other creatures, sharing some qualities, yet distinguished by some other elements which have been grafted on (Heidegger 1993c, 227). What this would imply is that the human body is very much the same kind of thing as the body of an animal, and that the only area of difference resides in some intangible sphere mysteriously connected with neurological activity. Indeed, in time science might prove capable of 'explaining' cognition in purely physical and chemical terms, such that culture would entirely have collapsed down into nature.

To provide an alternative argument requires some radical moves. In the first place, one must accept that human beings are not built 'in layers': a body providing the host for a mind, which conceals a soul (Heidegger 1993e, 228). The human body is not external and prior to history and language. While a human body can be studied by biology in the same way as an animal organism can, and will provide comparable results, it is important to note that what is acquired is knowledge of a particular kind. Its veracity and applicability will not be universal. Indeed, we might say that in order to scientifically treat a human body as an organism, it is necessary first to systematically forget that it is a human being. For what is most important about human bodies is that they represent the media through which a quite different kind of Being from animal existence is enacted. Only human bodies constitute the focus of the lived experience in which beings encounter other beings, and in the process interpret both themselves and others (Haar 1993, 29). The way in which animals come into contact with other creatures is categorically different, determined not by interpreting Being but by the animal's absorption in its instinctual drives. In the full sense, there are no 'other beings' for animals (ibid.). Nothing in the world 'shows up' in a meaningful way for any kind of creature which is not human. It is only through human beings that the world gains its intelligibility, and what distinguishes humans is not any positive attribute of their physical presence, but simply this way in which they allow other things to 'show up' (Dreyfus 1991, 12; Zimmerman 1993, 243). As we will see in Chapter Three, this does not mean that the material things which we recognise would not exist at all if we were not here to see them. Rather, it means that they would not be recognised as parts of a significant world, let alone be studied by science. Only human beings 'have a world', in the sense of allowing things to stand out as embedded in relations of meaning (Olafson 1993).

Existing in such a way that other things are recognised meaningfully, interpreting those things, and in the process interpreting oneself is defined by Heidegger as 'Being-in-the-world' (Heidegger 1962). We will discuss this notion in more detail below, but it is important to note that it allows no distinction to be made between a mind and a body, an external and an internal world. Human existence is thoroughly embedded in the world, yet this world is not simply a set of material objects and spaces, as Descartes would suggest. What makes the world worldly is its character as a structure of intelligibility: we occupy and are engaged in a context which is constituted by language and meaning. Our only understanding of this world takes the form of language and meaning. Thus to say that the human body exists first of all as an animal organism, and only later becomes a site of interpretation and a gendered object is to suggest that we can somehow know something about that body which evades the worldly conditions of the production of knowledge. Where would this knowledge have come from, if not the world? Human beings are always already enmeshed in a structure of meaning, and the interpretation of their bodies as one thing or another is constitutive of what those bodies *are*. In this sense, a tenth-century AD human body is quite a different thing from a twentieth-century AD body.

The distinction between humans and animals is, in these terms, categorical, although in a sense this argument does not preclude a creature with an 'animal' body from 'being human'. We may eventually have to accept that some species other than *Homo Sapiens Sapiens* are 'human', in the sense of being engaged in a meaningful world. The condition of Being-in-the-world cannot be derived from the corporeal development of the human physiology, since it has nothing to do with what is contained *within* the body: rather, it is concerned with the body's engagement in the world (Haar 1993, 10). Conventionally, archaeology attempts to think through the emergence of 'consciousness' in evolutionary terms, as the putting in place of the 'hard-wiring' necessary for complex thought. Once again, this attempts to find an explanation for human Being encapsulated within the body. At a certain point, human beings must have become 'anatomically modern', and thus capable of sustaining advanced forms of culture (Ingold *forthcoming*). The stratified model of human existence is thus presented in a chronological form, with evolution consisting of the 'adding-on' of attributes to the physical body. However, it could be argued that the image of detachable 'properties' which this conjures up is inappropriate to human beings. Rather than attributes, humans have 'ways of Being' which saturate their worldly presence (Heidegger 1962, 67). These are not added on top of a set of biological qualities. The human body does not have an autonomous existence in the world, moving around and collecting sensory information to send to a mind which is located somewhere else, at a distance. Physical experience and its interpretation are 'coextensive' (Haar 1993, 36). The sensations which we undergo can never be separated out from the moods, attunements and understandings in which we constantly find ourselves. It is through their particular way of Being that human beings first find themselves as human, and it is only because of the existence of this way of Being that particular humans have developed a concern with biology. Human existence makes biology possible, rather than vice versa.

NATURE, CULTURE AND MATERIAL CULTURE

If we are to recognise the concepts of 'culture' and 'nature' as products of an historically located mode of thinking rather than pan-historic categories, what is to become of material culture? My argument will be that a full appreciation of material culture has been effectively blocked by the culture/nature and mind/body dichotomies, and in later chapters I will hope to show that moving beyond these oppositions reveals the central concerns of archaeology to be more important than has generally been accepted. For the moment, the intention is to demonstrate the extent to which past forms of archaeological thought have been dominated by the Cartesian scheme. My contention is that archaeology has attempted to reduce material culture to an essence, which must then be located either within the realm of ideas or that of biological presences. In contrast, I will suggest that culture in general and material culture in particular span the mental and the material.

Culture can be thought of as knowledge, yet this knowledge is better conceived in terms of skills than 'belief' (Dreyfus 1991, 22). Knowledge is a part of our bodily engagement with our world, and may have as much to do with our skilled competence in getting on with the task in hand as with abstracted thought. Knowledge never exists outside of the world, in a sphere of pure thought, and material culture is not the manifest reflection of abstract cognition. Culture is situated and contextual, and realised in practice. This practice does not involve taking things out of one domain, called 'nature', and introducing them into a rarefied cultural world. Instead, it is a means of entering into the network of relationships which obtains between bodies and materials, and into the creation of meaning.

Within the Cartesian scheme of things, the human subject is a coherent whole, composed of a material body housing an transcendental intelligence. Nature is an externality, existing around us and composed of positive attributes, which the conscious mind can come to know. What this movement of encounter and experience requires is that this mind must somehow gain a knowledge of the outside through the sensory mediation of the body. It is as if the knowing consciousness must emerge from the depths of the person, collect information, and withdraw back into its fastnesses (Heidegger 1962, 87). The image which this conjures up is not so much that of the 'ghost in the machine' as a jack-in-the-box. Alternatively, we could say that the way in which we know the world is based upon our immersion in it: there is no 'inside' and 'outside' to the person. The body is not a container that we *live in*, it is an aspect of the self which we *live through*. Thinking is not clearly to be distinguished from action, and itself provides a means of involvement in the world. This involvement takes such a form that even a clear separation between the self and the world is difficult to sustain. Human beings do not first come into Being as complete intelligences, only to find themselves ejected into a world, or an environment which simply contains them (Zimmerman 1993, 261). As we will see below, there could be no human being without a world, and no world (in the specialised sense in which we will use the word) without human beings. Self and world thus cannot be prised apart: they are the necessary and complementary elements of the structure of Being-in-the-world (Dreyfus 1991, 67).

As a means of engagement in the world, knowledge is thus produced, reproduced and circulated through active relational involvement, rather than being hidden away in human braincases. The practices, relationships and contexts within which this takes place will not be homogeneous, and consequently cultural knowledge will not be evenly distributed between people (Lindstrom 1990, xi). It may be managed and restricted as much as it is shared. Human beings always find themselves locked in to sets of social relationships, which are both constraining and enabling, and it will be through their positioning in these relationships that they gain access to and manipulate cultural knowledge (Thrift 1991). Cultural knowledge will consequently be deeply implicated with power, representing the wherewithal to act meaningfully in particular contexts. This knowledge may not actually take a form which could easily be verbalised: it might include modes of address, and ways of standing, sitting and generally comporting oneself which are handed down from person to person in repeated everyday practice. Cultural knowledge in this sense is never static, but is constantly re-invented and re-negotiated, even without people being aware that they are involved in any activity at all (Marcus and Fisher 1986, 24). As the basis for acting rather than fixed code or underlying structure, cultural knowledge can be fragmentary, incoherent and self-contradictory (Rosaldo 1989). While cultural knowledge is a structure of meaning, it may not be meaningful in itself. Rather, it may represent meaning*less* tools for thought and social engagement, used contextually in the production of meaning.

Here we reach the crucial connection with material culture. For while some modes of involvement may be preserved as habits, body memories or traditions, others may maintain a physical presence. Ways of engaging in the world are not simply stored 'in the head': they are immanent in the relationships between people and things. This suggests that material culture is a constituent element of the structure of Being-in-the-world. Objects, whether or not they have been transformed by human labour, become bound up with human projects, and form a part of the web of relations in which we are embedded. We use knowledge to change things, and we learn from things. Things 'speak' to us about events to which we have no other means of access, and we 'read' things in order to produce meanings. This line of thought will be taken up again later, but for now it has set the scene for a consideration of past archaeological thought.

CULTURE AND NATURE IN CULTURE-HISTORIC ARCHAEOLOGY

The development of archaeology as a discipline was deeply lodged in the western intellectual tradition. While much of the early history of arch-aeology was concerned purely with temporal change, and with the establishment of universal evolutionary sequences, by the later nineteenth century a concern with spatial variability had begun to emerge (Trigger 1989, 148). Since human beings appeared to demonstrate considerable geographical variation, the distinctions between ethnic entities came to be of central importance. Given that this change in orientation broadly coincided with the national unifications of Germany and Italy, and with the imperial expansion of France and Britain, there does seem to be a connection between the creation of the archaeological 'culture' (or culture-area) as a discursive object and the increasing importance of the nation-state

(Jones *forthcoming*). To this we could add the administrative demands of overseas empires, and in particular the desire to conceptualise 'peoples' as bounded and manipulable units. Culture history, which dominated Anglo-American archaeological discourse throughout the earlier part of the twentieth century, and which remains a powerful force in many parts of the world today (Ucko 1995, 11), is based upon the notion that groups of people constitute sutured wholes, and produce bounded material assemblages which directly or indirectly reflect their distinctive identity. As such, it builds upon a more general association of culture with wholeness, continuity and growth (Clifford 1988, 338). However, I will argue that a much more specific heritage for the archaeological culture-concept can be found in Enlightenment thought. The model of culture-as-ethnicity is made possible by the culture/nature dichotomy, the isolation of analytical objects, and the notion of social totality. In the case of V. Gordon Childe, who probably more than any other writer formalised culture history as a system of thought, the debt to the modern western philosophical tradition is an explicit rather than a generalised one.

Martin Jay (1984) has very effectively documented the genealogy of the concept of totality, from classical Greek thought down to western Marxism. For our purposes, it is sufficient to note two points: that notions of the whole were particularly important in seventeenth- and eighteenth-century philosophy; and that Childe would have had access to two separate strands of holist thinking, from anthropo-geography and from western Marxist philosophy. A paradigmatic exposition of modern western holism can be found in Giambattista Vico's *The New Science* (1968), which presents the parts of any social totality as only being comprehensible through an appreciation of the whole (Jay 1984, 34). Consequently, the whole is prioritised over the parts, and the understanding of the motion of the collectivity is taken as being more illuminating than localised detail. Later, this stress on totality was elaborated in Kant's concern with historical entities as objects of contemplation, an 'aestheticisation of totality' (ibid., 48) which Foucault (1984b) would eventually characterise as a vain desire for 'apocalyptic objectivity'. Ultimately, the Marxist conception of the social totality originates with Hegel, echoing Vico in equating the whole with truth (Jay 1984, 54). Hegel's totality is relational, composed of lesser units, yet underlain by the unifying influence of the world-spirit, such that different aspects of human society would be transformed synchronously as part of the process of the unfolding of history.

It was reference back to Hegel which allowed the revisionism of the Second International to associate the totality with the state (ibid., 67). Thus, the nation-state as an entity might be held to be almost trans-historic, or at least to represent a unit which would survive any future social transformation. The perception of the state as a fundamental totality can perhaps be associated with a growing functionalism in social thought in the later nineteenth and earlier twentieth centuries, whose definitive proponent was Durkheim. In geographical thought something rather similar is demonstrated in the work of Friedrich Ratzel. Ratzel presented a picture of nation-states as organisms, locked in competition with one another for living-space (Bassin 1987a, 477). Ratzel's conception was one which drew upon the social Darwinist vision of human existence being characterised by a continuous struggle for survival. However, his particular version eschewed racism, suggesting instead that the basis for group identity was common occupation of a geographical area (Bassin 1987b, 118). This is particularly significant from the archaeological point of view, since Ratzel's *History of Ancient Times* (1884) was to pioneer the use of geographical distributions of artefacts as a guide to the extent of early civilisations (Trigger 1989, 162). For Ratzel, what made the Egyptians Egyptian, or the Phoenecians Phoenician, was their living together in a given geographical region.

Ratzel's view of societies as entities dominated by their environment was a legacy eventually taken up by Childe, who was to argue that communities could be seen 'as functioning wholes' (Childe 1950, 8). And certainly, culture history in most of its forms was to concentrate upon the shared cultural inheritance of collectivities, rather than the isolation of 'Great Men' (Flannery 1972). However, in Childe's own work there is a continuing tension between this view of social adaptation and a mentalist understanding of culture. For if societies use culture as a means of adaptation to their environment, his equal insistence that material culture is an expression of traditions that are fixed in the mind is difficult to reconcile with this. Childe seems to represent a chronic example of archaeology's indecision as to whether to locate material culture in the inner self or the physical world. A further source of Childe's hesitancy, though, lay in his desire to resist the racist implications of Kossinna's 'settlement archaeology' of the Germans. For while Ratzel's work had indirectly had a profound influence on western European archaeology, it was Kossinna who had refined his approach into a means of distinguishing discrete 'cultures'. For him, 'sharply defined archaeological culture areas correspond unquestionably with the areas of particular peoples or tribes' (quoted in Veit 1989, 37). According to Kossinna, different peoples produced artefacts in distinctive styles as a result of certain genetically fixed propensities. Naturally, the inherent racial superiority of the Germans led them to produce aesthetically superior artefacts (Veit 1989, 38). This genetic determinism contrasts starkly with Ratzel's view of human plasticity in the face of dominant environmental conditions.

In Kossinna's scheme of things, the relationship between people and material things is a direct and causal one. With Childe, the connection is less straightforward: 'cultures' are material assemblages which *correspond* with 'peoples':

Culture and race do not coincide ... there are no grounds for
assuming that the creators or bearers of a culture were always a single
race, all of whose members shared distinctive genetic characteristics.

(Childe 1950, 1)

It was the restricted degree of autonomy which Childe accorded to
material culture which allowed him to shift in the course of his career from
a concern with migration to an emphasis on diffusion (Renfrew 1979, 9).
As with predecessors like Elliot Smith and Ratzel, Childe's diffusionism
tended to underplay human creativity, implying that any cultural innovation
would be unlikely to be invented more than once in world history. Yet
rather than repeat their bleak prognosis that humans generally lacked the
ability to innovate, Childe stressed the role of social factors in restricting
the adoption of new cultural forms.

The remarkable uniformity of types in a given local and chronological
group or 'culture' just discloses the uniformity and rigidity of the
traditions actuating their makers.

(Childe 1942, 26)

Men cling passionately to old traditions and display intense reluctance
to modify customary modes of behaviour.

(Childe 1936, 30)

One reason why Childe may have been able to stand outside of the
Austro-German anthropo-geographical tradition within culture-historic
archaeology is that he was both politically and intellectually involved in
Marxism. While his Marxism is frequently dismissed as a vulgar materialism
(Trigger 1980, 15), it seems that through his association with R. Palme-
Dutt Childe had access to complex aspects of Marxist philosophy, and in
particular the work of Lukács (Gathercole 1989, 85). For Lukács, the notion
of totality is central to the process of history. The seeming flux of social
life is underlain by a coherent historical pattern, leading toward the eventual
emancipation of humanity (Jay 1984, 106). However, the overall structure
might only be appreciated from a particular point of view: by the prole-
tariat, who represented the universal subject of history (ibid., 107). Such a
concern with social totality as being at the heart of historical change might
have led Childe to see culture as a reflection of more fundamental processes
involving social and economic factors. In a similar way, Robert Braidwood
was to see material culture of the outgrowth of an inevitable process of
human advance through a series of 'cultural levels' (Braidwood and Willey
1962). Just as Braidwood's is a historical idealism which is comparable with
Hegel's account of the unfolding process of the world-spirit, so we might
see Childe's as a Hegelian Marxism which locates historical change within
the internal processes of the social totality.

Such an interpretation would explain Childe's statement that material culture represents 'the concrete expressions of the common social traditions that bind together a people' (Childe 1950, 2). Moreover, he contends that human social development has been made possible by abstract reason (carried out 'in the head') and the ability to transfer information linguistically (Childe 1936, 27; Childe 1942, 20). None the less, Childe is also willing to state that 'a culture is an adaptation to an environment. Hence a culture evolved in the Mediterranean is not likely to be transferred bodily to say England, without undergoing very drastic modifications' (1950, 2). These attitudes are seemingly contradictory, and yet they remain relatively stable throughout Childe's career, supported by the empirical observation that cultural traditions in prehistoric Europe appear to have been relatively stable over long periods, but that differences across space are clearly evident. As distinct from the processual archaeologists who succeeded him, Childe did not necessarily see cultural change in terms of a continual effort to maintain homeostasis between a community and its ecosystem. Instead, culture was transformed at the point of transfer between one group of people and another. Any plasticity in cultural tradition would thus have been the consequence of the process of diffusion itself. Thus a community would adopt a cultural innovation in a form that was appropriate for its own environmental circumstances: adaption rather than adaptation. Thereafter, the trait concerned would be reproduced through tradition and learning, re-created across the generations in a relatively slavish manner. However, by suggesting that the initial form in which innovation is adopted is related to geographical factors, Childe was able to refute connections between cultural advance and racial predisposition.

Childe's cultural theory thus appears to embody a notion of internalisation and exteriorisation: ways of doing things are inculcated into children in the course of a prolonged infancy, in the context of family life (Childe 1936, 28). Once lodged in the mind, cultural ideas are unlikely to be transformed: they continue to serve as a template for material production throughout the individual's life, and are kept in place by 'the dead-weight of conservatism' (ibid., 30). Cultural change is not denied, but is seen as arising from some combination of independent innovation and diffusion (Childe 1950, 8). What this seems to preclude is any notion that culture might be constantly in motion, with particular traits being adopted or discarded by persons in the course of day-to-day social action. Culture is consequently homogeneous and unitary. Moreover, since the critical forces of human development are generated within social and economic relations, material culture will never do more than reflect the emergence of a new social formation. At a particular stage in its development, a society will be 'ready' for more complex architecture, or metal tools, or enclosed settlements. Innovations will then either be adopted from elsewhere or (more rarely) be spontaneously generated. These material manifestations, however, are not an integral part of the social process: social change takes place

24

'elsewhere'. While as a Marxist Childe might have been expected to emphasise social conflict and contradiction, we could suggest that his adherence
to the Hegelian notion of the expressive totality had the implication that
culture was related to norms and values held in common by all members
of society. Culture was not an arena for the working out of class or factional
antagonisms. Implicit in this way of thinking seems to be the division
between style and function. Material objects which have a certain function
are adopted in keeping with the social and economic developments to which
they are appropriate, yet their stylistic variation flows from the peculiarities
of cultural tradition: idiosyncratic shared and transmitted norms held in
the head (Flannery 1972).

> The several types of knife or tomb each fulfil roughly the same function;
> the differences between them repose upon divergences in the social
> tradition prescribing the methods of their preparation and use.
>
> (Childe 1942, 25)

In consequence, Childe's archaeology is profoundly metaphysical. He has
succeeded in setting up two realms which cannot be directly addressed by
the archaeologist: the subjective space of the mind, and the intersubjective
space of social relations. Between them, the processes going on in these two
realms account for most of what archaeology would hope to understand. The
materiality of material culture seems to be of little consequence: Childe's
material culture is emphatically mental and cultural, rather than physical and
natural. Hence the physical presence of the things of the past is of limited
utility: the archaeologist must piece them together, in the awareness that the
elements which rendered them meaningful (minds and social relations) are
absent and beyond recall.

CULTURE AND NATURE IN PROCESSUAL ARCHAEOLOGY

Concentrating upon the work of Childe has allowed us to demonstrate the
way in which culture-historic archaeology is nested within the broader context of modern thought. In this section, it will be shown that the processual
school, which in many ways represented a radical break with culture history,
none the less reproduced the antinomial thinking of modernity. By focusing on the writings of Lewis Binford, we will see how material culture
remains an ambiguous category within processualism. As the central figure
in the New Archaeology of the 1960s, Binford's work concentrated on two
related yet fundamentally distinct issues: the need for an epistemology which
concentrated upon the archaeological record, and the project of working
towards an ontology of culture as it relates to human behaviour. As his
career progressed, we could suggest that the latter began to represent a more

distant objective, while the former fell into sharper focus. It would be the demand for a 'science of the archaeological record' that would lead him to call for the development of Middle Range Theory: generalisations developed in the present which bear directly upon the processes responsible for the generation of archaeological evidence.

> We must develop a theoretical understanding of certain properties of the archaeological record that will have unambiguous referents in the present and will be uniformly relevant in the past.
>
> (Binford 1982, 131)

That Binford considered that such a project was conceivable gives us a first indication of the way in which he views culture. In order to establish a body of Middle Range Theory at all, the relationships between cultural systems and their traces must be mediated through a series of formation processes which are constant, or are at least not culturally mutable. Certain aspects of the record which we observe can be disentangled from the cultural, and behave in a lawlike manner. While Binford would not deny that human beings inhabit a meaningful world, and communicate by means of structured symbolic systems, this has very little implication for the set of materials which are available to archaeologists.

> The archaeological record is not made up of symbols, words or concepts, but of material things and arrangements of matter.
>
> (Binford 1983, 19)

If the objects and substances that make up the archaeological record had meanings, those meanings existed in the past and exist no longer in the present. For Binford, the materiality of a thing seems to be fundamental, whereas its cultural significance is a secondary attribute which is added on top. Cultural meaning is an interpretation of a pre-given phenomenon which exists independently in the real world, and has a substance or presence which in no way depends upon human existence. This view, of course, parallels the conception of human beings as rational animals: biological creatures with something separate added. The archaeologist, encountering an artefact in the context of an excavation, sees the object purely as a material thing from which any meaning has been stripped away by time. When archaeologists study material things, they do so in a way which is analogous to the work of a natural scientist. In the laboratory, scientists conduct experiments and make observations which have the status of pure sensory experience, unmediated by social or cultural factors. Being mean-ing*less*, these observations have to be given meaning by the scientists themselves (Binford 1983, 22). Archaeologists, making observations on the dead, static traces of human behaviour, must find means of inference which allow them to render their raw material meaningful, and so enable themselves to make statements concerning the dynamics of the past. The initial means by which this is achieved is by addressing the question of how it was that the things which we observe as archaeologists came to acquire their present characteristics.

It follows from this that archaeology should not primarily be considered as being a social science. In the first instance, it is the task of the archaeologist to record material variability, and to assess the significance of the patterning of the archaeological record (Binford 1989, 56). Since the meaning of material things is always a secondary issue, one must proceed from a firm under-standing of the material record to an investigation of past people and their ways of life. The mistake of culture-historic archaeology had lain in assuming that the cultural behaviour of human beings was the consequence of normative mental predispositions which amounted to 'laws of the human mind'. Implicitly, accounts which dealt in migrations and diffusion were relying upon predictions of how human beings should respond in given sets of circumstances. For Binford, human behaviour was what archaeology sought to address, rather than a point of departure for archaeological analysis. Laws of behaviour should be the object of the inquiry (Binford 1972a, 116). Since culture history was concerned with cognitive norms, it viewed culture as the 'ideational basis for varying ways of human life' (Binford 1965, 204). If this were the case, the significance of any artefact must have been locked away in the brainboxes of long-dead people. Archaeology is then awarded an unappealing choice between the empty exercise of typologising presently existing artefacts, and indulging in 'palaeopsychology': seeking to extract the normative content of past human minds from objects. Rebelling against this pessimistic outlook, Binford argued that culture could not be reduced to ideas (1965, 206). Instead, culture was involved in the relationships between people and their environments.

Culture, then, represented 'man's extrasomatic means of adaptation' (Binford 1972b, 105). Having already declared that culture is not of the mind, Binford was now claiming that it was not of the body either, although it did represent a form of behaviour, or at least it served people 'as a clearly successful adaptive basis for the organisation of behaviour' (Binford 1973, 227). As such, it represented a far more flexible range of responses to environmental conditions than could be provided by genetic mutation.

> This view must not be thought of as 'environmental determinism' for we assume a systematic relationship between the human organism and his environment in which culture is the intervening variable.
>
> (Binford 1962, 218)

In answer to the question 'where is culture, if not in the mind?', Binford would thus answer that it exists at the interstice between a community and its environment. Cultural change is not simply triggered by environmental change: culture is one element in a complex system composed of numerous sub-systems, and the overall outcome of change in any one area depends upon the interactions of all of these subsystems. Moreover, the way in which any individual or group will respond to particular stimuli is not fixed. Culture represents a pool of variability from which humans can draw in their responses (Binford 1963, 92). This pool is not contained in its entirety in the brain of any one member of a community: culture is participated in rather than shared, and this participation may be differential. Binford's overall perspective is clearly Darwinian, yet he does not always claim that culture itself 'evolves'. The role of culture is primarily functional, facilitating the process of human evolution (Binford 1972b, 107). Culture does not 'do' anything: it is a means through which human beings carry out their actions.

All of the above serves to complicate the position of *material* culture. As archaeologists, we observe the *products* of human behaviour. This behaviour 'is the by-product of the interaction of a cultural repertoire with the environment' (Binford 1973, 229). Variations in behaviour are the consequence of the situation in which humans find themselves. The archaeological record does not represent a cultural repertoire, but the outcome of its use. Thus behaviour is not the same thing as culture: behaviour is the operationalisation of culture. So again, the material things which we excavate are not themselves cultural, so much as the traces of behaviour which itself draws upon culture. Within this scheme of things, the 'space' occupied by culture itself becomes more and more difficult to define. Culture is not in the head or in the body, or in the things which people make. Culture is neither in society nor in nature ('the environment'), but in a realm which exists between them. Through his investment in systems theory, in many ways the most extreme form of Cartesian thought, Binford has accepted that the world is a system composed of sub-systems, each of which possesses a certain autonomy. By defining a series of given objects which come to interact with each other in the evolutionary process, he turns culture into a phantasm. Culture is not 'in' other sub-systems, but constitutes a sub-system in itself. It is difficult to see how this sub-system is to be observed. Material things in the archaeological record are only the remains of behaviour, yet Binford was later to argue that ethnographic testimony represents no more than an informant's *explanation* of their culture (Binford 1987, 397–8). Hence neither archaeologists nor anthropologists ever 'see' culture. So, Binford appears to have as profoundly a metaphysical view of culture as Childe. Culture is an absent influence, visible everywhere in its effects, constantly drawn on in human survival strategies, but never directly observed. Because these effects can be recognised and yet culture cannot be tied down to any visible sphere, it must exist 'somewhere else'. Out there in the world, neither held in minds nor immanent in things, culture floats as a sphere to be 'participated in'.

It is possible to argue that Binford's archaeology represents a relatively orthodox Cartesian view of the world. Nature is seen as an exteriority, not a passive realm but a dynamic combination of forces which can be empirically known by science. As 'the environment', nature produces variable stimuli to which communities must react. People are seen as 'rational animals', biological organisms with something added. This 'something' may involve consciousness, lodged inside the organism, but its main constituent is *culture*. Culture, like Descartes' *mind*, has an existence which seems to be of a different order to the material things of the world. The proof of its existence lies in its effects: human beings exhibit cultural behaviour, therefore there must be culture. Material objects, like artefacts, are of the world rather than of this cultural realm. Objects *function*, 'together with ... more behavioural elements within ... cultural sub-systems' (Binford 1962, 219). Thus Binford was able to distinguish between *technomic, sociotechnic* and *ideotechnic* artefacts, which are used in coping with the environment, expressing social variation and signifying 'the ideological rationalisations for the social system', respectively (Binford 1962, 220). This seems to imply that although artefacts are composed of worldly materials, they can be caught up in cultural systems through the operation of human action. However, the relationship between culture and artefact is not so direct. The difference between these various types of objects does not inhere in the things themselves, but is a consequence of the different cultural sub-systems in which they were engaged. Even then, they did not enter into the cultural realm, but became patterned through human behaviour which was structured by those cultural sub-systems.

BEYOND MODERNIST ARCHAEOLOGY

Modernist thought involves the reification and radical separation of culture, nature, mind, body, society, individuals and artefacts. The conceptual frameworks for archaeology that have arisen within the modern era have been dominated by these distinct entities, and by a series of oppositions established between them which have allowed mutual evaluation and valorisation to be carried out between categories. Certain qualities have been attributed to abstract concepts, themselves perceived as essential presences. That which is material may be more real; that which is natural may be amenable to scientific enquiry; and so on. Furthermore, because archaeology deals with the relationship between past and present, another opposition has taken on a central role: between presence (in the present) and absence (in the past). In the way that it creates metaphysical entities which are locked away in the past, and which are severed from the physical materials that survive into the present, modernist archaeology is self-defeating. For Childe, the meaning of material culture lay in the normative content of minds and the unfolding of social relations across time. Yet both the individual consciousnesses and the collective social totality were beyond archaeological investigation. Material culture itself represented form without content, fulfilling particular functions and varying stylistically in accord with tradition, but lacking any meaningful content. For Binford, material culture is the product of behaviour organised by culture. Both behaviour and culture are of the past, and culture is a metaphysical, disembodied phenomenon.

The aim of this book is to challenge the pessimism which such an outlook breeds. However, this is not to be achieved by essentialist means, suggesting that material things contain meanings which can be 'read' out of them in an unproblematic manner. Instead, I will hope to show that cultural significance and the production of meaning are not encapsulated in any one sutured entity, whether mind, body, society or nature. Identity and meaning are both relational constructions, which emerge through the *process* of human Being-in-the-world. Identities are not located within any one entity, and are furthermore spread across time. For this reason, we must now turn our investigation to the issue of temporality.

TIME AND THE SUBJECT

———— •◆• ————

THE TIME OF THE WORLD AND THE TIME OF THE SOUL: KANT, ARISTOTLE, AUGUSTINE

What is time? Like many of the more fundamental concepts which we use to understand the world (art, Being, ritual, 'the social'), time appears to be self-evident. However, any attempt to clarify and schematise our ordinary everyday understanding of time appears to be fraught with difficulties (see Lewis 1980, 9–10, on the problems of terms which we customarily use but find difficult to define). In such circumstances, it is often the case that the more satisfactory definitions are counter-intuitive, and themselves help us to recognise why a particular understanding of a phenomenon has arisen. Those depictions of time which have attempted to elaborate upon the way that it is experienced by human beings, and have thereby moved on to general philosophical statements, have often found themselves in severe difficulties. A case in point would be Immanuel Kant, who, in his 'Transcendental Aesthetic' (1901) attempted an inventory of the grounds which underlay the human perception of phenomena. That is to say, Kant was striving to set out the logical preconditions for our experience of the world. Within this scheme of things, time and space were considered as a priori categories. Neither time nor space could be directly experienced in themselves, yet no other phenomenon could be experienced without postulating their existence. That we do have a sensible awareness of phenomena demonstrates the reality of time and space, yet this recognition is an intuitive one. Since they logically precede anything which can be encountered as sense evidence, there is no way in which their existence can be tested or falsified empirically. So time and space are objective, yet are never known as such (Ricoeur 1988, 23). Moreover, time is linear, and consequently different times do not exist alongside each other: they must constitute a unified sequence.

> It is, therefore, only under the presupposition of time, that we can be conscious of certain things as existing at the same time (simultaneously), or at different times (successively).
>
> (Kant 1901, 29)

From the above it follows that without time, we could not be conscious of other phenomena at all, and that no phenomenon could exist outside of time. Yet these arguments imply in some sense that time and space are 'containers', within which beings are located, even if these containers are infinite in their extent. So when we say that something is 'in time', the sense which is primarily indicated by Kant is that it is placed within some other 'thing', which is infinitely large. Kant's argument is essentially that time and space could be emptied of their contents, and yet would maintain their identity (Ricoeur 1988, 46). Thus their logical priority rests upon their constitution as boundless (and hence intangible) contexts for the location of other things. Space extends to accommodate things in three physical dimensions, while time adds a further axis of extension, a further means of defining relations between objects and events. However, whereas space is only the a priori condition of things which have a corporeal presence, time also *has to be* for us to be capable of inner perception. It was this point which Heidegger (1962, 374) isolated as a flaw in Kant's argument, since it implies that time is at once a precondition of all external events and yet in some way bound up with human subjectivity. In the first place, this uneasy position rests upon the radical separation which much of the western tradition has maintained between the outer world of things, and the inner world of the soul. As we will see, a more satisfactory understanding of *being in* time and space depends upon dissolving this division, such that human agency is always contextualised. But at the same time, it suggests that the temporality which we experience, and through which we gain access to the world is one and the same thing as the objective processes of nature (such as the decay of atomic isotopes, for example). Kant's time is both objectively existing and subjectively imposed upon reality. It is at once a being and a non-being.

Heidegger's criticisms are echoed by Paul Ricoeur (1988), who offers the insight that the conflict between objective and subjective conceptions of time can be reconciled by the historian through the recognition that the writing of the past has the character of narrative composition. This position can be pushed somewhat further than Ricoeur might have intended by repositioning it as social theory. That is to say, the human experience and perception and experience of time is story-like, and it is through such a narrative composition that individual and group identities emerge. They are negotiated readings of a past heritage. It is this perspective, which relativises identity, which enables us to reconsider the account of temporality provided by Heidegger and at the same time to avoid some of its dangerous implications. These issues can be satisfactorily opened by considering Ricoeur's treatment of the opposed conceptions of time championed by Aristotle and St Augustine.

For Aristotle, time was cosmological, an attribute of the external world. The existence of time in the world is registered by changes in phenomena, and by the speed of those changes. Events in the world take place in a sequence, and it is possible to add a numerical dimension to the relative order, duration and speed of events and processes. That is, we can measure time, because of the existence of objective standards (the solar cycle, for example), which exist outside of human consciousness. It is the inner self, the soul, which notes the changes in the world and contrives to measure them. But it can only do this because nature contains a pattern of instants which succeed each other in orderly fashion. As opposed to this 'time of the world', Augustine drew attention to the 'time of the soul', a phenomenological conception of time. Augustine held that for the human being, the quantification of temporal processes was entirely secondary to a fundamental orientation of existence in time. To the human subject, time is composed of past, present and future, and these cannot be identified in quantitative terms. The best that Aristotle could do would be to say that 'the present' is that instant which is currently taking place, an instant which is situated (Ricoeur 1988, 21). But for human beings, past, present and future are absolutes, conceptual categories for understanding personal experience and the fortunes of collectivities.

The 'time of the world' and the 'time of the soul' are thus polar opposites in the understanding of temporality that articulate with broader sets of philosophical and political concerns. If we emphasise the objective and worldly nature of time, we tend to promote a view of reality as a given, a set of physical conditions to which human consciousness must bend itself. It is a view of time which has much in common with the 'containment' aspect of Kant's argument, such that time is an exteriority against which we can chart the development of humankind. This is the time of science, of evolution and ecology, the time of 'objective' history, and the time of determinist materialism. The 'time of the soul', however, is a notion which can lead towards solipsism. Where one concentrates upon an inner experience which gives form to an outer reality, there is a tendency to reify that inner self into a transcendental subject. The subject becomes a primordial being, with certain fundamental characteristics, including the giving of temporality to the world. Hence it was, perhaps, that Husserl considered that the perception of time was one of the most pressing concerns of a transcendental phenomenology (Ricoeur 1988, 44). Ricoeur, however, sought to demonstrate that neither perspective was in itself satisfactory. For as Aristotle demonstrated, the soul cannot *create* the extension of time as a dimension of being, yet nature cannot divide it up into the threefold of past, present and future (Ricoeur 1988, 21). Integrating these two arguments requires a more detailed consideration of the way that human beings *are* on earth, but first it it will be instructive to investigate some of the frameworks for the understanding of time in the social sciences which are concerned with collectivities and historical processes. It has been these ideas which have been most influential within archaeology, and it is important at this point to demonstrate that what they lack is an appreciation of the temporality of human Being.

TIME AS PERIODICITY: BRAUDEL, ALTHUSSER, FOUCAULT

One of the central concerns of this book is the way in which we can think about the temporality of societies or social relationships. This question can be made to appear deceptively simple. The discussions of time which have proved most influential within archaeology have tended to be of the kind which concentrate upon its 'objective' character (see Gosden 1994). That is, they deal with the 'time of the world': time as a linear expanse along which events are dispersed. Where such an approach comes to focus upon the social, some fairly fundamental philosophical problems start to emerge. If time is considered as external, rather than as permeating social Being, social institutions tend to be given an essential and 'thinglike' character. They somehow exist 'before' time, rather than being articulated through temporality (Giddens 1987, 141). Thus the emphasis which will be placed upon the temporality of human existence in this account is not an attempt to place 'the individual' at the centre of social analysis, so much as an effort to avoid seeing societies and their constituent elements as absolute givens. It could be argued that the adoption of a concern with objective and external temporality leaves us with two alternative ways of conceptualising time, neither of which is entirely satisfactory. Either one can think of human collectivities as having a certain essential temporal character, or one can impose an artificial temporal structure upon past events, as part of the writing of history (Bailey 1985, 13). In the first case, social relations are understood through fixed categories which deny their historical nature, while in the second the only structure which time is allowed is that which is imposed upon it as if from outside by the historian.

This problem is particularly evident in the work of the historian Fernand Braudel, whose tripartite scheme of temporality has been adopted in one form or another by a number of archaeologists. Braudel's structural history, as exemplified by *The Mediterranean and the Mediterranean World in the Age of Phillip II* (Braudel 1972) is concerned to the motion of a series of worldly structures. In contrast to the notion of structure adhered to by Lévi-Strauss, Braudel's structures are empirical, and exist in the world of material things (Clark 1985). Environmental and economic structures of this kind are thought of as continuously unfolding, and provide constraints to (rather than determinants of) human action. Discrete human acts are dispersed within passages of time, which is considered to be both quantifiable and connected with the public interactions of human beings. Braudel's introduction of the threefold scheme of events, conjunctures and the *longue durée* thus allows ecological processes, socio-economic processes and the acts of individuals to proceed according to different temporal cycles. In practice, however, this means that perceptible changes (or events) take place at a different rate or periodicity in these three spheres. As Clark points out (1985, 182), this does not mean that these different 'kinds' of time are essentially different, merely that differences take more or less time to register. Consequently, it is difficult to see why Braudel's temporal structures are effectively kept so separate from each other: events slot into one time or another, acts are permitted or proscribed by enveloping structures, but these acts do not appear to have consequences which affect the further operation of those structures. Thus Braudel's world appears rather like a wedding cake, in which each of the three tiers is revolving at a different speed. The changing configuration of environments or economic institutions presents different sets of constraints for human acts, but changes within one structure do not affect the others. There is no interplay between structure and agency, and no dialectical movement between environment and economy.

It follows from this that Braudel's conception of time, while it proceeds at different 'speeds', is none the less rather similar to Kant's. Time is a container, a static backdrop through which the cycles of empirical structures of different orders flow. Economic and ecological processes may be continuously unfolding, but the time which they inhabit has no positive characteristics. Louis Althusser was later to argue that the failure of *Annales* history lay in the absence of an overall conception of an articulated social totality (Althusser and Balibar 1970, 96), but it is this negative theorisation of time which consigns it to a form of idealism. Braudel's is thus characteristically the historian's understanding of time, as containing past events and processes, which can be pegged to some point along the unfurling skein. In consequence, events are always considered retrospectively, and their significance assessed teleologically. What is required in order to advance beyond this position is a recognition that past acts took place in a present, and that past human subjects were historical beings. This recognition cannot be achieved where time is only the external calibration of events. It is because of this that Braudel is not presenting a perspective on the experience of temporality, so much as the historian's writing of periodicity. Moreover, while he is prepared to recognise that human beings have, at various times in the past and in different cultures across the world, conceptualised time in dramatically different ways, he considers that these cultural constructions of temporal experience are only active in the short term (Clark 1985, 184). Human agents may act on the basis of understandings which are culturally installed and historically specific, but this is a false consciousness which is specific to the time-of-the-event. In other words, the longer-term the process that one is studying, the more empirically sound one's understanding of it is likely to be. Thus the argument ends up by reifying nature into the realm of a grounding reality.

This prejudice towards the long term and the enduring, and against the vagaries of human consciousness and contextual action thus lead Braudel to focus upon the *longue durée*. Within archaeology, it has had still more serious consequences. In recent years, the history of the *Annales* school has become a fashionable façade for some of the more determinist forms of ecological archaeology: 'palaeoeconomy with a French accent' (e.g. Bintliff 1991b). This has proved possible on the basis of a series of arguments which actually push Braudel's position to its logical conclusion (Bailey 1981, 1983; see Shanks and Tilley 1987, 120–5 for criticism). From this perspective, not only are meaning, context and significance limited to the short-term, but the coarse-grained character of the archaeological record determines that they cannot be addressed. The prehistorian's domain is thus exclusively the *longue durée*, and the only meaningful context for archaeological evidence is the background record of ecological change. The environment thus takes the centre of the stage, as the subject of prehistory. The environment is both a place, into which human beings come at intervals to carry out acts which register as archaeological traces, and an objective scale of time. Only those human acts that have a material consequence are to be considered, and these only in their relationship to the environment, as adaptation and modification. Since these acts are seen 'objectively', outside of their short-term context of meaning and signification, they need not be evaluated as manifestations of human projects, and the human beings themselves can be considered as wholly biological entities, shorn of their cultural integument. So while no attempt is made to legislate against anthropological, sociological or historical understandings of human behaviour, these are simply considered irrelevant to those who study the deeper truths of the long term. They are concerned with humans as natural, rather than cultural beings (Shanks and Tilley 1987, 120), since culture is so much froth riding on the great waves of ecological process. As John Cherry put it, in his study of the colonisation of the Mediterranean islands,

> Man, after all, is an animal. ... Looking at man from this rather mechanistic perspective, as an initial exploratory strategy, is not to demean his achievements, but rather to sharpen the focus on his cultural achievements in the past.
>
> (Cherry 1981, 64)

It is unclear, however, how this 'initial exploratory strategy' could eventually be made to give way to a richer perspective, given the qualitatively different understandings of the world which are involved. In reaction to this point of view, Tim Ingold (1986a, 167) has argued that human acts (as given to the archaeologist in the form of clusters of knapping debris, hearths, butchering deposits, etc.) cannot simply be considered as isolated events, giving commentary upon the state of adaptation in respect of the environment. On the contrary, Ingold insists that human acts are linked by intentionality, such that events (in 'micro-time') are contextualised within a continuous stream of human conduct (defined socially in 'meso-time', Braudel's time of the conjuncture). Ingold's rather gloomy prognosis, however, seems to assume an entirely positivist model of the potentials of archaeological research:

> In short, barring such unlikely eventualities as the invention of a time machine (which would effectively convert prehistory into anthropology anyway) it seems that the object of prehistory must be cultural adaptation rather than social evolution.
>
> (Ingold 1984, 12)

The implication is, then, that because they can talk to living informants, anthropologists have a monopoly over discourse on social relations and their transformations within 'meso-time'. Here Ingold appears to overlook a fairly straightforward point: while anthropologists talk to informants in order to gain information about social relations, they never actually 'observe' a society, because a society is not a thing. We can argue that social relationships are *real*, in one sense of the word, but that they are only recognisable in their effects. Another way of putting this is to say that social structures only exist in and through their manifestations, but that this does not make them any less objective than the natural forces that are invoked by physicists or chemists (Bhaskar 1989, 79). We can only achieve an adequate understanding of human phenomena by hypothesising the existence of social relations and socially defined projects, and it makes no difference whether we do this on the basis of informants' accounts or archaeological traces. What links together purposive human acts is not the presence of the environment as a continuous adversary, but the network of expectations and retained memories which provides the context for the projecting-forward of agency.

While Braudel had attempted to break time down into separate rhythms largely for the purpose of description, the superficially similar partitioning of time proposed by Louis Althusser was perhaps more analytical in intent. Althusser's objective in this respect was to evict any remaining traces of idealism from Marxist theory, and hence his interest was attracted by Hegel's account of historical time. In that Hegel was describing the unfolding into the world of processes which were essential and spiritual in character, he clearly presents social and cultural development as unified and homogeneous. One is not dealing with a dialectical engagement of worldly forces but with ideal forms, and consequently all of the aspects of the human world proceed forward at a uniform rate. So while Hegel's totality was complex, it was none the less unified by being underlain at base by the development of an Idea (Laclau and Mouffe 1985, 97). Hence, at any given time, all of the elements of the totality can be appraised at once, given that they are integrated into a 'spiritual unity' (Althusser and Balibar 1970,

94–5). In contrast, Althusser suggested that a materialist dialectic involved not simply the relative autonomy of the different levels and instances of the social formation, but their development within different historical times. Thus the legal system, ideology and the like might be determined in the last instance by the processes of the economic base, but they none the less had histories of their own which might be expected to be divided up and understood in ways which were specific to themselves. Hence, 'it is no longer possible to think the processes of the development of the different levels of the whole *in the same historical time*' (Althusser and Balibar 1970, 99). The picture which this conjures up of different institutions and practices being played out in quite different temporal cycles, and of the consequent fragmentation and disjuncture of reality, is an interesting one. For archaeologists, who have too often sought to divide up the past according to a single aspect of society, namely technology, it is a sobering notion. Archaeology sets up temporal blocks called 'the Stone Age', 'the Iron Age' and so on, expecting change to take place in uniform sequences (so that we can talk about 'Bronze Age agriculture', or 'Iron Age society', for instance). This is very much the kind of idealism proposed by Hegel.

However, it is possible that Althusser's conception of time might have proved more fruitful had he placed less store in the determination of all in the last instance by the economy. Had he maintained his earlier focus upon the overdetermined and symbolic nature of social relations (Laclau and Mouffe 1985, 95–6), these might have been conceived as more thoroughly historical in character. As it is, the criticism that Althusser's picture of the social formation resembles a kind of clockwork model of the universe with gears and cogs spinning at different speeds (Thompson 1978) is not unfounded. The infrastructure and superstructures of the social formation themselves become reified categories, so that Althusser places them above and outside of history, as ideal constructs. In a way reminiscent of Braudel, time is the container of this orrery, recognised through the changes in its state of development (Giddens 1981, 30). By contrast, the kind of historical time that the abandonment of 'relative autonomy' and determination in the last instance might lead to would be rather similar to that implicit in Foucault's 'genealogical' history (1984b). For Foucault, the consequence of the recognition that the historian is never external to the history that she writes is that the past can never be grasped in its entirety as a completed development. Not only the heuristic categories which we use to describe the world, but even the most fundamental givens of our thought (the human body, emotions, instincts) need to be historicised and shown to emerge out of something else. Genealogy, then, sets out to write a history which tracks these entities back to their emergence, producing an account which is directed rather than totalised. It is concerned with discontinuities, ruptures and reversals, rather than orderly and progressive evolution. Things become different with time, but they also irrupt and disappear, and cohere into formations which are transient, yet which develop logics of their own. Multiple paths can be traced through the scattered phenomena of the past, and each will bring to light forgotten voices which have been buried by the efforts of 'official' history. In order to describe this kind of history, Foucault frequently employs a range of spatial metaphors: thus events are 'dispersed' in time (Lemert and Gillan 1982, 96–7). Historical time is consequently a weblike network, within which events possess a particular singularity as articulating boundless relationships between unstable phenomena.

Foucault's history is thus productive in its antitotalisation. It insists that our analytical categories are never adequate for writing a 'true' and complete past, that human beings are *in* history and that human beings are fundamentally historical. Moreover, since his conception of space is one that is deeply connected with the exercise of power and knowledge, his use of spatial metaphors to discuss time is suggestive. Seeing time as a 'fourth dimension', within which relationships are spread out, is no more satisfactory than a geometrical notion of space. Foucault's understanding of time is one of fragmentation and heterogeneity, but perhaps one which is underdeveloped. For Foucault is more concerned with history than temporality, with being in history than being in time, and with being historical than with being temporal. So while Foucault is a source to which we will return repeatedly, understandings concerning the temporal character of human beings will have to come from elsewhere.

HEIDEGGER ON DASEIN'S TEMPORALITY

Probably one of the most sophisticated treatments of temporality in the western tradition was that presented by Martin Heidegger in *Being and Time* (1962). This is a complex work, which attempts to hold a series of different philosophical arguments in check by undermining the commonplace understandings upon which they are erected. The central argument, however, concerns the phenomenon of *Being*, and the way that it has been 'covered over' as a problem since the time of the Greeks. As a means of addressing the question of Being, Heidegger investigates the Being of one particular kind of entity, 'a being which does not just occur among other beings. Rather it is ontically distinguished by the fact that, in its very Being, that Being is an *issue* for it' (Heidegger 1962, 32). Putting this in very un-Heideggerian terms, he is concerned with beings which have a particular kind of consciousness, in that they are self-aware in such a way that their own existence *matters* to them. This may perhaps serve as a more satisfactory definition than those customarily given in the literature for what separates humanity from other animals ('a conscious subject', 'a tool-user', 'a culture-bearing organism', etc). However, as we will see, this is not an inclusive definition of humanity which covers all of the characteristic aspects of personhood, nor does it apply to all beings that can biologically be defined as human. Heidegger's term, *Dasein*, refers to the characteristic Being of this kind of creature, which can more or less be equated with a human being (or with 'the way that human beings are': Dasein is a way of Being or a *practice* more than a *thing*). Bound up with this characterisation is the understanding that Dasein's Being fundamentally involves self-interpretation (Dreyfus 1991, 24). Thus there is rather little to Dasein that is fundamental, beyond its reflexivity. The logical outcome of this argument, put baldly, is that Dasein's Being is time (Wood 1993, 138). How Heidegger comes to this conclusion will require some consideration, since it paves the way for a clearer understanding of how human beings are in time, and of the nature of personal and group identity.

An important aspect of Dasein's way of Being is that it constantly interprets itself in certain ways which cover up the more disconcerting aspects of its nature. Thus Dasein tends to consider itself as a thing, or object, which has a certain essential and unchanging nature (Dreyfus 1991, 41). This kind of interpretation is the foundation of Dasein's ordinary everyday understandings of the world, which we might call common sense. These common-sense notions underlie much philosophical thought within the academy, although Heidegger argues that the ability to think in this way is without exception founded upon the more fundamental characteristics of Dasein's Being. Part of Dasein's thinking of itself as a thing alongside other things lies in the understanding that it is contained within a world which can be described in the language of the natural sciences. Thus it thinks of itself as contained within a world of geometrical extension, while, as Hubert Dreyfus admirably puts it, being in the world is actually more akin to 'being in love' (ibid.). The character of the world which Dasein inhabits will be considered in more detail later in this book, when we come to discuss the relationship between human beings and material culture. The significant point at this stage is that in a similar way we think of ourselves as contained within a limitless expanse of featureless time, but that this understanding is in turn built upon a far more fundamental experience of temporality. If we return to Ricoeur's argument concerning the time of the world and the time of the soul, it is Heidegger's contention that human beings are fundamentally temporal. They have time written into their constitution, in that they have a past, a present and a future. The time of the world, public time or measurable clock time are abstracted from this basic temporality. The world of nature might have processes going on within it which proceed at a given rate, but no one would think to measure them in the first place if their attunement to existence were not one which was fundamentally temporal.

This temporal character of Dasein is connected with what we might choose to call the structure of human consciousness. Heidegger (1962, 264) would put this another way: Dasein is disclosed to itself. Dasein is 'there' for itself in its disclosure, which takes place through its understanding, its mood or 'being affected', its falling, and its telling (Blattner 1992, 102). These rather specialised terms require a good deal of explanation. Dasein becomes aware of itself as being already in a world, it gains self-identity only to find itself already enmeshed in a series of social and material relationships. Indeed, Dasein-ing as a practice is only possible as a bringing-together of self and world (Haugeland 1992, 35). So Dasein is already in a set of circumstances, it never has time to catch its breath before it is 'thrown' into the world, and it is always already-thrown because it never exists without a world. But its self-disclosure also involves the way that it is attuned toward its experiences in the world according to the *mood* that it is in at any given point: fear, angst, joy, being impartial or whatever. As Dreyfus (1991, 169) points out, these moods should not be thought of as essential psychological conditions so much as cultural sensitivities. By being a white, middle-class British male I am so attuned that I am likely to react in certain ways to particular phenomena, and these reactions reveal something about myself to me. My embarrassment in particular social situations, for instance, is not something that I have the option of adopting or discarding at will, but it tells me something about the way that I am. I do not choose my mood, and I do not choose my reactions: indeed, I am 'delivered over' to my mood, as Heidegger puts it. Understanding, by contrast, refers to the way that, even as I am becoming aware of myself, I am having to cope with the world around me. This understanding is not something that is exclusively cerebral: it is far more to do with having the skills (perhaps non-discursive skills, in Giddens' terms) which allow me to use equipment and negotiate social inter- action. But just as it implies a skilled coping with things, it also involves a skilled coping with myself as a social being. So I am disclosed to myself as already coping with social relationships.

Dasein's *telling* refers to its use of language, in the sense of telling others things, but also of telling things apart. Dasein is disclosed as a language- user, or a being which is already caught up in language. It might not be too far-fetched to draw a parallel here between the role of Dasein's telling in its disclosure and the significance of language or the symbolic in Lacan's arguments concerning the emergence of self-identity in the 'mirror stage' (Lacan 1977). According to Lacan, a young child reaches a certain stage of cognitive development at which it will recognise itself in a mirror, which coincides with the child's entry into the symbolic order, and language. Having recognised this first category of Self, however, the child must go on to oppose it to the second category, the Other. Rather than a unified world of self, the child must enter the sundered realm of Self and Other, signifier and signified, where it becomes possible to classify the things of the world (including the self) as discursive objects. In a similar way, Heidegger is suggesting that Dasein's disclosure emerges in part from becoming a language-user and using symbolic means to categorise world and self. The parallel with Lacan also provides a clue as to why the specialised term 'Dasein' is preferred over 'human being', in that it removes any possibility that what is being referred to is something which is first and foremost a biological organism. For while Dasein is always embodied and never pure consciousness, Dasein is also a particular way of engaging with the world, including the symbolic. This sense of *engagement* is also being referenced with Dasein's *falling*. By this, he means the way in which human beings tend to slip unthinkingly into habitual practices which are held in common by the social or cultural group. 'Falling' is a notion which is difficult to disentangle from Heidegger's concern with a distinction between 'authentic' and 'inauthentic' Being. For reasons which will be explained below, this duality is one which we might wish to regard with some caution. Moreover, there is a sense in which Heidegger always failed to adequately theorise the social, since he tended to see society as the common herd into which Dasein finds itself absorbed if it is unwary (Gosden 1994, 8). Heidegger argues that just as Dasein is delivered over to its moods, it is also of its nature drawn into the social world that surrounds it. Thus, for him, falling is falling-away from Dasein's possibility of authentic Being. Dasein gets fascinated by the glittery ephemera of life, gets caught up in idle gossip and speculation with others, and gets absorbed with itself, in the sense of worrying about its health or its appearance. Whether this falling requires there to be an authentic (and hence essential?) Being for Dasein to be fleeing from is another question, however. If we wish to resist the essentialist notion that Dasein can ever achieve some kind of wholeness or total self-identity, we could simply say that falling is one amongst a number of self-interpreting ways of Being in the world.

The character of Dasein's disclosure to itself is thus such that it always finds itself already hedged around with a series of constraints on how it acts, speaks and relates to the world. Of course, these various factors are enabling as well as constraining, and represent skills for coping with everyday existence. Taken together, they demonstrate the way that Dasein's situation in the world *matters* to it.

> Dasein is incapable of taking control of its being from the ground up, because the way that things matter to it guides the way it projects itself onto possibilities.
>
> (Blattner 1992, 111)

Dasein is disclosed to itself as a language-using, mood-ridden, culturally constructed social being, who has constantly to *get on* with its life. This condition of finding oneself already enmeshed in a series of social, cultural and material circumstances we might call *Dasein's thrownness*. That this disclosure is always concerned with the set of relations in which Dasein is engaged and with the way that its presence in the world matters to it means that Dasein is disclosed to itself in *care*. That is, all of these factors are unified in representing the way that its own Being 'gets to' Dasein: Dasein cares. Moreover, the nature of these different sources of care is such that they are temporal, that care is deeply bound up with Dasein's temporality. Understanding, the skilled coping with life, involves the formulation of projects for action, or being-ahead of oneself. Falling involves being-amidst the world, being with other persons and engaging with them or becoming absorbed with oneself and one's immediate circumstances. It follows that falling is a means of disclosure which is connected with the present. Mood, however, is concerned with the past. Being in a mood is to a greater or lesser extent to do with the continuity of one's person through time: one is already-in a mood. This being-already-in is an indication of Dasein's thrownness, such that Dasein always is as having-been (Blattner 1992, 102). Taking Dreyfus' perspective, it is also an indication of the cultural construction of Dasein's sensibilities: Dasein is as having-been-constructed. In its care, then, Dasein is revealed in a familiar and inconspicuous way as being temporal. This impression is increased by telling, or language-use. Language does not draw attention singularly to past, present or future, but involves all three in its constitution. Speaking, or using language as a means of classification, forces us to order our thoughts temporally. Our speech and writing are fundamentally narrative: they require that we deploy information in linear sequences structured by grammar and syntax. Moreover, language makes use of tenses, so that when we tell something we tell it as having-happened, as happening or as not-yet-having-happened. This connection between language and temporality is one which is of the utmost significance, since it is the ground of the notion that the sense of selfhood is found in narrative.

Heidegger (1962, 377) refers to past, present and future as the three 'ecstases' of temporality. Temporality, as a fundamental characteristic of Dasein, temporalises: it makes temporal. Thus temporality cannot be thought of as a thing or an externality: it is something that Dasein does. This making-temporal involves an orientation toward one's future possibilities, back to one's past, and a 'letting-oneself-be-encountered-by' (ibid.). This 'outside-of-itself' character of temporality, fundamental to disclosure, is the sense of ecstasis, taken from the Greek εκστασις. As in Augustine's argument, the three ecstases are seen as qualitatively separate in their significance for Dasein's care, rather than simply being arbitrary divisions of a linear, objective and external time. So in the sense that temporality is a feature of Dasein's Being, Heidegger is closer to the 'time of the soul' perspective. However, while conceptually separable, the ecstases form a fundamental unity bound together by the structure of care. If Dasein did not care about itself, there would be no temporality. Dasein cares in its thrownness, and this requires that all of the aspects of its disclosure must be present alongside each other. Care is always ahead of itself, already in the world, and alongside other beings. Thus there can be no future without a past and a present, and so on. Temporality is disclosed because of Dasein's care, but at the same time care is also made possible by Dasein's temporality (Gelven 1989, 179).

Because Dasein has this fundamentally temporal structure, it is possible for it to understand that past events have been, to recognise its co-presence with others, and to formulate its specific projects for the future. Thus the temporal structure of Dasein, which we might refer to as 'existential time' renders the temporal character of the things of the world comprehensible. In this sense, existential time grounds pragmatic time, the time of the world. Things that go on in the world can be dated, but that dating depends in the first instance upon the fixing of an event in a 'now' or a 'then' (future or past). The existential time of Dasein possesses what Heidegger calls a 'mine-ness', a certain immediacy of direct relevance to the person and their existence. In existential terms, the three ecstases are all coexistant. We commonly think of the past as dead and gone, and of the future as 'not yet now', but this refers merely to the concrete possibilities and happenings of future and past. While a specific event may or may not happen to me in the future, I 'have' a future which is as real to me as is the present. Equally, particular events have passed me by and are lost, but I am who and what I am, and I am in a particular mood because I 'have' a past. Existential time is also finite: the past is conceivable in terms of my having-been, and the future is significant as 'not yet'. The basis of human existence is finite time (Gelven 1989, 184). Once one extends time beyond the span of my past having-been and my future possibilities it is no longer connected with my care. In all of these particulars, pragmatic time differs from existential time. Pragmatic time is not 'mine': it is shared by society, it is a public time. Since public time is not tied to the existence of any one Dasein it is infinite: it can extend onward for ever and ever but I don't *care* about it. Because it is not directly connected with the projects and experiences of the person, its divisions can be quantitative. Particular 'nows' can be dated and the distance between them can be measured. Time can thus be conceived of as a series of dateable 'nows' clicking past like the pages of a flick-book. This kind of time, however, can only be constructed because we have a more fundamental, existential time to base it upon. According to Heidegger, where we go wrong is in believing that we can understand time in a fundamental way in terms of this derived and secondary public temporality. Thus a science of time, dedicated to explaining time as a natural phenomenon, is always dependent upon existential temporality. Dasein commonly believes the opposite to be true, that science gives a more fundamental understanding of the world, because of its *fallen* character. Dasein flees from its own temporal character into a belief that time is an attribute of the world.

Having a temporal character, and being positioned in a historical world as well as having characteristics which it has taken on from its culture,

Dasein's Being is historical. This historicity can be linked with Foucault's more recent arguments concerning the contingent character of human existence. In addition, Heidegger presents a series of notions which begin to make connections between Dasein's personal history and the history of human groups, or of the world. As we will see, these are concepts which have to be handled with some care, given both the unhappy connotations which they may convey and the ends to which Heidegger himself later turned them. Given Dasein's state of thrownness, and the way that it is always already-in a world and a state of attunement, it always has available to it a set of possibilities for future action, which are described as the 'heritage' (Heidegger 1962, 435). Dasein does not choose these possibilities, but they do not represent a straightjacket either (Ricoeur 1988, 74). Dasein has handed its possibilities down to itself, and this is an operation which is only open to a historical being (Murray 1970, 19). An animal, for instance, is not in the position of being able to act on the basis of accumulated knowledge: the animal exists purely in the now. This handing down of possibilities from the self to the self has the effect of 'stretching' Dasein's Being across time. The movement of self-stretching across time is the source of a person's self-identity, in that the person one is now has a historical connection with the person whom one was yesterday.

Paul Ricoeur (1991) has pointed out one of the fundamental paradoxes of identity: are an acorn and the oak tree that it grows into the *same* thing? In one sense, of course, they are fundamentally different, and yet they are linked by the continuity of process by which one thing becomes another. Thus they share an identity. In the case of a human being, one might say that one is a different person to the one which one was ten years ago, and yet the sense of identity is maintained by the handing down of possibilities. Sets of events in the present are linked with memories of the past, so that one is able to construct a narrative which runs through them. Self-stretching, self-constancy and narrativity thus lie behind the possibility of self-identity: the self is a story which it tells to itself. Having to remain the same person as one has been, and having to accept the set of possibilities which one hands down to oneself is what Heidegger refers to as one's *fate*. Just as the existential future refers to one's having a future rather than any content of that future, so 'fate' implies no predestination other than in having to accept and take up the burden of one's own past, which provides the resources for the negotiation of future projects.

THE SUBJECT AND THE SELF

Having followed Heidegger's arguments concerning time and personal identity this far, it should be clear that there are affinities between his 'anti-humanism' and the 'de-centred' conception of the human subject that prevails in much contemporary social theory. This being the case, it may be useful to draw out some aspects of these understandings of subjectivity, before considering temporal dimensions of identity and selfhood in more detail. Several different schemes of social thought have chosen to draw attention to different aspects of human existence, and it may be possible to find echoes of Heidegger's thought in several of them, while at the same time the degree of their elaboration is such that they can add something to an understanding of the way that human beings are in time. Within Cartesian thought, the human being is composed of a body, which obeys the laws of nature, and a mind lodged within the body yet somehow distinct. Both of these aspects of the person are given in their entirety. However, the development of structural linguistics, and the recognition that the signifier (word or symbol) and the signified (the thing or concept being referred to) are never identical, did considerable damage to this conception of a self-contained subject. For it follows that 'I' can only come to know 'myself' through the medium of language. The subject is not a fully formed consciousness that comes into the world and takes up language as a means of expressing its primordial thoughts and experiences. Rather, as we have seen, it is necessary for the subject to be inserted into language in order to develop a sense of self-identity (Lacan 1977). In so doing, however, the subject must take on board a symbolic system, which is given by the culture to which it is becoming attuned: identity depends upon recourse to an externality. Moreover, the sense of selfhood can only be achieved at the cost of the recognition of the alternate category, the Other. According to Lacan, the consequence of this recognition is a sundering of the infant's world, which, through the transitory 'mirror stage', has maintained a certain unity. Where there is only a recognition of Self, there is not yet any Other. But as soon as the categories by which we classify the world begin to emerge, it begins to fragment and lose its unity. This fragmentation, as the price of reflexive self-identity, sets up a fundamental drive to achieve a return to an imaginary state of wholeness which, by definition, can never be reached.

In that it must insert itself into the networks of the symbolic system in order to become a 'Self', the subject is always fundamentally absent from itself, always dispersed and fragmented in webs of signification. The self is constructed in language. The externality from which it must emerge is the sphere of the social rather than the individual, and will be historically and culturally contingent. The subject is thus constructed in a realm which is outside of itself, and this realm is one not simply of language and culture, but also of power relations (Hacking 1986). Some, like Althusser, have presented this process as one in which the subject is created as a helpless dupe, whose own identity is an illusion forced upon it, which serves to integrate it into the social formation and the process of material production. Foucault, however, came to stress the production of identity as a self-formation which was distinctively reflexive and hermeneutic in character. Here one is close again to Heidegger, and the notion that Dasein's Being lies in self-interpretation. Dews (1989, 40) suggests that this perspective implies a paradox, whereby the self must somehow already exist in order to begin to interpret itself. A partial answer to this problem lies in the understanding that personal identity is inscribed upon the existing matter of the human body, so that the self is at once outside of itself and anchored in the physicality of being a person. Society and culture provide a historically specific 'technology of the self', through which identity is crafted temporally in the process of self-interpretation. Hence there is nothing fundamental about the self; its identity is interpretation 'all the way down' (Foucault 1988a). Moreover, it is not that 'a subjectivity', as a whole object, is grafted on to a body at a certain stage in its development. This would imply another retreat into the Cartesian mind–body duality. Rather, the body forms the site from which subjectivity is exercised, and through which the practice of self-interpretation is lived and experienced.

The real paradox of human existence is thus that subjectivity is at once dispersed, and outside of itself, and yet embodied and located spatially and temporally. The self is the developing site of this enterprise. Thrift (1991, 461) usefully draws out some of the implications of such a conception of subjectivity. In that identities emerge from a self-interpretation which is inscribed upon the physical body, subjects can be seen as texts, and as being positioned in relation to power and space. In that this interpretation and inscription is a construction, it is one which is spread across time: thus the self is a narrative text. Thrift acknowledges the way that subjects are dispersed, fragmented, outside and beyond themselves, and that this dispersal is located in the realm of the symbolic. Thus subjects are bound up with discourses (a conception perhaps similar to Foucault's concern with technologies of the self), yet this immersion is not one within which they are powerless. They constantly 'test' those discourses: 'subjects are dialogical, bringing specific personas, discourses and voices to contexts of negotiation and domination' (ibid.).

The subject, the self, and Dasein represent three ways of conceiving different aspects of human Being. The subject is constructed in the symbolic realm, through a process of self-interpretation. That identity which emerges in the process is the self. Dasein, as a concept, draws attention to the way that subjectivity is always lived in an embodied form, so that a person encounters herself as always already constituted as a subject. One further aspect of the person is emphasised by Anthony Giddens when he writes of the 'agent', in that a human being is also a site from which agency is exercised. The agent acts, but it does so under conditions over which it has very limited control. Hence Giddens talks of a 'stratified model of agency', such that the agent will only be able to account verbally for a proportion of their acts. Over and above the unconscious, a person will partake of a discursive and a nondiscursive consciousness. Thus many of the acts of the agent will be routine and unconsidered, employing skills which are not learned in words and which would be difficult to verbalise. Indeed, the act of trying to make what one is doing at any time explicit can interrupt the flow of action: one thinks here of falling off a bicycle as a result of attempting to 'hold in the mind' the operations of turning the pedals, steering and changing gear (Giddens 1991, 36). While there is a Freudian inflexion in what Giddens is suggesting here, it also connects with Heidegger's description of the way in which equipment 'recedes' from our conscious awareness when it is engaged in the enactment of a project. As long as the hammer is successfully hammering nails, we cease to be aware of it as a thing, and concentrate instead on the task in hand (Heidegger 1962, 98). For Giddens, acts can be undertaken at a discursive or nondiscursive level, and can have unintended consequences as well as being based upon unacknowledged conditions (1984, 7). Yet actions and their consequences are continuously monitored by the agent, who can modify her conduct reflexively. What is perhaps most helpful about Giddens' account is the recognition of a connectedness between a certain form of conscious agency and the ability to formulate and describe projects in language. Hence even those projects characterised by 'mineness' depend upon the agent's cultural construction and affiliation for their constitution. Similarly, the way that even tasks which are learned discursively may in time slip into the realm of the routine and the nondiscursive carries echoes of the 'falling' into the 'they-self'. This, perhaps, allows us to return to Heidegger in such a way as to avoid the essentialism of the appeal to authentic Dasein.

This same point could perhaps be pressed further by connecting Heidegger's notion of the 'they-self', *das Mann*, with Bourdieu's concept of the *habitus*, thereby giving some strength to Heidegger's assertion that falling should not be seen in entirely pejorative terms. In that one is disclosed to oneself as already-fallen, it could be said that one has always already acquired certain habitual ways of acting at a nondiscursive level, 'a matrix of perceptions, appreciations, and actions' (Bourdieu 1977, 83). Bourdieu's point is that much of our everyday practice takes the form of a stream of improvisations that are grounded upon structuring principles absorbed in the person's early youth: 'a spontaneity without consciousness or will' (Bourdieu 1990b, 56). The classic exposition of this hypothesis is the study of the Kabyle house (Bourdieu 1970), in which the cosmological layout of domestic space provides a mechanism for the internalisation of the principles of a cultural order, simply through the enactment of everyday life. Without having to have the 'rules' of behaviour explained to them verbally, children gradually build up an instinctual knowledge of cultural categories, learned from experience. Because this knowledge is learned through the encounter with the world, what is taken in is a product of collective history, yet its unconsidered character enshrines it as that which is taken for granted. If and when it is ever reflected on or questioned, it has the character of common sense, the 'natural attitude'. So arbitrary and culturally contingent ways of doing things are incorporated into habitual practice, and are thereby reproduced. Because the internalised set of principles that allow improvised action, the *habitus*, originates in shared conditions of being-alongside others, persons in social or spatial proximity who share certain experiences will share elements of the same *habitus*. It is this holding in common of an unuttered basis for action which makes the practices of the agent comprehensible to others, and thus forms the basis for the coordination and integration of collective action (Bourdieu 1977, 80). Again, this unconsidered knowledge, learned nondiscursively, bears a similarity to Heidegger's description of the primordeal understandings which provide the ground of the possibility of scientific 'objective knowing'.

While it might be misleading to suggest that all of these different under-standings of human Being could be integrated into a new synthesis, it may be that each helps to light up particular points which pertain to human temporality. Moreover, one point which they largely hold in common is the suggestion that the formation of human subjects is not a process which has had the same form, or been carried out through the same agencies, at all times in all places. As Foucault in particular demonstrates, the regimes of power, knowledge and bodily control which constitute the space within which the subject emerges have been radically different at different times in the history of the west. This is all the more so when we come to consider a broader range of human diversity, as represented in ethnography and prehistory. It is not merely that the human subject is constituted by different mechanisms, but, as anthropologists have repeatedly demon-strated, the business of being a human being is conceptualised, experienced, managed and lived through in radically different ways (e.g. Geertz 1973; Battaglia 1990). As has often been pointed out, archaeologists would do well to avoid inflicting the western, capitalist, modernist conception of the individual as a sovereign, self-contained decision-maker onto pasts to which it is probably highly inappropriate (Shanks and Tilley 1987, 62). Human subjects become aware of themselves as positioned in both space and time. In the first place this means that they have available to them as resources for self-formation other human beings and a range of material things. At one point, Heidegger would have described the things at least as an 'equip-mental totality', but it might be equally useful to consider a notion of the later Heidegger: the way that each thing on earth *gathers* the world around itself in its own way (Heidegger 1977b, 329; Dreyfus 1992, 180). While Heidegger uses this term largely to consider inanimate things, we might suggest that in the same way as the bridge over the river gathers earth and sky around itself, so a human subject as a site of interpretation gathers its selfhood from its involvements in the world. So it is not the case that each human subject is merely a node in a uniform global network: the work of self-disclosure gathers the world into sites. In the second place, human beings are positioned in relation to their own temporality: they bear the burden of having a particular heritage which they have handed down to themselves, and this set of possibilities gives them a future. Groups of persons as well as individuals have a sense of identity that is generated by history, and this in turn creates a set of local resources for the formation of subjects.

These points are well illustrated by Brenda Clay's study of the creation of Mandak Big Men in New Ireland (1992). As Clay points out, anthropologists have tended to interpret the institutional positions of non-western societies as if they were occupied by western individuals. Thus the discourse on Big Men and Great Men in Melanesia is dominated by the distinction between individuals who achieve status and others who have status ascribed to them by inheritance. All of this assumes that the individual exists as such in advance of the acquisition of authority, as if this authority itself were a thing which was to be passed from hand to hand. For the Mandak, personhood is more relational than concerned with individuality, such that people are conceived of as manifesting aspects of cross-cutting sets of relationships. None the less, persons are thought of as sites from which agency is exercised. Agency, however, is clearly something which is vested in persons by virtue of their production as agents of a particular sort, which in turn is a relational practice. Thus 'becoming a Big Man' is better described as 'being constructed as a Big Man', and depends upon the establishment of a set of relationships with a group of 'witnesses': other Big Men (Clay 1992, 723). Thus the production of the Big Man as agent is an event which is enacted in the setting of a mortuary feast, in the presence of a gathering (I use the word here in Heidegger's sense as well as the conventional one) of Big Men, and of ancestors who are being evoked. It is not society at large that confers agent status upon the aspirant Big Man; it is a gathering that is localised in both space and time. The production of a certain kind of person is thus contingent upon synchronous relations with others who constitute a network of power, and narrative relations with others who have been, who have made a particular set of possibilities available. As Clay points out, it is the calling to mind of ancestors that establishes each witness as such (ibid., 725), so that the whole gathering might be seen as drawn together around the event of the mortuary feast, and yet boundless, potentially unravelling at its edges. The relational network runs off through social space and back into ancestry, since no person is a fixed and bounded identity at which the running-on of relational identity can come to a halt. It is this character of the gathering as a knot within a fabric which constantly slips away into dispersal which demonstrates the unstable character of the material from which personal identity must be crafted.

IDENTITY, NARRATIVE AND MEMORY

Heidegger's account of the temporality and historicity of Dasein has brought us to an understanding of human identity as being stretched across time. It is the fate of a person to accept a heritage of possibilities which is drawn from one's own past, and to pass it down to oneself (Ricoeur 1988, 75). As a result, human beings have a constancy through time. In *Being and Time* Heidegger is able to dismiss any notion of a subject who is whole and self-contained at each moment of a time conceived as a series of 'nows'. What one might infer from this is that human beings are not merely de-centred within webs of signification, but that their Being is dispersed through time. One is never a whole in that the whole of one's possibilities are never simultaneously present to one. In practice, Heidegger suggests exactly the opposite, by introducing the notion of an authentic Being which can be grasped by facing resolutely towards one's ownmost possibility. That is to say, as Dasein is a finite being who must die, the single possibility which is at once its most intimate, non-transferable and unavoidable is the certainty of its own death (Heidegger 1962, 304). This does not concern the particular character and circumstances of death, but the inevitability of ceasing to be Dasein, and it is this possibility from which Dasein constantly flees by burying itself in the everyday. However, Heidegger argues, if one can resolutely grasp and face up to the inevitability in a 'moment of vision', what becomes possible is an authentic Being-towards-death. This fundamental orientation makes it possible for Dasein to grasp its own possibilities in such a way as to draw together past, present and future into an authentic whole: a moment of total Being. The essentialism of this view is relatively clear, but it is also this notion of grasping one's fate and destiny which, when transferred from the singular Dasein to the collective, surely provides the means by which Heidegger's ideas became susceptible to the perversion which aligned them with Nazism. Thus I will argue that Heidegger's ideas are best used by pushing them beyond themselves, and purging them entirely of the 'metaphysics of presence'.

One way this can be achieved is the means employed by Paul Ricoeur in *Time and Narrative* (1988), in which he stresses the collective and cultural character of the process of drawing on the past in order to achieve a sense of selfhood. For Ricoeur, the drawing-together of the ecstases of temporality is not a mystical and lonely moment dragged back from the levelling influence of the crowd, but a dialogical practice connected with Dasein's telling (Clark 1990, 164). Dasein can produce an account of itself as an entity, but it is only a story. Yet if we take this argument a step further, we can argue not merely that Dasein produces a narrative as an understanding of its historical Being, but that it is the process of passing down possibilities from the past to the present which *produces* the subject. The narrative of selfhood is constitutive rather than reflecting an essential self. By drawing upon past experiences and ordering them in such a way as to make sense, the self is constantly bringing itself into existence. This narrative or autobiography may be selective, such that it will be connected with what Foucault might call an aesthetic of the self, and at the same time it will involve a public giving account of the self.

Dasein *has* a past, but not all aspects of this past contribute equally to the sense of self-identity and self-constancy through time. How the personal and public past can be drawn on in the formation of identity (whether personal or of the group) is clearly related to the issue of memory. Autobiographical and social memory take on considerable significance once we acknowledge their role in constituting persons and social collectivities. Memory is a complex phenomenon, concerned with language in that what one remembers is the significance of experiences (Giddens 1984, 45), but also involving the hauling-back of sights, smells and other sensory experiences (Fentress and Wickham 1992, 36). Since memory is a representation and interpretation of the past to oneself which is linguistically mediated (even if we may find it difficult to put it into words) it is also socially constructed. Just as we experience the world we inhabit through the 'as-structure' (we feel something *as* the west wind on our face, as Heidegger says; we do not feel a stream of molecules), so the past is remembered-as: it always already has a significance and is pieced into narrative accordingly. However, while a part of the story of the self is given by the reordering of past events and experiences, it must be emphasised that memory is incorporated into a present in which the self is embodied. As John Berger points out, the body through which we live is ageing, rotting away from day to day (Berger 1984, 36), and part of the significance of memory is to make us aware that we are not as we were. Similarly, following Julia Kristeva (1986a, 187), this embodied experience of time is not the same for all persons. Everyday time is gendered, in that women are forcibly and repeatedly reminded of the cyclical character of their own biology. In consequence, the way in which women order and understand their own autobiographies may be rather different to that of men. Similarly, the imposition of cultural schemes of time organisation onto the everyday experience of persons will impact upon their conception of past and present. As Berger suggests (1984), the introduction of clock-time and work time associated with the alienation of labour in industrial capitalism may sever people from the older rhythms of everyday experience. All of these factors suggest that the way in which the narrative of self is constructed will be highly context-specific.

The self is thus rather like a narrative text, which involves a poetics (in the sense of a construction) (Ricoeur 1988, 4). Fentress and Wickham (1992, 6) put forward the suggestion that the remembered past may be seen as a text – yet their model of the text is very much the historian's one, a bounded physical piece of writing. By contrast, the kind of text described by Roland

Barthes (1977) is a space of productivity, a site of engagement and labour: it is not a work. This is not a thing in a place, but a methodological field. 'The work is held in the hand, the text in language' (ibid., 39). The text is a site for the production of, exploration of and struggle with meanings: 'a polysemic space where the paths of several possible meanings intersect' (ibid., 37). The potential meanings of a given set of signifiers are limitless, and textual practice involves the crafting of an individual meaning from the raw material made available, by following the networks and chains of connection through which the text explodes out beyond itself. Within archaeology, the model of the text has perhaps been understood in too literal a way (see Buchli 1995). Particularly in recent critiques of the approach, the 'textual analogy' is reduced to no more than the suggestion that material objects can be read like written texts (but see Olsen 1990 for a more subtle approach). Following Barthes, text is a quality or process which is engendered by all forms of signifying practices. Indeed, textual practice does not require the presence of a written work at all: one can simply place oneself in front of the world and engage with it in such a way as to undertake the labour of meaning-production. This is precisely what the practice of archaeology involves (Shanks 1992, 178).

Memory can be compared to textual practice in so far as it provides an archive of past experiences, which can be summoned in a labour of inter-pretation which is simultaneously a process of self-construction. Moreover, memory is intertextual. Personal experiences become intertwined with public events in the creation of autobiography (Rubin 1986, 13). Thus in the modern west, our personal pasts involve the remembering of dress codes, commercial products which were available at particular times (and their packaging), popular songs (which 'define an era') and historical happenings. In Britain, people of a certain age remember vividly their doings on the day of the last coronation, while in a larger arena thousands of individuals can recall the precise moment at which President Kennedy was assassinated. Memory is thus a text which is continuously being re-worked in the present and, as I have hinted, is bound up with material things as well as past events. Material objects were in the past, yet continue to exist into the present, and thus can call the past to mind. The role of objects in memory and biography will be considered in more detail in the next chapter.

In this chapter we have suggested that archaeology's explicit concern with time (as dating, seriation, sequence) has served to cover over the more fundamental role of temporality in human existence. Since time provides the framework of our investigation (which is necessarily an externality), it has proved difficult to recognise the way that time is implicated in human social life. By the means of a reading of Heidegger, I have hoped to demonstrate the temporal character of the existence of human subjects, in that their whole sense of personal identity depends upon having a past, present and future. These three ecstases are absolute, yet their content is far more fluid and negotiable. Moreover, it is inherently to be interpreted. The character of a person's future is clearly indeterminate: it is a matter of possibilities which are projected forward. Yet the past also is indeterminate, in that it provides a resource which we deploy in a selective and strategic manner. Our own past is necessarily something which we have to reconstruct from fragments, and these fragments may have to be juggled and played off against each other if we are to construct a story which is coherent. Some of our past actions may have to be dismissed as aberrations if the self is to be thought of as something which has a definable character. It may be that, in doing this, we are actively producing that defined essence. While this account has striven to work 'from the bottom up', in concentrating on the experiences of temporality and personhood at the level of the subject, it has not been the intention to suggest that the individual has any fundamental and essential character which precedes the constitution of the social or cultural collectivity. I have hoped to emphasise the way in which the formation of personal identity is contingent upon the existence of social context and cultural tradition. It is to the material aspect of context and tradition that we now turn.

MATERIAL THINGS AND THEIR TEMPORALITY

——— •◆• ———

INTRODUCTION

In this chapter I will extend the analysis of human temporality offered in Chapter Two to consider material things and the way in which they exist through time. I will suggest that in many ways the temporal structure of things bears a similarity to that of human beings, and that this is a consequence of their being encompassed by the structure of human care. However, it may be useful to introduce this discussion by relating these issues to a continuing debate regarding the way that archaeologists conceive of the material world. Where we look on material things as the consequence of human action in the past, it may be that society comes to be reified into a metaphysical entity divorced from materiality. By contrast, recent work which places the concept of 'the archaeological record' in question does much to remind us that social life is lived out *through* the material world. However, I wish to add to this perspective the suggestion that when we use material traces as evidence for past human activities, we are adopting a quite specific attunement toward material things. Although this way of dealing with materiality is characteristic of the discipline of archaeology, and I will refer to it as 'the archaeological imagination', it is not restricted to members of the archaeological profession, and it may represent one way amongst others in which people habitually cope with their world.

ON THE ARCHAEOLOGICAL 'RECORD' AND THE ARCHAEOLOGICAL IMAGINATION

Necessarily, what follows will paraphrase two important recent considerations of 'the archaeological record', which have been presented by Linda Patrik (1985) and John Barrett (1988a), although with the aim in mind of qualifying both. Patrik's opening argument is that while many archaeologists may use the term 'the archaeological record' as a shorthand for the range of materials, deposits and other information which serve as the raw material of their craft, they often mean quite different things by it. In particular, Patrik draws a distinction between two understandings of the notion of a record: a fossil and a textual record. These two models form the grounds for two quite different forms of archaeology: one processual and scientistic, one contextual and symbolic. As Schiffer (1987, 5) indicates, the New Archaeology of the 1960s relied upon a notion of correlation, whereby past human behaviour could be related directly to a set of physical outcomes. The task of the archaeologist was then simply to comprehend the lawlike and universal processes by which dynamic actions were transformed into a static record. In Patrik's terms, this is the model of the fossil record, in which the creation of archaeological remains is seen as the equivalent of a natural, physiochemical process. Thus, in the case of palaeontology, the existence of the fossil remains of an animal's skeleton is taken as the basis for the inference that a particular kind of animal once existed. In these circumstances the 'recording' referred to is the outcome of the operation of natural agencies. In a similar way, much of the archaeological writing of the processual school assumed that the relationship between human action and its archaeological correlates was an equally straightforward one. However, Schiffer (1972) was to present a rather different conception of the archaeological record by instituting a distinction between *systemic context* and *archaeological context*. That is, Schiffer held that objects and materials are taken out of nature and circulate in a series of engagements with a social system until such a time as they are discarded, deposited or lost. They are then transferred into the archaeological context (figure 3.1). This archaeological context is a record of sorts, yet it is a record that requires translation. Indeed, the central phenomenon with which archaeologists should concern themselves is the constellation of 'formation processes' that give rise to and transform this record (Schiffer 1987, 7). Both prior to and subsequent to their deposition, objects and materials are being affected by natural and cultural processes which have physical consequences. So, following the arguments developed in Chapter One, it would seem that 'behavioural archaeology' is another example of a mode of archaeological thought which is firmly embedded in the culture/nature dichotomy.

Schiffer's later work perhaps represents an advance from this position, in that it begins to erode the division between the traces which an object accumulates in its 'life' and those which result from post-depositional processes. None the less, one could argue that Binford's central criticism, that Schiffer appears to consider archaeological remains as being a record of a functioning system which is somehow stopped in time, has not been answered satisfactorily (Binford 1981). Indeed, it seems possible that any adherence to a belief that archaeological evidence represents a record as such falls foul of this so-called 'Pompeii Premise'. The very notion of a 'record' implies a separation between an absent past and the here-and-now present. The past is something which has stopped, is ended, and its boundedness from the present seems to guarantee its integrity as a sutured entity.

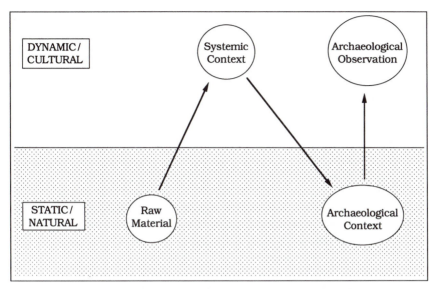

Figure 3.1 Michael Schiffer's 'behavioural archaeology'

In other words, the past is a 'thing', which can be reduced to an essence, which is contained within the record. Hence it is highly revealing that Schiffer (1987, 3) draws a categorical distinction between the archaeological record and the *historical* record, which represents for him not merely written texts, but artefacts that 'remain part of an ongoing society' (ibid.). Schiffer clearly makes this division in order to distinguish between the relative sets of epistemological problems faced by those working in the historical and prehistoric eras. Despite this, it demonstrates the way in which he thinks of the prehistoric past as a remote entity which we must recover as a functioning whole – the behavioural context. Schiffer's world is one of essences, which are overtaken at various times by discontinuous events that leave behind their traces. In this respect, his thinking is curiously redolent of 'normative' culture-historic archaeology. The object, the arte-fact, is first taken from nature by an act of transformation which brings it into the social system, or the world of culture. From then on it is animated by human purposes until such a time as it is discarded. It dies. Yet as an element of the archaeological record it can undergo further transformation, by human or natural intervention. Implicitly, though, the impression is that these 'transformations' are distortions which need to be filtered out in order for us to arrive at the primal truth of the artefact and its behavioural context.

In discussing the means by which traces are mapped onto objects, Schiffer recognises four dimensions in the variability of artefacts: formal, spatial, quantitative and relational (1987, 15-16). This suggests that his understanding of things fits into two of the traditional philosophical modes of defining thingness: things as bearers of traits, and things as formed matter (Heidegger 1971a, 30). So an artefact is seen as a piece of raw matter which has been fashioned into a cultural form, and which can then serve as a repository for subsequent marks, scratches and stains that may distort or obscure the original design. As Heidegger suggests, such approaches are flawed in representing things as *mere* things: that is, as isolated and alienated objects to which things can be *done*. On this objectification is built the separation of systemic context and archaeological context, and of past and present. As we have seen, this way of thinking makes the ethnocentric move of dividing nature from society, and of seeing nature as a given realm from which materials are extracted and transformed into artefacts. In Heidegger's terms, this means that the world has come to 'stand reserve', as a giant storehouse of resources. This can be argued to be the product of a historically and culturally specific, technological, understanding of Being, which allows things to show up in a distinctive way: not necessarily a way which bears very much relation to the prehistoric past. According to this view, nature is inert and passive, and has to have life breathed into it by society. When things exit from the behavioural context, they thus return to a static condition, passively impacted upon by cultural and natural processes. In this chapter, I will suggest that a more complex set of relationships exists between persons and things, and that social relationships interpenetrate with the material world in ways which negate any notion of nature as an entirely separate realm from which things are translated and to which they return.

Significantly, Lewis Binford, who castigates Schiffer for presenting the archaeological record as a representation of a frozen social system (a behavioural context which has stopped behaving), none the less conceives of that record as something static and object-like (Patrik 1985, 38). The archaeological record is immobile, yet records a vital and changing adaptive process. The record is something material, which exists 'here with us in the present' (Binford 1983, 19), and our task is to decode or translate it into statements concerning past ways of life: the generalities of adaptive process rather than the specifics of history. However, Binford's approach results in a far more categorical division of past and present even than Schiffer's. The archaeological record for him is totally object and objective. It is at once ontologically separate from the past and epistemologically distinct from present-day social relations. Archaeological remains do not contain any 'pastness' that can be extracted from out of them, but neither do they have any involvement in contemporary values and understandings. So the archaeological record may not have 'stopped', in mid-motion, like Pompeii, but it is just as dead. This separation from past processes and from present observers means that the archaeological record becomes something hermetically sealed, and it is this move which allows the construction of a 'science of the archaeological record'. We can undertake research in the present to consider what happens when dogs scavenge the carcass of a wildebeest, or when a person walks over a scatter of potsherds, and these actualistic investigations can give meaning to the contemporary observations that we make upon the archaeological record. Middle Range Theory, which constitutes the archaeological record as a world in itself, thus relies upon its disengagement from any other world. The past has happened, and any subsequent happenings are simply sources of distortions which need to be removed from the surface. The record may be scratched, but the tune in the grooves remains unchanged.

In recent years, the evident weakness of the fossil record model of Binford and Schiffer has given rise to a competing framework, in which the archaeological record is conceived of as being text-like (Hodder 1986; 1988; 1989; Patrik 1985, 42). Within this scheme of things the evidence studied by archaeologists represents less an imprint of past actions than something which has been encoded. All human practices are considered as signifying practices, and all human acts convey significance. Since any action contains sense, and has consequences which are separate from its 'author', the methodologies of textual analysis (whether structuralist or hermeneutic) are appropriate to acts and their material consequences (Ricoeur 1981). Even acts as simple as the disposal of rubbish, the building of shelters, or the making of a pot are meaningfully constituted, because in carrying them out agents deploy cultural categories, traditions, symbolic connotations and associations. In making and depositing things, people may be seeking to convey some message, or they may simply be reproducing cultural encodings at an unconscious level. Like words, the significance of things is arbitrary, conventional and slippery (Tilley 1989), and it follows from this that material things may have a plurality of meanings. The material world around us is inherently to-be-interpreted. So, in day-to-day life, human beings are routinely monitoring and interpreting their material surroundings, picking up meanings from material things which give them clues and cues regarding how to act from one moment to the next (Moore 1986).

The textual analogy suggests that the materials we call the archaeological record are ambiguous and polysemic, and there is no straightforward relationship between the thing in the past and the record in the present such as we would associate with the fossil. The issue is complicated by the play between signifier and signified: the ultimately undecideable meaning of the symbol (Derrida 1986). Following this argument, we are obliged to read the archaeological record as we would read a written text (although perhaps not a text in the Barthesian sense mentioned in Chapter Two above). We do not simply read an unambiguous message *out* of the record, we read an interpretation *into* it. Moreover, because this text is one which was encoded in a different cultural context (or series of contexts) from that in which it is to be read, our archaeological engagement is an hermeneutic one which involves trying to flesh out that alien context (Johnson and Olsen

1992). One way in which it has been suggested that this might be achieved is by considering the networks of relationships which give meaning to artefacts (Hodder 1986, 124-34). That is to say, an object never signifies in and of itself, but through a web of relations with other things which makes up a context, a signifying field, the material equivalent of a language. Far from merely reading off the meaning of the archaeological record, we become caught up in a complex running-on of material signifiers.

This notion of the archaeological record as a text is an attractive one, yet Barrett (1988a) is able to develop some important criticisms. Barrett's doubt 'that such texts are capable of adequate translation' (ibid., 6) is perhaps only relevant where one contends that an originary and unitary past meaning can be read out from material culture. It may be more germane to suggest that the interpretations of material culture which we create belong to the present rather than the past, and must be seen as partial and situated (Shanks and Tilley 1989, 4). More crucial is Barrett's observation that the whole notion of a record implies that one is concerned with a static outcome of past dynamics (Barrett 1988a, 9). This way of thinking inevitably leads to a picture of societies as metaphysical entities, which leave the lifeless record of their actions behind them as an animal leaves behind its droppings. As Barrett argues, social practice is in no way separate from the material world: material things are media which are drawn upon and deployed in social action. Consequently, the material world is continuously reworked in the unending performance of social life.

Such a perspective also confirms that Schiffer's division between the systemic context and the archaeological context is an illusory one. There is no hard division to be made between those objects and materials which are engaged in social relations and those which have been laid to rest. Rather, human beings are constantly re-encountering and re-evaluating their material surroundings, perhaps awarding them altered significances in relation to the formulation of their projects. Material things are consequently repositioned and reincorporated into society as they become absorbed in our circumspection, slip away from us in neglect, or return to our notice. Things are not at one moment 'in' a social system and at the next moment 'out' of it. Indeed, the mere fact of having become waste material, discarded or cast aside does not sever a thing from human concern, since the very category of rubbish may be significant in structuring cosmological divisions between purity and defilement (Douglas 1966; Moore 1986, Chapter 6). Waste materials can mark out restricted locations, and defiled substances can perform important roles in society (Parry 1982). The notion of an archaeological record implies that one is attempting to recover a particular state in which these materials fitted together to constitute a unified system which we can describe in its totality. Yet the relationships between persons and things are constantly in motion. As Heraclitus had it: everything flows.

The erasure of a division between the 'living' social system or behavioural context and the 'dead' archaeological record in turn does away with the gulf between the present and an utterly distant past. I am not claiming here that the past is directly accessible to us. Binford was wholly correct to point out that the material things which we study exist in the present and are no longer engaged in a particular set of past social relations which we as archaeologists might be interested in. The past has gone, and archaeological remains gain their particular significance in alerting us to the having-been of past human beings (Heidegger 1962, 431-3). They stand as evidence of past Being. But between those past persons and ourselves there has been no radical moment of severance, in which a 'past' has given way overnight to an utterly separate 'present', as would be implied by the 'Pompeii Premise'. There has been no point at which the evidence which we study has been 'unworlded', totally decontextualised and stripped of any significance whatsoever. Rather, things and their meanings have been handed down as a heritage, from one generation to another, losing something in their significance but also gaining something. The process by which the past context has *become* the present context will have been gradual and incremental. The world which is composed of human beings and things is continuously in motion, handing itself down to itself. Even if a particular object has lain buried for thousands of years, what intervenes between burial and recovery is a period of history, not a blank or void. Social relations and cultural traditions will have been transformed over this time, but they will not have been altogether absent. While the specific artefact may not have been in use or even in contact with human beings, it will still give indications to its discoverers of its character *as an artefact*, of some kind. A thing will rarely become so alien as to be literally meaningless, or culturally neutral. Hence we will only infrequently come to archaeological evidence in a condition of dispassionate objectivity towards it.

So when we come to interpret archaeological evidence, we will rarely find ourselves looking at something which outwardly *appears* so completely 'Other' that it escapes being immediately recontextualised through our prejudices and assumptions, before we have any opportunity to interrogate it analytically. No artefact ever truly dies, in that as long as we can recognise it as an artefact at all it is networked in a series of complex ways with all of the other artefacts which have ever been. That is, all equipmental things belong to a 'world of things' (Vycinas 1961, 119). This is the sense of what Heidegger means by the 'equipmental totality': things which have a connection with human purposes can be recognised through their myriad relationships with other equipment, even if we can never know this totality in its whole or grasp the entire significance of any one element. Since this equipmental totality has been passed down continuously by humankind, constantly changing and transforming in the process, we are not at liberty to look at the material evidence as a total object. While the particular configuration of social relationships within which an object was crafted is gone (was gone immediately, since such relationships are never stable), and the people involved in those relationships may all be dead, we cannot say that the evidence does not today exist in a social context. This is not to say that that social context is fixed, or that the significance of an artefact is in any sense essential. If a particular buried object were dug up and reburied once in every century, the set of relationships in which it would find itself would be different on each occasion, and so would be the successive ways in which it would be interpreted. But it would never mean *nothing*. Each time it would be recontextualised, since it would exist in a present and yet carry something of a past with it. This is the paradoxical nature of archaeological evidence; it finds a place for itself into our contemporary understanding of the world, some part of which is inherited from the past, and yet it has also a certain Otherness by virtue of what is *not* there: the past contexts of which it has formed a part. One aspect of archaeological analysis must therefore be the struggle to recognise the difference implicit in the artefact, in the face of the tendency to recognise it as something familiar.

In that all material things, as part of the equipmental totality, are passed down, reworked, and their significance renegotiated, they are always already involved in social relationships when we come to excavate them. When we undertake archaeological analysis, what we are doing is taking some part or parts of the material world out of the continuous stream of history and constituting them as objects. Thus although the model of the textual record may be flawed, the nature of these things as 'evidence' is not automatically given. Rather, in order to 'do archaeology' we have to recognise certain things as representing evidence. Archaeological analysis is consequently a specific form of 'clearing' which enables entities to be recognised in a very specific kind of a way. To put it another way, we have to recreate entities as evidence, by transforming them from things into objects. This objectification is always a political act, since it is performed upon materials which already exist in a social context. If, like Binford, we assert that these objects which we have created can be viewed objectively, we deny that social context and seek to negate the continuous process which links past and present. Thus in contemporary Britain, the monument of Stonehenge is held to have had a single, originary meaning which is lost to us since it existed in the far past (a point contested by Bender 1992; 1993). This meaning would have been authentic, yet because they are separated from it by the unbridgeable divide between past and present the meanings attributed to the site by present-day groups like druids and travellers are inauthentic (Chippindale 1990). Only objective science holds out the promise of being able to recover the authentic meaning of Stonehenge. However, I would argue Stonehenge never had *a* meaning. It was constructed by a society which already had a deep and rich heritage, and the multiplicity of meanings which those builders might have created in and through the monument would have been contingent upon that deep tradition. Through the Neolithic and the Bronze Age the site was reworked, reconstructed, its meanings altered. Yet there would have been no point at which it was meaning*less*. Nor was there some point in the Iron Age, or Roman, or early Medieval times when Stonehenge levitated off from the Wiltshire downs, or became invisible, returning to reality in time for its 'discovery' by the literate classes of the sixteenth century. The antiquarians did not fill a void by attributing meanings of their own to Stonehenge: they entered a hermeneutic battle against folklore and the habituated spatial knowledge of the local people.

Or to put the same argument into a more humble context: imagine that we excavate a sherd of pottery from the site of a Roman villa. This is a material which is familiar to us, and from the moment when it is turned up by the trowel the way in which we understand it is already constrained by a range of prejudices and understandings. We know certain things about how pottery is made, what it can be used for, and the conditions under which people can routinely make use of pots. Before we begin, these will inevitably colour the way in which we will interpret the artefact. When the artefact is recovered, it is already a part of a world. Furthermore, if the artefact is not recognised as an artefact, the likelihood is that it will not be recovered at all.

To undertake archaeological analysis is to wrench some part of the world out of the flow and constitute it as evidence relating to the activities of past persons. This is, in a sense, a scientific practice. However, it would be a mistake to assume that this practice is categorically different from anything which is engaged in by ordinary people. When someone has worn their muddy boots to walk across our carpet, or when there are crumbs but no cake in the cake tin, or when the front door has been left open, we use these traces of past actions in order to infer their character. In everyday life, human beings grasp elements of the material world, and constitute them as evidence for past human practice. The 'scientific' enterprise of archaeology is based upon this prescientific way of being attuned to the world, which I will call 'the archaeological imagination'. Just as geographers have argued that their discipline elaborates upon a 'geographical imagina- tion' through which human beings negotiate the role of space and place in their own biographies (Harvey 1973, 24), so academic archaeology builds upon this more fundamental orientation toward materiality. While Barrett is correct to suggest that the material world is not static in the way that we might expect a written text to be, archaeology requires us to *make the world static*, to freeze it in order to interpret it. By constituting things as evidence, we render them susceptible to reading, in very much the way that we might read a text. However, we need to cultivate an awareness that in doing this we are relating to the world in a rather unusual way. We require a sensitivity to the material which recognises its having been integral to past social relationships and historical processes. As I have already suggested in Chapter Two, the conception of the text which is most useful to us in this enterprise is that proposed by Roland Barthes (1981). Here, the text is not an object but a practice, a labour of engagement with some material in which we create meaning. So if I agree with Barrett that the rubric of 'the archaeological record as a text' is an inadequate one, it is not because the notion of textual practice is inappropriate to archaeology. Archaeological evidence can be a text without being a record, in the full sense. Archaeology is a textual practice, which is performed in the present upon materials which speak to us of the past. What we produce is an interpretation, which is not of the past, but which stands for the past (Ricoeur 1984). It is an account of the past which is itself inscribed, and as such the fluidity of the past must always escape it. The danger is that the appropriation which is necessary in order to speak about the past at all tends to encourage us to present it as having been composed of a set of fixed and stable entities.

ENCOUNTERING THINGS IN THE WORLD

This notion of the archaeological imagination can open the way for a discussion of the human relationship with the material world. Doing archaeology requires that we place ourselves in front of the world in a particular way, and read it as evidence. What this implies is that there are a number of different ways in which we as human beings can comport ourselves towards our material surroundings, and just as this insight illuminates our practice as archaeologists, it may help us to understand the relationships between persons and things which have existed at various times in the past. This train of thought might seem to imply that we will be considering the relationships which obtain between three bounded categories of phenomena: 'self', 'world' and 'thing'. Following Heidegger, however, I will suggest that each of these categories needs to be broken down to some extent, in order to arrive at a way of thinking which we might describe as being 'relational'. In the first place, it may not be helpful to think of these engagements as being grounded upon a fundamental relationship between a self-contained human subject and a worldly object. World and self are never two separate entities which exist side-by-side with each other. Rather, they are inextricably linked parts of a structure of Being (Heidegger 1962, 81). This structure is Dasein. Thus the particular way of Being which characterises human beings is one which necessarily involves being *in* a world. It is not the case that human beings first somehow exist as decontextualised intelligences which then enter the world: human Being as Dasein emerges in and through a world. As we have already seen, this is the sense which is conveyed by the term 'thrownness' (see page 42): that we always find ourselves already in a worldly situation.

If being human involves being in a world, it should perhaps be restated that this sense of 'being-in' is by no means to be understood as geometrical containment. Human beings are engaged in a world through their concern: through the way that they care about their own situation. People *care* about what has happened to them, where they are, and what will happen to them. So Being-in-a-world has the character of being absorbed with that world, abiding in it, being accustomed to it (Heidegger 1962, 92). It is important to recognise that the sense of 'world' conveyed here is a rather specific one. 'World' is not intended to suggest a particular planet, or a collection of objects, or the totality of all of the physical things which exist. On the contrary, we will use the word to relate to a *structure of intelligibility*. When human beings encounter phenomena on a day-to-day basis, they can make sense of them by assigning them to a meaningful context. We know that a spade is a spade because we may have used one to dig a hole, may have seen depictions of spades in gardening magazines, we are acquainted with the concept of 'spade', and so on. As soon as we encounter the physical object, this network of meaningful contexts allows us to render it intelligible. Or to put this more strongly: things always 'show up' to us as already being intelligible. It is the complete set of meaningful contexts which a person or group of persons has available to them, a matrix of relations of intelligibility, which we can call their world. It follows that it is quite possible for material things to exist which are not 'in the world' as far as a particular person or group is concerned: but only in so far as they have not yet been encountered. As soon as a thing has been experienced, it will already be a part of a world and be understood in a particular way. Before the European arrival in the Americas, then, horses would not have been 'in the world' from the native American point of view. None the less, once those people actually encountered horses belonging to conquistadors or running wild on the plains, those animals would have found a place for themselves within an extant structure of intelligibility: they were identified as giant dogs, demons, or mythical beasts. Human beings cope with the phenomena they encounter by slotting them in to the understanding of the world which they have already developed: nothing is perceived without being perceived 'as' something. It is therefore the phenomenon of world which determines the character of perception. When we encounter things, we never experience their presence as pure and uninterpreted sense data, tones and noises (Heidegger 1971a, 26). Our engagements with things are always mediated through the 'as-structure'. When we listen to things, we tend not to hear 'noises or complexes of sounds, but the creaking wagon, the motor-cycle. We hear the column on the march, the north wind, the woodpecker tapping, the fire crackling' (Heidegger 1962, 207). What we perceive is thus a function of a structure of pre-interpretation, which itself is predicated upon the phenomenon of world. In a sense, we are *closer* to the things which we are coming into contact with than the bare sense data. Since we have to strip away the significance of the things in order to experience sound waves, chromatic tones and gradations of texture, our awareness of the things of the world is more fundamental. The world which we dwell in, then, is a world of meaning and signification. In Lacan's terms, our everyday world is the symbolic order. However, as we will see below, even by operating within a world human beings can gain an awareness that there are things which escape or defy this symbolic order: the Other, or what Heidegger refers to as *earth*.

It follows from this that there can be no human beings without world, and no world without human beings. This is not to imply the idealism in which the universe is a product of the human mind: the position which I am advocating here is not a solipsism but a *perspectivism*. This point of view holds that there may be a single, real material world, but that it will be experienced and understood from the multiple perspectives of human beings whose grasp of reality is always imperfect. Solipsism would require that the world issues from a primordial and hermetic mind. I suggest instead that if there was no Dasein, no person, there would still be rocks, trees, mountains ... but no one to recognise them as such or to call them by those names, and no connection between them as parts of an intelligible structure. Even the 'objective' structures of natural science, of ecology and geomorphology, have no meaning without a human presence. Of course, human beings are also physically located in relation to all of these purely physical things. But it is a mistake to imagine that by attempting to describe human beings merely in respect of their physical, chemical and biological attributes and surroundings one can gain access to a more fundamental level of reality. This is precisely the fallacy of Cartesianism. For all human practices and projects are conceived and played out in a world. Humans are fundamentally worldly beings – to remove them from their worldly context is to impoverish our understanding of ourselves. Natural science, which achieves such an 'unworlding' of material things in order to understand them in abstraction from human projects is a perfectly legitimate and useful undertaking: but it is also something which is only done by human beings. Those human beings themselves live in a world, and hence natural science involves wrenching things out of contexts of meaning and sense in order to render them as objects for a particular form of investigation (Dreyfus 1991, 113). Those things which are studied by natural scientists, then, first show up within a world. This is the fundamental point: world is a precondition of anything whatsoever showing up to us as an object (Heidegger 1962, 92). By definition, without a world things are quite simply unintelligible, and in these terms it makes no sense to think of world as an entity which we exist separate from and alongside.

Natural science and the use of material things as archaeological evidence are both ways of relating to the world which involve looking upon it as object. It could be argued, however, that this is a rather unusual thing to do. To think of oneself and of another thing as two entirely self-contained objects is actually to disengage both from their worldly context. This disengagement has to be developed out of a more basic way of being in the world, in which one is more immersed and engaged in one's surroundings. Such an immersion is not merely a mental state, but is also a bodily comportment towards the world (Dreyfus 1991, 41). As we have argued, the separation of mind and body which seems basic to much of western philosophy can be seen as a secondary and derived way of thinking. Most of the while, human beings 'get on with things' (in both senses of the term) in such a way that mind, body and world are totally enmeshed. But to be more precise, mind, body and things do not first exist and then become enmeshed; they have to be created and abstracted from the fundamental interconnectedness of Being-in-the-world. When human beings encounter things in this basic state of everyday Being, they do not look at them in an analytic way, as if listing their qualities and dimensions to themselves. Instead, they become aware of them through their inconspicuous familiarity: things are simply 'there'. This way of routinely taking account of things without a distanced, analytic looking we can call 'circumspection' (Heidegger 1962, 98). 'Getting on with things' in this state of Being is by no means a kind of somnambulism, but tends to involve skills which are routine and which are not verbalised (Giddens 1984, 7). Those skilled practices which allows us to carry on our lives without having to stop at each moment and analyse our next move represent a form of knowledge, but here knowledge cannot be thought of as a collection of verbal statements. Instead, knowledge involves competence in coping with engagements in the world (Dreyfus 1991, 62). Much of this knowledge is acquired through circumspective activities rather than through formal learning, so that we are often capable of carrying out actions which we would find it difficult to describe in words. In terms of our relationships with material things, this means that we understand them better through making use of them in some task than by any analytical looking. Those material things which we are most closely connected with will therefore be those which serve as equipment: things-for (*zeug*) (Heidegger 1962, 97). This status as equipment, however, is not inherent in the thing itself so much as bestowed upon it through its involvement in some human project. In this way, our connection with material things is bound up with the structure of care: things are equipment in that they are engaged in our concernful dealings in the world.

The implication of this argument is that there are actually different ways in which we can engage with the material things that surround us. In the first place, where we make use of something as a piece of equipment, we may find that we are concerned less and less with the thing as an object, and more and more with the task in hand. If we write a letter, we are focused upon the message we are hoping to convey and the characters we are inscribing, rather than upon the pen that we use to do the job. If we use a hammer to hammer in nails, the tool itself *recedes* from our notice as we concern ourselves with the project of hammering.

> The less we just stare at the hammer-thing, and the more we seize hold of it and use it, the more primordial does our relationship to it become, and the more unveiledly is it encountered as that which it is – as equipment.
>
> (Heidegger 1962, 98)

Paradoxically, then, we become more closely involved with things the less we are conceptually aware of them. When the hammer is totally absorbed into our projected purpose, it ceases to be an object at all. Things with which we have this intimate relationship of concernful engagement can be described as being *ready-to-hand*. In contrast, we will encounter a great many other things in the course of our day-to-day activities. These are a part of our world, and we can recognise them as things of a particular kind, even if we are not actually making use of them. Circumspectively, we may take note of them as potential items of equipment, and by focusing upon them as objects (of analysis and discourse) we can render them intelligible (Dreyfus 1992, 174). These things which we see, feel or otherwise become aware of but which are not yet engaged in our projects can be called the *present-to-hand*.

When we take up something which is present-to-hand and begin to make use of it, it starts to become less object-like and more ready-to-hand. So individual things are not fixed in the mode of present-to-hand or ready-to-handness; they slip back and forth in their relationships with persons. What enables a piece of equipment to recede from our notice is our confidence in its capability to do the job, so that it is reliability which forges a particular kind of bond between persons and things. The opposite is also possible: when things fail to do what we expect them to do, we become aware of them as objects, so that they once again become something present-to-hand (Heidegger 1962, 104). Failing things 'announce' themselves, by making themselves conspicuous as not working, by obstinately refusing our efforts to make them work by repair, or by obtrusively making the task break down, forcing a complete reformulation of the project (Dreyfus 1991, 71). When things fail, they draw attention not only to their own presence and materiality, but to their context and the relationships in which they are enmeshed. It tends to be the case that equipment is tacitly accepted as part of the background through which the world operates as long as it is functioning smoothly. Yet the failure of a thing tends to announce its social and political context. In this connection, Pfaffenberger gives the example of the Challenger space shuttle disaster, which exposed the political and financial manoeuvres which lay behind the project (Pfaffenberger 1988, 249).

World, as a structure of intelligibility, is something which can only be engaged in by a certain sort of being. It is the capacity for language and signification which renders a being as Dasein. Language, as something which is not contained within a single mind but into which we have to be inserted (and yet which is only maintained through people's *speaking*) contributes to the fundamentally relational structure of Being-in-the-world. World is a space which is opened up through the human introduction into language. In a way, world can be thought of as something which has an interconnected structure, since the sense and meaning of each phenomenon which we are likely to encounter is networked to that of limitless other things. However, this is not to suggest that human beings are equipped with something like a totalised map of their world. If world is structured, it is not because it is something which is static and fixed. World is also a process: world *worlds*, through the concerned activities of human beings. World consists of everything that Dasein is capable of apprehending, and its networks of relationships are constantly being restructured through the operation of Dasein's skills and practices. World is that which Dasein can cope with. As Dasein carries out its everyday activities, the things of the world show up to it as unconcealed. By encountering things in circumspection or in analytical looking we achieve an awareness of some constantly changing portion of the world. The event of things showing up in this way can be termed the 'clearing'. Human beings, by being linguistic creatures, are engaged in a complex network of relationships, in which the material and the symbolic cannot be disentangled. Their grasp of this network at any given time is limited and regionalised, since it spreads out from a located spatial centre. This is the clearing. The clearing, which constitutes our ongoing understanding of the world, is not something which we choose to effect (Taylor 1992, 258). We do not control the way in which the things of the world reveal themselves to us, nor is this revelation something which takes place inside our heads. The clearing is a feature of the Dasein's Being-in-the-world, through which a region of the world 'lights up' around a centre. This lighting up, however, does not necessarily take the form of explicit objectification. The clearing may take place at a non-discursive level, and may have the character of rendering things amenable to our skilled coping practices (Dreyfus 1991, 22). Nor should the 'spatial' character of the clearing give the impression of a Cartesian mind looking out into a geometrical world from inside its fleshly carriage. Dasein *is* the clearing, in that it is not a thing in itself: Dasein itself is a space or process in which things can be made to show up. The 'weirdness' of being a human being thus lies in not being something which has a fundamental essence at all, but in being a 'nothingness' which allows things to appear (Zimmerman

1993, 243-4). Stranger still, it is a nothingness which is lived through a physical body. Only as a secondary result of this characteristic do human beings come to (mis)understand themselves as objects.

THINGS, WORLD AND EARTH

So far our discussion has concentrated upon the way that human beings encounter material things *in a world*. Given that the world thus defined is characterised by its meaningfulness or significance, it might be suggested that the argument is likely to take us towards a form of solipsism in which the universe consists exclusively of those things which can be rendered intelligible through a particular symbolic ordering. As opposed to this, I hope to suggest that our relationship with material things actually involves us in some kind of encounter with the Other, with that which cannot be entirely accommodated by the symbolic order. We have already suggested that when we come to know things through circumspection we do not think of them as analytical objects (Vycinas 1961, 119). Further, it will be those things which we engage with in this way that we find ourselves most closely connected with. An analytical approach, because it involves a distanced way of focusing on things, severs a particular bond between ourselves and material things. The specific problem which this avenue of inquiry sets up is that we are attempting to understand through analysis the character of a connection which is itself dispersed by analysis. This is all the more of a problem since the way in which we encounter archaeo-logical evidence will be overwhelmingly analytical in character. Our understanding of materials relating to the past will be generated through a mode of knowing which is qualitatively different from that which charac-terised its use in past contexts. There is much at stake here, for it can be claimed that things have a 'thingly' character which goes far beyond what-ever we can learn about them as objects, and that it is in the nature of the human relationship with things to establish a more profound involvement in the world (Alderman 1973, 159).

In the modern west, technological society has attempted to explain and gain mastery over nature by penetrating, classifying and dissecting the things of the world (Heidegger 1977b). Heidegger suggests that this programme of aggression ultimately fails, for it never manages to unlock the essence of things, which always recedes and slips away. By objectifying material things, we eventually reach the position where they 'stand reserve'. That is, they come to be seen as bare materials whose only significance is as resources to fuel the continual expansion of capitalist production (Taylor 1992, 265). An alternative way of 'getting on with things' is found in some non-western societies, where people *spare* the things of the world, and dwell alongside them. That is to say, people may live in a state of embeddedness within their local surroundings, where the option of treating land and living things as alienated commodities does not occur. The relationship with place and with things is a social one, in which people belong to the land as much as the land belongs to people. By turning the material world into a mere stock of resources, we sever ourselves from the possibility of this kind of dwelling. Science annihilates the thing, since it denies the rich networking of the thing's gathering (Heidegger 1971b, 170). Interestingly, Heidegger's argument is effectively an ecological (or at least 'green') one which none the less raises grave doubts regarding the practice of scientific ecology. By investigating our surroundings as 'environmental systems' characterised by succession and climax, we run the risk of contributing to their definition as environmental resources, which need to be 'managed' by humans. In sparing things by dwelling in a way which lets them be, and which implicitly recognises that we are deeply connected to them, we become attuned to them in a non-objectified manner. This kind of attunement allows us to obtain a sensitivity to the manifold connections which run through material things.

The fundamentally relational character of material things is manifested in their involvement in a network of multifaceted connections which spreads out from them limitlessly. At one level, things form parts of symbolic systems, interrelated by metaphorical association and metonymical connotation (Kristeva 1986b). But a thing also manifests a raw material, bears traces of its transformation (by human or other means) and its ageing, and has a history which may include a series of past involvements with persons. Given a way of thinking conditioned by a technological society, we tend to consider material things in terms of cause and effect, as a play of material forces. This kind of influence of one thing upon another can then be thought of as discontinuous. However, another way of conceptualising the causality immanent in things could be found under the rubric of *responsibility* (Heidegger 1977b, 9). While the logic of cause and effect implies chains of singular events like the collisions of billiard balls, the responsibility for the character of a thing indicates a more complex and enduring set of connections. A thing will have been formed from a particular material, whose characteristics it will continue to exhibit. Thus a snowman is not severed from the condition of being made of snow, and will still melt if the temperature rises. A thing will also have taken on a particular form or shape, which is clearly responsible for the way that it shows up to us. The end which is to be achieved is also responsible for the way that a thing is. Thus the end of holding water bears responsibility for the character of the pot. However, even where a thing is not an artefact it may have been caught up in natural processes which are responsible for it. Finally, some agency is responsible for bringing a thing about: in the case of an artefact, the artisan who fashioned it. The mistake would be to collapse all of the other connections of responsibility down and conflate them into agency. What this means is that each of these modes of occasioning adds something to the networking of the thing, enabling another facet of the way that it shows up. Things may be rocks or clods of earth, connected to a series of physical and chemical processes, but they may also be caught up with and animated by a series of human projects (Shanks 1994). Thus a thing is a conduit through which flows a rich web of material and signifying practices. Following Benjamin, Shanks (ibid.) refers to the quality that things have of resonating with these many entanglements as 'aura', and the thing itself can be the location where the disclosure of those connections takes place (Heidegger 1977a, 320). Our sensitivity to the thing as a thing allows us some degree of access into its world. This is not to suggest that material things possess some kind of inherent mystical substance, but that we are affected by things in a certain way because of the way that they themselves are involved in the structure of human care. Attending to things is thus attending to the way that we are with things.

The thing is a doorway into a web of relationships. Moreover, as a locus through which these relations flow, a thing can be said to *assemble* different aspects of world. The world which surrounds us is not composed of distinct and separate processual entities or systems (material, economic, ecological, social, cultural, spiritual). Rather, the relationships which connect persons and things might be said to have social, ecological, economic and spiritual dimensions to them, which can nevertheless not be prised apart without doing a fundamental damage to our understanding. Heidegger approaches this issue in a rather gnomic fashion by describing world as the outcome of a 'mirror play' carried on by 'the fourfold': Earth, Sky, Divinities and Mortals (Heidegger 1971b, 179). Without at this stage attempting to deal with the significance of these terms, what is implied is that each aspect of our surrounding world permeates each other, and that their interconnection is a dynamic one which brings about the process of 'worlding'. By constantly working upon one another, material, symbolic and spiritual aspects of the world create the conditions under which things can be rendered intelligible.

As anthropologists have begun to make us aware, a view of the world in which separate analytical entities cannot easily be pulled apart may be more appropriate to understanding non-western communities than the objectified categories of modernist/capitalist thought. For the modern west, persons become individualised identities while objects are alienated from social contexts as commodities (Kopytoff 1986, 64). We could suggest that this way of thinking is not merely a recent development, but that it actually requires that things and persons be severed from a background of inter-connection through acts of objectification. It may be that many aspects of non-western thought can be understood as manifesting a greater sensitivity to the embeddedness of things. Australian Aboriginal descriptions of landscape, for instance, often involve the belief that ancestral beings have entered directly into the land and the substances which are encountered day by day. It is this association with ancestral beings which makes present in places a spiritual and symbolic significance. Similarly, the iridescence of rock paintings and lithic material used for stone tools is attributed to the direct influence of the supernatural (Taçon 1991, 195). On the face of it, this would seem to offer us the unpalatable choice between accepting the reality of ancestral spirits, or rejecting outright the indigenous under-standing of the world in favour of a 'rational' western account. Following Heidegger we could suggest that attending to places and things through dwelling allows the Aborigine to enter into the rich networking of persons and materials which they embody. This would include remembering the persons who had been in places or who had used particular things, being reminded of past events, stories and myths, sensing aesthetic qualities of the materials present, and also perhaps catching a glimpse of some aspect of reality which lies beyond the capacity of symbolic systems and cosmology to encompass totally. What this suggests is that through their engagement with the material world, human beings can gain some contact with alterity, the cultural Other. That this encounter is always then inter-preted (in terms of ancestral spirits or whatever), such that it is accommodated into the worldly scheme of things, should not necessarily lead us to reject its reality out of hand.

The way that things and persons are held in encompassing relational webs is equally expressed in the non-western understanding that material items are very much like human beings. For the Sabarl islanders, stone axes have 'bones', 'flesh' and 'heads' (Battaglia 1990, 133). Axes are analo-gous to the person as a member of a clan: they are 'born' as a result of human activity, and they circulate from hand to hand just as persons move from one social context to another through marriage. In societies where a relational rather than individualised notion of personhood prevails (e.g. Josephides 1991; Strathern 1988; Clay 1992), both persons and things circulate in exchanges, which contribute to the formation of the identities of each. This perhaps helps to emphasise the point that 'the social' cannot be thought of exclusively as a sphere of relations between human subjects, but that the relationships which connect persons with things are social in character (Shanks 1994). By the same token, it is a mistake to think of technology as a separate 'system' which 'impacts' upon the social, so much as an aspect of the marrying and binding of things and persons (Pfaffenberger 1988, 241-9). And as Bourdieu has demonstrated (1970, 153) it is equally wrongheaded to think of the symbolic as a metaphysical substance which is somehow grafted onto an already oper-ating substrate. As we have already seen, the supposed 'empirical reality' which underlies the symbolic has actually to be approached (and constructed) from out of the world in which we operate. The capacity of things to be symbolically ordered is fundamental to their showing up as a world.

In that the kind of thinking which is being proposed here is one which emphasises the interconnectedness of the things of the world, it is important to draw a clear contrast with the systems theory associated with processual archaeology (e.g. Clarke 1968; Bertalanffy 1969). While systems thinking is concerned with relationships, it is essentially monadic in that it proceeds by establishing a series of objects (the cultural sub-system, the ecological sub-system, the economic sub-system, the religious sub-system and so on) and then investigating the 'connections' between them. Individual phenomena can be slotted into these categories as they are encountered. Thus the objects or sub-systems take on a 'given' character, their integrity is not questioned and their separation from each other is total. In distinction to this, I would suggest that these networks of relations actually provide the context for the creation and emergence of anything which can be defined as an object. Something rather similar is advocated by Foucault (1972; 1981), who presents a picture of objects created by discourse and emerging out of power/knowledge relations. However, I would wish to emphasise the embedding of power and knowledge in a more encompassing structure of relationships.

The way that these interconnections spread out endlessly from any given point from which we choose to begin to explore them invites a form of analysis similar to Foucault's (1984b) 'genealogy', Deleuze and Guattari's (1988) 'rhizomatics' or Shanks' (1992, 22-5) 'tree thinking'. That is, we follow connections from point to point, unravelling a strand which we define for ourselves. This exploratory groping fits with Heidegger's 'clearing', in which only a part of the vast dark world 'lights up' before us at any given time. Again, the contrast with systems theory is evident, since it is a first principle of cybernetics that the salient features of any totality can be adequately expressed as a simplified whole. The subtle part of this argument is that on the one hand it dissolves the categorical division between society and nature, yet on the other it retains the difference between linguistic mortals (humans) and other beings. It has often been argued that the belief that the social and cultural capabilities of human beings separate them from other animals implies a gross anthropocentrism, and that we should thus continue to apply ecological and behavioural approaches to people (O'Connor 1991). This would seem to be self-defeating, in that it effectively requires us to ignore the consequences of language and culture and present an entirely mechanistic account of reality. We should not perhaps think of human beings as separate from the rest of the world, yet their being there brings a different quality to the world. Linguistic capability allows humans to reflect upon the richness of their experience, but also to sever themselves from it through abstracted analysis. We might argue that it is inadequate to simplify matters by treating human beings as if they merely behaved, like automata, and that we should also consider that animals are engaged in social relations with people (Ingold

1986b, 35). In other words, we place human beings back in the world not by 'behaviouralising' people but by 'socialising' animals. This approach may take on more importance as we begin to recognise that some animals engage in conscious social action, and that conventional behavioural ecology is quite incapable of offering a full understanding of their lives (Strum and Latour 1987). In terms of the two arguments developed in Chapter One, we might find that we need to treat such creatures as being more 'human' than 'animal', without lessening the important distinction between the two.

When we investigate the connections between people and things, it is reasonable to refer to aspects of these relationships as being 'social', 'cultural', 'ecological' or whatever. However, it is much less clear that we can draw a line around a group of objects and define it as 'a society' or 'a culture'. The existence of a community as a bounded and self-contained entity is a form of self-interpretation on the part of a number of persons. It is clear that in the case of most such entities social relations actually extend outside of the 'society' (Friedman 1976). However, the recognition of this state of affairs has generally led to the recommendation that analysis should take on an ever-widening scope, eventually encompassing that collectivity which can reproduce itself without recourse to outside agency or resources. The disadvantages of such an approach have been thoroughly rehearsed: the tendency to displace fine detail in favour of global general-isation, the failure to recognise the heterogeneity of the persons and things involved (and the dubious belief that these can be expressed from a single point of view), the implied distancing of the observer from the object of study (e.g. Foucault 1984b; Deutsche 1991) (see Chapter Five below). Beyond this, it can be argued that conceiving of society as a bounded whole is to render it as an object, a timeless and closed entity which is in turn connected to other entities of similar status. Here again we are dealing with the monadic thinking of systems theory.

> This is a mathematic, if you will, that sees the world as inherently divided into units. The significant corollary of this view is that the relationships appear as extrinsic to such units: they appear as secondary ways of connecting things up.
>
> (Strathern 1990, 5)

If we are to think of both things and persons as being caught up in a mesh of relations which cannot be prised apart without reducing our understand-ing of its character, we should recognise that this network is no more homo-geneous than it is static. The fabric which holds entities in place is regionalised, it has a geography, and this heterogeneity is deeply concerned with the way in which relationships are invested with power. If knowledge is to be thought of as a means of skilfully engaging in the world rather than a set of ideas enclosed in a mind, the location at which that engagement takes place will tend to condition its outcome (Lindstrom 1990, xi). We should thus think of a geography of knowledge and power which both conditions and enables the character of practice (although 'geography' should not be taken here to refer exclusively to measurable geometric space). The competence of given actors will thus be related to their access to the potentials afforded by particular configurations of interconnection and interaction.

It is the process by which all of the knotted strands of these networks work together, then, that we can call 'worlding'. By dwelling alongside things in a state of inconspicuous familiarity, getting on with them, using them without using them up, human beings enter into this worlding. Human beings as mortals are thus one essential element in the movement of world. In manifesting their many connections, things allow us access into the different aspects of this worlding. One aspect of this connectedness is the way in which things *stand upon the earth*. The word 'earth' is here used in a very specialised sense, as a materiality which remains dark in respect of the clearing. The concept represents a way of recognising that there is something about reality which is not encompassed in language, and which escapes the structure of pre-understanding. This, of course, is precisely what natural science would like to believe it is investigating, but for reasons already discussed, this is an illusion. Earth is the Other, something which cannot be adequately expressed in language or ordered by culture. Yet in attending to things, we can gain some experience of the earth: 'the world grounds itself on earth, and earth juts through world' (Heidegger 1971a, 49). What this means is that the phenomenon of world as a field of disclosure could not be manifested if there were not something material holding back to be disclosed, and this is earth. Any material thing comes from the earth and bears the traces of earth, but in alienation and objectification we sever its ties with this origin. The earth is dark and concealed, and resists any attempt to penetrate it. It cannot be objectified, since as soon as some part of earth is wrenched forth it becomes both worldly and an object. Thus earth continually resists and withdraws, and cannot be appropriated by science. Despite this, earth can be recognised through *co-disclosure*. When we attend to things in such a way as to bring them near circumspectively, earth shines through, but only *as an absence*.

The more that we attempt to grasp the essence of earth by addressing it directly, the more that it withdraws from us. Cutting a thing in half, probing it with x-rays, revealing its atomic structure makes it all the less likely to reveal anything of earth. Instead, we might say that dwelling in harmony with earth involves acknowledging its opacity as the Other. That form of expression which tells us most about earth, says Heidegger, is poetry. The task of the poet is not to tackle earth head-on, but to 'get the measure' (Heidegger 1971c, 227), finding metaphors to express the way in which the inexpressible cannot be expressed. Getting the measure means opening up the vastness of what cannot be directly grasped. In a curious way this also describes the task of the archaeologist, since our job is also to engage with an Other (the past). An archaeological poetics involves finding ways of expressing and taking the measure of something which is absent.

Technology severs the thing from earth, and modes of production which are purely technological disperse the earthly quality of a thing's material. None the less, the possibility remains that some forms of production may transform a raw material but at the same time disclose something about the material which is already present. The potter or the woodcarver, by working 'intuitively' (that is, circumspectively) with a material instead of setting themselves against it and breaking it to their will, may do just this. For Heidegger, the defining characteristic of a work of art is that it is able to combine the establishment of a set of worldly relations of sense and meaning with the ability to convey some indication of the unworldly (the earthly) through its materiality. The artwork hints at something beyond itself by enhancing and framing its earthly qualities. The raw material from which the work is crafted is not 'used up' in the way that industrial production exhausts resources: on the contrary, it is freed in such a way as to allow us to enter into a closer communion with earth. While Heidegger attributes these characteristics exclusively to the work of art, it may be that in the non-western world, and in prehistory, this division between works is not so clear-cut. Indeed, we could argue that the world of art represents a last refuge in the west of things which are attended to aesthetically. This being the case, the qualities of crafted things or artworks are not inherent to them, but reside in the way that we as humans relate to the material world. Thus it may be quite possible to 're-enchant' a rusty iron cog or a Styrofoam cup by attending to it in a particular way.

Heidegger himself acknowledges that there is a history to the relationship between people and artefacts (Dreyfus 1992, 174), which runs from *technē* to industrial production, and finally to cybernetic control over an objectified nature. For the ancient Greeks, *technē* was a way of assembling or crafting things, which was an aspect of *poeisis*, and hence there was no categorical distinction to be made between the arts and technology. Nor was art thought of as a separate realm of cultural activity (Heidegger 1977b, 34). Yet as human beings have gradually ceased to dwell with things and have tended more to act upon them as objects, 'using' has turned to 'using up' and an exploitation of things as resources. As production has ceased to attend to its materials, craft has declined into industry. However, it is worth considering that in many non-capitalist societies a range of the things which are used day-to-day may have a character which in the west is restricted to artworks. Just as Heidegger describes the Greek temple as a form of architecture whose fashioning allows its materials to shine though, and to hint at the spiritual, so things which are fashioned by hand and which are fully engaged in the matrix of gift and debt relations may have a place in 'worlding'. In making, using and circulating artefacts made of particular materials, people may be opening up a heterogeneous network of persons, things and the Other. A good example in this context is the role of cloth in Oceania, which may bind together a material or set of materials, while serving as a powerful and explicit metaphor for the interconnection of social relations (Schneider and Weiner 1989, 3).

THINGS, TEMPORALITY AND IDENTITY

In the last chapter, the character of identity as narrative was discussed. It was argued that selfhood could be seen as a pathway which establishes connections between a sequence of experiences, in such a way as to draw together a comprehensible account of a person. In the creation of these narratives of personal and collective identity, people and things come to be closely bound together. Things are instrumental in the setting up of the world which we live through: they bring the past to mind; they are alongside use; they are implicit in the formulation of future projects. It is through our involvements with things and other persons that we come to take a stand on ourselves, so that identity is less an already given individuality than a particular way of engaging with the world. Identity has to be taken up, and has to be crafted: hence Foucault's celebrated notion of the self as a work of art (Foucault 1988b). As we have seen, this way in which human identity emerges is based upon the fundamentally temporal character of human existence. What distinguishes human beings is their having-been, their being alongside others, and their constant projecting-forward of themselves through their projects. A consequence and precondition of this temporal way of existing is care, the way in which one's own Being becomes an issue to oneself. This in turn means that human beings alone are *mortals*. That is, they have the capacity to die, whereas other creatures merely perish. Death implies more than the ceasing of the body's biological functions. It is the recognition of one's own mortality which allows one's own Being and that of other things to *matter* to one (Heidegger 1971b, 179). On the face of it, this argument seems to draw a very rigid line between human and other beings, and would appear to be out of keeping with the case which has been made in this chapter: that the relationships between people and things are social in character and that things may have a role which is akin to that of social actors. But this would be to overlook the point that whatever it is that distinguishes human beings is not an essence held inside a corporeal body, but is a characteristic of their Being-in-the-world. The things of the world are thus engaged in the structure of Dasein and caught up in human care. Because of this enveloping in care, we could argue that non-human things will also have a temporal structure, which is in some ways analogous to that of human beings. Clearly, this is not to suggest that inanimate entities are conscious of existing in time. What it does indicate is that things have a pastness, are present alongside us, and are projected into a future because of the interest that we take in them.

Human beings can be identified as subjects through their personal biographies. We can achieve a particular kind of understanding of them by following them through the series of events that overtakes them in the course of their lifetime without necessarily assuming that the 'person' involved represents a self-enclosed consciousness to whom things are simply 'happening'. Rather, we are considering how particular events have the effect of inscribing an identity onto a body. In a similar way, we can talk of the biographies of material things as accretions of meaning. Like human beings, the unity of material things in social terms is to be found in their temporality. As archaeologists, we tend to split things up into a series of separate attributes, which are studied in different ways by different specialists. Thus the style of an artefact is studied through formal or structural analysis; its materiality may be approached through spectroscopy, neutron activation analysis or petrological thin sectioning; its technological character can be investigated by experimental replication, or use-wear analysis in the case of a stone tool. All of this implies an analytical separation and segmentation of the thing. If we follow the arguments developed in this chapter, it may be that this probing and dissection loses track of the 'thingness' of archaeological evidence. Instead of breaking things down through the more and more precise description of separate attributes, we should perhaps be considering how artefacts explode out into other things, exploring their networking or following their genealogies. This kind of thinking resists the practice of considering artefacts as being composed of some attributes which are primary ('function') and others which are grafted on top ('style') (N. Thomas 1991, 29). On the contrary, every material thing is connected in numerous ways to other things, and which of these connections are drawn on in the way that it shows up to us depends upon the way in which they are disclosed. Thus there is no inherent 'toolness' to an artefact which dictates that it is first of all something to throw at deer and secondly something which carries a message about the identity of the owner. The recognition of a thing as a tool depends upon the configuration of a world, and the character of human involvements in that world.

What makes a material item more than just a constellation of disaggregated attributes is its temporality. In its worldly dimension, a thing is revealed to us as having-been, being-alongside and projected forward. But at the same time, because much of their integration into a world depends upon the way that human beings engage with them, things can also be present-to-hand or ready-to-hand. This in turn shows up another aspect of their temporality. That is, when we are using something in order to perform some task, its failure in that task may alert us to its ageing. The handle of an axe may be rotten, or the rubber of a hose may have perished. In this way, we come to recognise that things are not static, but are changing in various ways, and may require maintenance.

Objects are revealed as having-been in that they have a history. This may involve the physical evidence of manufacture and an awareness of the processes of manufacture. So the flake scars on a stone tool, or the burnish on a pot tell us something about its past. At the same time, a thing may also have acquired the 'personal' history of having passed from hand to hand and place to place. Marks of wear may also be traces of personal history – objects which have been used for particular tasks have diagnostic characteristics. In the case of Melanesian Kula valuables, signs of age are a mark of worth. The patination of shells, for example, is taken as a sign of great age. Over time, these shells may acquire personal names and histories. By being used and classified in particular ways, the shell valuables become involved in a network of material and symbolic connections. They are thought of as male or female, representing partners in a marriage, while their classification according to colour introduces them into a much wider matrix of associations, concerned with age, death, desire and sexuality (Cambell 1983, 236-45). Objects may bear traces of persons, who may have made or altered them, or be represented by them, or have owned or used them. Thus they articulate, reproduce and bring to memory social relationships. The circulation of things from hand to hand thus has a role in the acquisition of knowledge, including knowledge concerning past, distant or mythological persons. In many contexts, the practical engagement and involvement with material things are much more effective ways of learning than verbal telling (Borofsky 1987, 136).

In crafting new artefacts, people may consciously refer to things which have survived from earlier times, and which have acquired some significance that may not originally have been intended. One could think of Renaissance efforts to evoke a lost classical age through architectural style, or of reproduction furniture which may even be 'distressed' to give a spurious impression of age. One consequence of this process is that ideas drawn from the past and carried by material things may interact with new elements in unforeseen ways. Thus the mix-and-match of contemporary post-modern architecture is facilitated by the survival of structures built at different times, which constitute a stylistic resource. Because things erode or rot, they gain in scarcity, and the fact of their continued existence becomes steadily more remarkable. The peculiar character of old things lies partly in the way that they have been used and handled by persons who may by now be dead. By enduring, material things may seem to have transcended death, and may represent a strand of continuity. In this way, things can stand as evidence for past lives, identities and relationships. A ring can bring to mind a past union between two families, a point from which presently living persons can chart their descent. Aged Oceanian cloths can carry with them the history of past social relationships, in some cases becoming closely associated with a particular descent group and its continuity through the generations (Weiner 1989, 35-52). Where an artefact's identity starts to be so closely bound up with that of a person or group of persons the nature of its value may be transformed. While both things and persons may be exchanged between groups of kin, the association of a thing with the continuity of the group as a whole may render it inalienable (N. Thomas 1991, 18).

As having-been, then, things can serve as witnesses to a human past, evidence which substantiates particular narratives. Their mnemonic character is a facet of their part in establishing a world: things can evoke the presence of certain persons and qualities at a non-discursive level (Ray 1987). However, the presentness of things is as significant as their evocation of a past. Things are alongside human beings, and consequently we are continuously encountering them, being surprised by them, and having our actions channelled and modified by them. The hammer may recede from us in the act of hammering, but it is none the less the conduit through which the project of hammering is achieved. Similarly, if we are to say that we can enter into an engagement with the world through the connectedness of things, this is only possible because of their material presence. Objects are also projected forward, in that they are engaged in our projects. Projecting-forward may involve relocating things, designing things, setting out to acquire things, making things. The creation of material things presumes future contexts of interaction, so that things are futural (Battaglia 1990, 6). Future interaction can be seen as a project or intention.

Any material thing can have a place within a world which it helps to constitute. Circumspectively, or by means of objectification and scientific inquiry, we can obtain a knowledge of it. Yet there is no sense in which either an intimate acquaintance with a thing, built up over a lifetime perhaps, or an exhaustive list of its qualities, attributes and contributory elements can represent a total knowledge. There is always more that could be said, more ways in which the thing could be experienced, more associations and connotations that could be investigated. In this sense, there will always be something of the thing that draws back from us. Consequently, the thing in the world must remain an assemblage of fragments rather than a whole whose limits can be defined. As with a human being, these fragments can best be integrated in telling, so that our understanding of a given artefact is likely to be narrative in character. If we are called upon to give an account of a thing's identity, it may well take the form of a narrative which knits together the events of where it has been and who it has been involved with, to what purpose; where it is now and what end it serves; and what it may be expected to do in future. Both people and things might usefully be thought of as having a life-path, similar to those depicted in the web diagrams of time geography (e.g. Carlstein 1982; Gregory 1989; Pred 1977). Thus the process through which persons and things come to mutually constitute each other's identities could be thought of as a series of inter-connecting pathways winding through space and time.

PLACE AND TEMPORALITY

—— •◆• ——

GEOMETRIC SPACE VERSUS
SIGNIFICANT SPACE

In a world constructed as nature, each object is a self-contained entity, interacting with others through some kind of external contact. But in a landscape, each component enfolds within its essence the totality of each and every other.

(Ingold 1993, 155)

The opening chapters of this book have amounted to an attempt to grasp the inseparable parts of a structure of human Being, which links together identity, materiality and temporality. Throughout, there has been another element which has demanded some consideration, and this has been space or place, since human existence always involves Being-somewhere. In this chapter we will turn to consider place more directly. Places, as referred to here, represent locations which are implicated in a human world. Just as the stretching of persons and material things through time is the means by which they acquire their identities, so I will hope to show that the identity of place has a narrative and accretional quality. This does not simply mean that places which are first given as arrangements of geometrical planes and surfaces later have a layer of cultural meaning spread over them. This much is suggested by the understanding that 'space' can be transformed into 'place' by human activity. Instead, the suggestion is that places emerge *as* places through their involvement in structures of understanding and practice. Places are always already place-like as soon as we are aware of them, use them, and consume them.

The notion of place has long held considerable interest for archaeologists, who have always concentrated their attentions upon 'sites', which are generally assumed in some way to have formed foci for intensive human interaction in the past. In advocating an 'archaeology of place', Lewis Binford argued that in order 'to understand the past we must understand places' (1982b, 6). With this I concur, although his concern was largely with the way in which localised assemblages of artefacts come to be modified by human mobility patterns and the more or less intensive re-use of locales. The archaeology of place which is proposed here is one which investigates the production of place through the *inhabitation* of spaces by human beings. As with some of the other arguments already outlined, we can make this understanding of space a little clearer by opposing it to that which is found in Cartesian philosophy (and, by implication, in much conventional archaeology). For Descartes, the physical world was characterised by its spatial *extension*, which was composed of both shape and motion (Heidegger 1962, 124). So, aside from the things of mind and spirit, everything in the world could be expressed in terms of its shape and speed of movement. Since the intangible aspects of human existence were utterly separate from the corporeal, all that can be, or needs to be perceived can be grasped through its substantiality, rather than its significance. Movement itself represents no more than the change in location of objects. This being the case, mathematical geometry was judged capable of describing all of creation. No location within geometric space could be argued to have any kind of priority over any other, and spaces which contain human beings are in no way different from spaces into which no human being has ever set foot (Dreyfus 1991, 139). This conception of space is one which has characterised both 'spatial science' within locational geography (Gregory 1978) and 'spatial archaeology' (Clarke 1976; Hodder and Orton 1978), which existed as a means of expressing formal relationships between archaeological traces.

Cartesian understandings of space reduce the world to the occurrent, and reject any concern with spatial meaning. By contrast, I will argue that meaning and significance are diagnostic of human existence, and that space is rendered meaningful by virtue of its involvement in human worlds. The mere happenstance that we can measure any object which we come across does not necessarily imply that the size or extent of places is a grounding reality which only later allows us to recognise them as being familiar or strange. The contemporary western understanding of everyday geography is that the spaces we inhabit have a fundamental nature which allows a cultural super-structure to be constructed as a secondary and derived phenomenon. It is not surprising, then, that the concept of 'nature' is so often associated with place or landscape. Nature, or 'the environment', is taken as having a set of essential characteristics which precede any human presence (Zimmerman 1993, 261). When human beings begin to build houses and monuments, they impose something upon 'nature'. This geographical nature is composed of 'eco-systems', which behave according to the laws that can be discerned by natural science. 'Environmental perception' on the part of human beings thus comes to represent the distorted and perverse ways in which people construct cultural edifices which *cover over* the firmer ground of scientific reality. However, we could equally argue that for some location to be measured, or for its ecological characteristics to be determined and fed into a flow-chart, it must first 'show up' as a place. Without our recognition that the world is internally differentiated and broken down into regions according to the character of human interest and involvement, no location is any more worthy of our attention than any other. We first choose to study a particular moorland or desert or limestone pavement because it already holds a certain interest or meaning for us.

SPATIALITY AND THE HUMAN BODY

If places can only emerge by means of the worldly involvement of human beings, it follows that we need to reconsider the spatial character of human existence. We have already pointed out the mistakenness of perceiving our being in a world as representing the same kind of thing as being 'in' some kind of container. But despite this, our worldly existence does have a spatiality (Heidegger 1962, 134). We *can* measure our physical bodies and express our proximity to other things in quantitative terms, but this is really only a secondary issue. The measurement of space in relation to the human body relies upon a much more fundamental understanding of things: the qualitative distinction between that which is 'closer' and that which is 'further away' from us. When we say that we feel emotionally distanced from something, or that we have become very close to someone, we are not simply using a spatial metaphor in order to express more metaphysical relationships. On the contrary, our perception of space relies upon a more fundamental human ability to experience relationality. This results in a spatial order which is centred on the human body, as opposed to a homogenous space of endless extension. This spatial order, which we might call 'experiential space', has a certain priority, in that geometrical space can only be discovered through first existing in experiential space. So we can measure the distance across a valley because we can first of all recognise the difference between its near and its far side.

Heidegger describes the fundamental characteristics of human spatiality as 'de-severance' and 'directionality' (1962, 139). Human attunement to material things is directed or spatially focused. This directionality is only possible where a physical body finds itself in a physical world (Jager 1985, 215). Such an orientation is fundamental to understanding the world, and demonstrates that what is often considered as abstract thought would not be possible in abstraction from a physical world. Once again, the world appears to be integral to the constitution of the human subject. But at the same time, human beings are orientated in relation to the world as it is *understood* rather than as it is revealed by empirical science. De-severance refers to the way in which human beings can allow the things around them to 'show up' as distinct entities. Things have first of all to show up as *things* before they can be recognised as close or distant, or as being in any particular relation to the body (Dreyfus 1991, 132).

While the human body as a solid object exists in a single defined locus within geometrical space, human beings are *stretched* and dispersed through experiential space, in the sense that particular places remain 'close' to them. So our spatial understanding of the world does not depend exclusively on our present location. The things which are 'closest' to us are not necessarily those which are in geometrical proximity to us (Heidegger 1962, 135). Our nearness to a place or a thing might be a consequence of the way in which it contributes to our personal history, like the exile who continues to feel close to her homeland. The spectacles on my nose, which I look through without noticing them, are in one sense very distant from me, yet a house many miles away can be very close as I recall it to memory (Heidegger 1977a). As our concern shifts from one thing to another, our closeness to them ebbs and flows, although this process is not purely mental and is in no sense independent of the materiality of the world in which we find ourselves. Rather than simply being determined from outside by the geometrical form and configuration of things, our concern with our material context is *directed*. The distinction which we have already made between that which is ready-to-hand and the present-to-hand, or in other words our degree of involvement with different things, directly affects our spatiality and orientation within the world.

Despite this, it would be too simple to say that experiential proximity amounts to no more than the 'distance' of a thing or place from our conscious mind. There are different ways in which we can be close to things. Once we know something or somewhere deeply, it may begin to recede from our explicit concern, and become a matter of *bodily under-standing*. Walking to work across a square every day, it ceases to be necessary for someone to ponder each change of direction, and their body simply comes to negotiate the space. This intimate form of closeness is the outcome of *inhabiting* a space, and it is through inhabitation that a space becomes a place. In this way the quality of place emerges out of incon-spicuous familiarity (Lang 1985, 202; Bachelard 1964, 4). All of this implies that the experiential distance between the human body and the things that surround it is not fixed. Just as places can recede from notice as we become familiar with them, so objects can recede from conspicuousness when we use them as tools, and concentrate on the job for which we use them (Jager 1985, 219). A hammer becomes almost a part of the person as it bangs in the nails, a pen disappears into the act of writing, and a walking-stick becomes a third leg which supports our weight in walking and conveys sensations of hardness and softness to the hand. Equally, the body itself can slip away from our notice. When we touch something and become interested in its texture, the touching hand recedes from notice in relation to the touched thing (ibid., 200).

Particular parts of the body, like hair and fingernails, have a rather ambiguous character, in that they continue to grow and yet they do not directly feel sensations any more than does a walking-stick. Whether or not hair cuttings or fingernail clippings are considered to still constitute parts of the body appears to vary from culture to culture, and is related to conceptions of the self. So although in the contemporary west it is conventional to think of the self as a tightly-bounded entity, and of the body as being absolutely separate from its surroundings, it is possible to present anomalies which are difficult to reconcile within this way of thinking. Tools and discarded bodily materials (even milk teeth and exfoliating skin) demonstrate that there is a flexible boundary between the person and their environment. The self 'shades off' across experiential space, and the closeness of things and body parts is variable across time. The consequence of this is that the distinction between the person and the places which they inhabit is not hard and fast, just as it is a mistake to divide mind from body. The human body is the medium through which people gain their understanding of the world, yet this always takes place from a position of being bound to that world and saturated by it. Humans experience the world physically, but through a body which is attuned by mood and understanding (Haar 1993, 36). In other words, the body is not simply a piece of sensory apparatus which relays pure data about the environment to the mind. Sensuous activity and perception, conceptualisation and affective attunement are equiprimordial in the sense that they do not lead one to another in a lawlike chain of cause and effect. Each is socially and culturally constructed and inherited, and neither can be easily dispensed with. Mind and body are together thrown into a physical situation which affects understanding directly. This direct involvement of physical Being in the experience and understanding of the world means that the human body is categorically different from the physical bodies of other kinds of animals (that is, non-Dasein beings) (Haar 1993, 12). Experiential space can only be lived through a *human* body (Dovey 1993, 249). We can choose to look on the human body as just so much meat, glands and reflexes, but this requires that we *purge* it of its social and cultural constitution.

ENGAGEMENT AND DWELLING

The quality of place emerges out of the way in which spaces are inhabited by human bodies, gaining in familiarity through interpretation and sensuous experience. Place involves 'a specific landscape, a set of social activities, and webs of meanings and rituals, all inseparably intertwined' (Relph 1993, 31). Places cannot be dissociated from the events which take place in them. But at the same time, those events cannot be derived from the geometry of the space alone (Tschumi 1994, 139). This presents an immediate problem for archaeological analysis. Archaeology has traditionally investigated architecture and landscape as if they represented abstract forms, viewed from a distanced and disengaged perspective (Barrett 1994; Thomas 1993). The analysis of structures created by human beings has tended to choose between typological approaches, which would reject any hope of assessing their original significance, and projects inspired by structuralism, which search for a conceptual template beneath the visible form (e.g. Fritz 1978). These approaches start from the supposition that the material evidence represents an outcome of human action, which can relatively easily be separated out from the action itself (see Chapter Three above). Following the line of thought which we have developed here, the significance of places cannot be inherent in their form. Meaning is not held within an entity, but develops in the relationships between things and human beings. The meaning of a place is always in flux, and is the outcome of a dialogue in which people are 'testing' spaces and meeting resistances. In this sense, our relationships with places are rather like relationships with other human beings (Jager 1985, 221).

Of course, if the human beings who fashioned and lived in ancient architectures are now dead, the connectedness of bodily presence, place, and interpreting Being is by no means evident. At a minimal level, traces of human activity must make us aware that a certain kind of existence was present in the past, although we cannot 'read off' the meaning of place from spatial configuration alone. That is, one cannot reconstruct a past world of meaning from a Cartesian template of geometrical form. As Gregory (1990, 49) indicates, 'it is impossible to recover human geographies from a contemplation of their abstract geometries'. This could lead one to argue that the only legitimate form of archaeology is one which relies entirely on those inferences which can be made directly from the evidence. As Bell argues,

> Explanations should be 'close' to the data. They should be directly testable themselves or they should entail other statement(s) that are directly testable.
>
> (Bell 1994, 20)

In terms of spatial archaeology, this would mean that we could only contemplate analyses which involve the measurement and description of spaces and structures as they are revealed to us in the present. This achieves the status of scientific respectability which Bell evidently approves, but it yields no real understanding at all. Something of the past is missing from spaces and places investigated by archaeologists, and yet that *something* cannot be regained by method alone. Quite simply, an archaeology of place can never provide the guarantees of verification which processual approaches seem to demand if it interprets beyond the evidence, but it cannot provide a satisfactory understanding of the past if it does not. If human beings no longer inhabit the spaces we excavate, we must *put their bodily presences back*, through interpretation, if we are to say anything of consequence whatsoever. This kind of an interpretation is not a reconstruction or a recovery of a past meaning, but a plausible account produced in and for the present. This is not an *excuse* for an interpretive prehistory: it is an argument which explains why any more 'scientific' archaeology will never succeed in producing the understandings of the past which we require.

In that it is a feature of people's relationship with their world, place is something which can emerge anywhere. As soon as we are aware that we are *somewhere*, it is already a place. It is not necessary for somewhere to be physically altered for this to happen. Where people are 'at home with' their surroundings, and can go about their business in a state of familiarity, a relationship with place exists which we can call *dwelling* (Heidegger 1977a). However, when human beings do make a deliberate and lasting change to a place, something quite important takes place. *Building* involves a transformation of place in which a location becomes the 'place of' something. When people set up a structure or dig a ditch, the resulting evidence of human activity identifies a place with something historical, an act of construction. In this way, the location comes to visibly manifest the interconnection between people and their world. Building opens up a site as an embodiment of a particular way in which people exist in a world (Mugerauer 1993, 125). Architecture both founds a relationship between people and place, and allows that relationship to manifest itself. However, Heidegger's argument is that for people to exist in a kind of harmony with their surroundings, they must have first learned to dwell before they start to build. Building should be an outgrowth of dwelling, rather than an exercise in opposing and subduing a world which is conceived of as 'nature'. Building may then involve an alteration of place, but one which adds to its significance rather than wiping away previous meanings.

PLACE AND NARRATIVE

The identification of locations as the 'place of' something demonstrates the relational character of place. Human lives thread their way through spaces, and in the process our memories of having-been are localised. Bachelard (1964, 7) points out that although we can rarely remember how long a past event or process took to transpire, we can generally locate where it took place. If one of the roles of memory is to act as a guarantee against the fragmentation of personal identity, a principal means by which this is achieved is through the locatedness cf dwelling. Thus in a real sense we can talk about humans as having 'life-paths'. But just as the inhabitation of space contributes to human identity, and just as the identity of a group may be founded upon their common inhabitation of a place, so the relationship of dwelling-in contributes to the identity of place. When we think of a modern country, only a part of the image which we have of the place is directly related to its topography, vegetation and natural resources. And even these 'material realities' are understood in a particular way because of the way in which they are lived out or dwelt through. Mountains in Switzerland and in Japan might empirically look very similar, but we understand them in quite different ways.

Very often, in the context of built space, this meaningful character of place comes to be seen as something which is added on to a more funda- mental material presence. Thus Hegel considered that architecture itself represented a supplement which was added to shelter in order to invest it with a distinctive identity (Tschumi 1994, 221). This would suggest that house-builders in Bali and in the German Black Forest first establish an enclosed space and then render it Balinese or German by adding detail. In practice, it has been this model of the 'Hegelian supplement' which has given us an architecture of 'decorated sheds', found in the post-modernist tendency to add anachronisitic trimmings to blocky forms (Harries 1993, 42). It reality, places are meaningful 'all the way down'. We do not add meaning to meaning-less locations: we discover places through their meaning. Hence it is difficult to maintain the categorical distinctions required in order to see space as a container of persons, whether as physical bodies or as social beings. Both bodily presences and social relationships are embedded in meaningful space. Social relations are reproduced and identities are formed through movements in space as they are played out through time (Gregory 1989, 354). Thus the dispersal and fragmentation of identity with which Bachelard is concerned is potentially a dispersal in space as well as time. Human beings are involved in sets of relationships which are constantly mobile through both space and time (Thrift 1991, 458). The intimate knowledge of place mentioned above grounds human identities in the world, but the sequencing of experiences between particular locations has a narrative structure which parallels the narrative of personal identity. Personal histories are also 'spatial stories' which draw places together in sequence (De Certeau 1984), and places enter directly into the sense of selfhood. Place thus comes to have a temporal character through its intertwining with human identities, as well as through its own ceaseless change.

This way in which experiential space is ordered in narrative sequence demands that we reconsider the notion of landscape. While western under- standings privilege an understanding of landscape that is primarily visual, perceived synchronously from a distanced vantage point (Cosgrove 1984), landscapes as they are lived are experienced sequentially. We might do well to imagine human landscapes as made up of innumerable braided and inter- secting pathways. While people often move in cyclical patterns in the course of routine activities, returning to the same location again and again, and synchronising their presence with others (Ingold 1986, 176), it is not the case that the points to which they return are fixed and given. The places which represent the stations within our personal histories are themselves continuously being physically altered and decaying, as well as continuously being re-evaluated and re-interpreted by their users. The relationships which tie human mortals to their world do not involve any fixed points. Everything which surrounds us is in motion, so that the rhythms of human existence are nested in a broader range of rhythms (Ingold 1993, 164). While it may be tempting to separate this range into separate categories, so that geological, ecological and human time are seen as different strata in the temporality of landscape, this might be a mistake. Everything in landscape flows and is constantly in motion, but to say that the lapse of time over which change becomes perceptible within a given phenomenon represents a categorical distinction between *types* of change artificially disrupts the integrated and nested character of worldhood. Hence while Ingold (1993, 160) describes the temporality of landscape as being composed of a series of superimposed rhythms, these rhythms are in practice locked and meshed into one another. This is not least the case because the ways in which place is experienced and produced are associative, so that the character of place derives from elements which might unwarily be described as parts of different 'sub-systems'. Places are hybrids, relational webs of meaning and material.

This web-like character of places and landscapes means that they are capable of sustaining multiple meanings, and that multiple narratives criss-cross and thread through them (Duncan and Duncan 1988, 123). While physical interventions in landscape, such as architecture, may involve the attempt to impose a unitary understanding upon a place, the resulting configurations will always be used 'against and despite' themselves (Tschumi 1994, 19). Places are consumed as well as produced in strategic ways, and all of the relations of meaning in which human beings are enmeshed are also relations of power. It is a common mistake to imagine that power itself is a phenomenon restricted to relations of force, rather than a quality which is immanent in relations of all kinds. The interpretation of place is a struggle for position within the meaningful world. Furthermore, the ways in which places are linked together in personal narratives may play a subversive role in undermining dominant interpretations of space.

PART TWO
THREE HISTORIES

CHAPTER FIVE

THE DESCENT OF THE BRITISH NEOLITHIC

—— •◆• ——

INTRODUCTION: SCALES OF ANALYSIS

In the second part of this book, I will present three studies which make use of the ideas which have been developed in the earlier chapters. These studies are arranged in broadly chronological order, since they are concerned with the earlier Neolithic, the later Neolithic, and the end of the Neolithic and the Early Bronze Age respectively. Additionally, the scale at which the analysis is pitched is different in each case: the first example involves developments which took place across the whole of the north-west of Europe, the second is restricted to the British Isles, and the third is focused on a single site and its surroundings. This kind of an exercise demands some discussion of the issue of scale, since it could easily be construed that what is being presented here is a series of approved 'scales of analysis'. This might imply that 'the site', 'the landscape', 'the region' and 'the continent' represent given entities which are host to particular forms of social interaction, and which constitute the spatial equivalents of Braudel's temporal scales. Thus face-to-face interactions would be expected to take place in 'micro-time', while continent-wide social transformations might be a feature of the *longue durée*. However, I would argue that such an understanding would be both flawed and simplistic. Particular social and cultural phenomena have a spatial range or extent over which they operate, and this range may expand or contract across time. As a result, these phenomena will not fit comfortably into any pre-given entity such as a 'region'.

The scale of archaeological entities is contingent, a dimension of histor-ical process in itself. A predictable response to this state of affairs is to argue that the appropriate level of analysis for historical phenomena is the closed system: whatever social entity can reproduce itself without significant input from external agencies (e.g. Friedman 1976). Yet networks of human interaction are rarely as system-like or 'sutured' as this formula would suggest (Laclau and Mouffe 1987). Historical change may involve ruptures and discontinuities, events in which relatively isolated groups of people are suddenly (and perhaps briefly) drawn into contact with a wider world. It will be perfectly possible to find ways in which the webs of interconnection in which any person or community is embedded spread outward limitlessly, so that the only feasible basis for investigation lies in a consideration of a 'world system'. This position none the less rests on the assumption that historical analysis should proceed 'from the top down', and that it should attempt to encompass any or all of the influences which might be salient to a given set of events (Friedman 1976; 1989). Such a 'totalised' account of the past has been criticised on the grounds that it requires us to have a full and objective knowledge of what has happened and its relative significance, as if we ourselves were external to processes whose repercussions are still being felt and whose meanings are still being reconsidered (Foucault 1984b). Totalisation argues that by grasping the thing in its entirety, we can see it as it really is. Furthermore, an emphasis on the global and systemic aspects of change tends to underplay the ways in which historical conditions were experienced and negotiated, and the extent to which people were able to act, albeit under circumstances of limited understanding (Kaye 1984).

These critiques of totalisation are by no means nihilistic, and they allow a number of different approaches. The 'genealogical' method advocated by Foucault (1984b), for instance, involves tracing the descent of institutions and practices, through a tight focus on particular cultural manifestations and a concern with the instability and historicity of all aspects of human experience. Genealogy represents a recognition that human history is endlessly rich and complex, and that it may not be possible to present an account of the past whose truth is complete and universal. As such, it constitutes a form of Nietzsche's 'useful history', a history which has a distinct role to play in the present, as opposed to 'monumental history', which presumes to represent an objective record of 'what really happened'. A similar imperative lies behind the notion of a 'history from the bottom up', which begins from the detail of located human experiences, only later addressing wider issues of causality (e.g. Thompson 1963). Unfortunately, within both archaeology and history, a disadvantage of studies which focus on the immediate circumstances within which human beings find themselves has been a degree of under-theorisation. Marxism, evolutionary ecology, structuralism, functionalism and *Annaliste* approaches have all tended to favour the investigation of macrosocial processes (see Skinner 1985), while an interest in the minutiae of human existence has often been associated with empiricism. However, the growing influence of cultural studies within academic thought, and the emergence of feminism, structuration theory and phenomenology as significant elements in archaeological analysis have all increased the extent to which everyday life can be minutely scrutinised.

The result of these developments has been a growing tension within prehistoric archaeology, which has none the less been remarked upon relatively rarely. Andrew Sherratt evidently considers that archaeological analysis has become far too myopic:

The spatial scale of phenomena such as the Bell-beaker culture or the Lapita complex render inadequate any methodology based solely on 'case studies' which privilege local understanding at the expense of wider settings. By continuing this procedure of New Archaeology ... and foreclosing research into 'grand themes'... such a methodology actively impedes an understanding of the larger structures within which such local manifestations occur.

(1993, 126)

The implication of Sherratt's argument is that these 'local manifestations' are representative of broader patterns which are relatively homogeneous and which can be grasped in their entirety. We can certainly agree with Sherratt's formulation of the problem: world prehistory documents the existence of material forms which are relatively uniform across vast areas, and we do need to understand how these similarities arise. However, it is another question whether the shared morphology of pots, or house plans, or metalwork necessarily means that the *significance* of these objects is homogeneous as well. Consequently, an explanation which operates at the level of shared material form may be no explanation at all. It seems to be a characteristic of accounts of prehistory which deal with very large-scale entities that they tend to presume a fixed relationship between material culture and human identity. It may be for this reason that European prehistory is still largely written in terms of 'cultures', decades after the Childean model has been rejected.

This is not to deny that innovative attempts have been made to write 'archaeology as long-term (and large-scale) history'. In *The Domestication of Europe* (1990), Ian Hodder interprets the European Neolithic sequence as representing the playing-out of a long-term structure which underlies architectural form, artefactual style and funerary rites. This structure, involving an opposition between the *domus* (the house and the domestic world) and the *agrios* (the wild) thus constitutes a set of rules or codes which underpins a 'story which unfolds gradually across Europe' (Hodder 1990, 42). Hodder's structuralism contrasts oddly with many other recent prehistories (e.g. Edmonds 1993; Richards 1993), which many would categorise together with his work as representative of a 'post-processual archaeology'. These works are far more concerned with detail and with the specificity of the local context, but they are sometimes reluctant to place themselves in a broader picture like that constructed by Hodder. We might choose to argue that Hodder's vision of a structure of meaning which determines thousands of years of prehistory is questionable, on the grounds that meanings are unlikely to maintain this degree of stability over time. Meaning, we might suggest, is not a structural quality contained in a mental template or a cultural form, so much as an interpretation which people create through their engagement with the material world (Barthes 1981; Olssen 1990). However, this does not free us from the necessity of accounting for the large-scale patterns of material regularity which distinguish (amongst other areas) the European Neolithic.

It seems that focusing on the global or the local scale encourages one to prefer particular kinds of interpretation. This suggests that, considered in 'close-up' or from a distance, historical phenomena may disclose different aspects of their character. At the least, they involve us in different kinds of thinking. To reiterate, this does not imply that these different 'scales' have an absolute value. Nor can we argue that meaningful social phenomena obey some pseudo-evolutionary logic when considered in the long term (e.g. Bailey 1981). But it *may* suggest that our understanding of how material resources are used on a day-to-day basis might be different in kind from grasping how those resources are deployed and reproduced over great expanses of space and time. Moreover, rather than accept a choice between 'top-down' and 'bottom-up' approaches, we could argue that while the two are incompatible, they none the less presuppose and require each other. That is to say, there is little point in our constructing a radical re-interpretation of a particular site, involving subtle readings of gender and ethnic identities, if it can have no impact on a large-scale under-standing of the past which is still written in terms of 'cultures'. This means that while we have to have concepts and language which are adequate to describing different aspects of historical processes that have different extents and durations, there is a need to 'tack back and forth' between these different accounts, so that each informs and contextualises the other.

This chapter is intended to address this set of issues by investigating a particular archaeological problem which seemingly demands a consideration of very large scale entities. At the start of the Neolithic in the British Isles, a range of material forms emerged which are similar to artefact and monument styles current on the European continent (Kinnes 1988). The European material, in turn, is lodged in a complex set of regional sequences and processes which extend back for hundreds of years. It seems to follow that understanding the British Mesolithic–Neolithic transition requires some form of explanation for this vast pattern of prehistoric change. This demands an analysis which accepts on the one hand that material culture is implicated in the ways in which people construct meaningful worlds, but on the other that there may be no trans-historic structure underlying long-term developments. In deference to Foucault's 'genealogical' histories, I will suggest that what is under consideration is the 'descent' of the British Neolithic: a concatenation of numberless events by which a particular set of material resources came to crystallise and to be widely adopted in a particular place at a particular time.

THE *LINNEARBANDKERAMIK*

In what sense might the first Neolithic communities north of the Alps, the *Linnearbandkeramik*, be said to have contributed anything to the formation of the British Neolithic, hundreds of years later? This seems to be a question which presumes the operation of long-term historical continuities. Admittedly, in that domesticated plants and animals, pottery and polished stone tools were introduced into central and western Europe by these communities, there must have been a certain connection with subsequent developments. But it seems to be difficult to ask the question at all without implicitly accepting the framework of culture history. The task is a more subtle one than simply distinguishing which elements were held in common by the two temporally separate entities. It requires an investigation of the means of descent by which a cultural inheritance was passed on from one set of hands to another, in the process being transformed in form or significance. In order to do this, it is first necessary to consider exactly what sort of an entity the *Linnearbandkeramik* (LBK) might have been. This is not a straightforward issue, for although the LBK is one of the classic archaeological 'cultures', in which pottery styles, funerary practices and house forms were remarkably homogeneous over vast geographical distances, it need not follow that all of the people using this material represented a single social entity, kinship network, language group or ethnic unit.

The LBK appeared in the areas around the Danube, Rhine and Elbe at around 5350 BC/4500 bc, initially occurring in Bavaria, Bohemia, Moravia, southern Poland and the western Ukraine (Bogucki and Grygiel 1993a, 403; Kreutz 1990, 249; Kukzycka-Leciejewiczawa 1983), but gradually spreading to encompass parts of Holland, Belgium and eastern France (figure 5.1). Across the whole of this area, material culture showed a high degree of uniformity which is most notable in the case of the distinctive timber longhouses (Coudart 1991, 404). Polished stone adzes, too, are virtually indistinguishable from one region to another, and the chipped stone assemblages of Bavaria, Poland, Hungary and the Dutch Limburg are more or less interchangeable in respect of their technology (Modderman 1988, 104; de Grooth 1987, 37). This homogeneity has sometimes been taken to denote 'an almost pathological conventionality' (Keeley 1992, 82). In other words, it is implied that similarities in material culture reflect uniformity at a structural level. Thus in relation to house design, Coudart argues that 'by its very high degree of conformity to a specific model, the Bandkeramik architecture reveals the strong cultural unity of the Bandkeramik populations' (1991, 404). In contrast to these arguments I will suggest that LBK material culture was not necessarily the manifestation of a commonly held system of belief, structure of meaning, or way of life. Instead, we might

think of these material things as a *technology of meaning:* a technology which allowed meanings to be produced. While it was composed
of forms which were stable across space, its significance was realised in
quite different ways in different contexts. Each artefactual style might have
a meaning which was lodged in tradition, yet this would be open to negotiation and re-encoding at the local level. It is not necessary for an object
to change its appearance for its meaning to be transformed. Only much
later, when they had been fully bound up in the creation of a series of
localised group identities, did the material forms themselves begin to
change. If we wish to find a long-term process in the development of the
LBK, it may lie in the emerging tension between increasingly defined local
systems of meaning and the global repertoire of material forms.

The spread of the LBK from central to western Europe is difficult to
date accurately, but may have taken less than a century (Modderman 1988,
68). Given the relatively low densities of settlement involved, it is difficult
now to see this expansion as the consequence of runaway population
growth, as Ammerman and Cavalli-Sforza's (1973) 'wave of advance model'
might suggest (Milisauskas and Kruk 1989, 406). Indeed, this interpretation
begs the question we have already posed, concerning the precise kind
of entity which we can recognise spreading across Europe through the
changing distributions of potsherds, domesticates and houseforms. One
argument *might* be that the unity of the LBK was maintained as a result
of shared economic practices, and that the uniformity of material culture
consequently reflects a more fundamental unity. In broadly this spirit,
Bogucki describes the LBK as an agricultural adaptation to temperate conditions (Bogucki 1988). A less determinist (if somewhat normative) form of
the same argument would be to suggest that settlement form, artefact style
and agricultural practice represented integrated elements of a total 'way of
life'. Since LBK people across Europe shared the same routines and rhythms
of life, they might also maintain the same material culture. Admittedly, the
evidence does suggest that the artefactual conformity of the LBK is matched
by a regularity of settlement location and preferred resources. In many
parts of Europe, LBK settlements were established on the edges of loess
plateaux, within comfortable reach of lesser watercourses flowing into
major rivers (Bakels 1982; Lüning 1982a). This implies a preference for
locations which allowed access to hillslopes with light soils for agriculture,
and valley bottoms which provided grazing for livestock and oak for
building material, but which were not susceptible to inundation (Louwe-
Kooijmans 1976, 235; Lüning 1982, 14).

A perennial problem of economic archaeology has been the difficulty
of integrating faunal, botanical and locational evidence, since the relative importance of animal and plant resources to a community is almost
impossible to assess. Recently, Alasdair Whittle (1995) has suggested that
the consensus view of LBK people as having practised a form of mixed

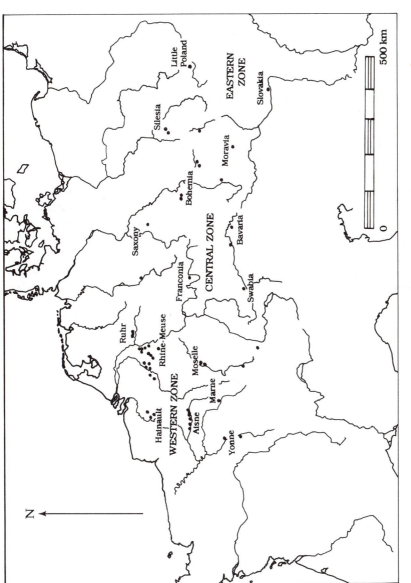

Figure 5.1 The extent of *Linnearbandkeramik* settlement in Europe (after Coudart 1991)

agriculture, which has largely replaced the model of slash-and-burn horticulture, can itself be questioned. Rather than imagine that LBK settlements
were the equivalent of medieval farmyards, Whittle emphasises the central
role of cattle, and stresses the potentially high degree of mobility which a
pastoral way of life would involve. Other authorities have previously argued
that livestock were of critical importance to the LBK, and that this might
have required a high degree of residential mobility (e.g. Bogucki 1987, 7).
However, any notion of LBK people following their herds from place to
place seems ostensibly to conflict with the evidence of stable and long-lived
longhouse settlements just as much as does the original swiddening hypothesis. Whittle's counter-argument is that the settlements might represent
fixed places within a cyclical and seasonal pattern of movement, and that
consequently the everyday lives of these Neolithic communities were very
similar to those the hunters and gatherers whom they might periodically
have encountered. Both would have been mobile societies, regularly
returning to particular key places. This is an attractive picture, and it
demands that some of our questions concerning long-term cultural inheritance be recast. If the economic practices of Mesolithic hunter-gatherers
and Neolithic herders were relatively compatible, why did they maintain
their separate identities for so long? Conversely, if as this suggests livestock might have been introduced into the Mesolithic way of life without
causing a major disruption of the spatiotemporal rhythms which enable
the reproduction of such societies, how is it that we can distinguish the
Mesolithic-Neolithic transition in Britain and several other parts of the
north-western fringe of Europe as a significant horizon of change?

I will suggest that some part of the answer lies in the material culture
of the LBK and subsequent Neolithic groups. However, I will not argue
that this 'Culture' enabled Neolithic people to distinguish themselves from
the 'Nature' surrounding them. Instead, artefacts and architecture may have
represented means of intervening in and transforming the world, without
in any sense abstracting oneself from it. The most salient quality of LBK
longhouses is, of course, that they are *buildings*. As such, they embody the
distinctive activity of building, which as Heidegger describes it is a form
of transformation, but also a means of dwelling, of abiding with things,
sparing them, and entering into a relationship with them. Through building,
people establish a connectedness with their world, which lays the conditions under which the unconsidered and habitual practices of everyday life
may proceed. My argument will be that Neolithic material culture did not
consist of materials extracted from the natural world and set against it, but
that in engaging with materials in certain ways, people were drawn into a
connectedness with their world. Timber houses represent only the most
obvious case in which the Neolithic constitutes *building*. The making of
pots, or of particular kinds of stone tools, are also means by which human
beings might engage with worldly substances, and establish relationships

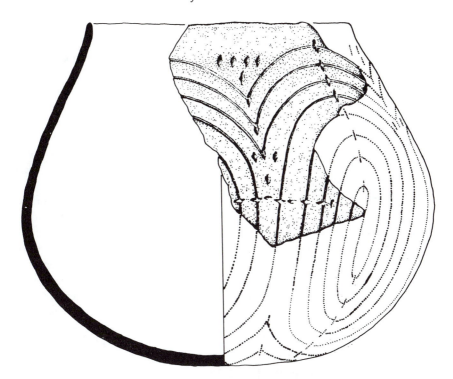

Figure 5.2 *Linnearbandkeramik* pot

with them in the process of changing them. And beyond this, houses, pots and tools all persisted as permanent witnesses to these relationships, which actually entered into the way in which people dwelt in their world. A building is both a project of construction and a means through which people dwell. Neolithic material culture both brought a world into being and continually reproduced human relations in and with that world.

It may not be entirely helpful to attempt to set up a view of the LBK in which a particular economic base enabled the maintenance of a cultural superstructure. The ecological potential of temperate Europe was quite adequate to have allowed any one of a number of different subsistence regimes, which might easily have been tailored to the localised resources of different regions. Moreover, the evident emphasis on cattle can hardly be presented as an optimising economic strategy, since the keeping of larger numbers of pigs would have provided more meat for less effort in a largely wooded landscape (Keeley 1992, 86). From their earliest appearance in central Europe, LBK communities appear to have kept cattle almost to the exclusion of other domestic species, and the characteristic which is most variable from one faunal assemblage to another is the representation of wild species (Kukzycka-Leciejewiczawa 1983, 54). However, rather than suggest that cattle husbandry represented a cultural predisposition of the LBK peoples, which was simply imposed upon a permissive ecosystem, we could argue that like the building of houses, the following of herds represented a particular kind of dwelling in a landscape. By enacting a certain set of economic practices, people will have developed patterns of mobility and rhythms of work through which a familiarity with places and landscapes will have been promoted. In these terms, the distinction between subsistence economy as the production of a certain number of calories of energy and culture as a means of understanding the world makes no sense whatever. Neither has a priority over the other.

One aspect of the analysis of LBK subsistence patterns which has proved instructive has been the attempt to establish 'exploitation territories' around sites. On the loess, LBK settlement sites have a markedly discontinuous distribution. Clusters of sites like those on the Aldenhovener Platte, in the Dutch Limburg and the Belgian Hesbaye and Hainault may be separated by as much 100 km of loess upland (Keeley and Cahen 1989, 159) (figure 5.3). The relative density of these *siedlungskammer*, or 'settlement cells' might easily indicate that the hamlets, villages or isolated houses of which they are composed were integrated by ties of exchange, interaction and kinship. These ties overrode any imperative to spread out over the untouched land between the settlement clusters. On this basis, Bakels suggests that each site in the Dutch Limburg would have had a 'territory' of 60–170 ha (Bakels 1982, 37). Bogucki (1988, 88) argues that for a herd of cattle to be biologically viable, to survive disease and predation, provide meat and reproduce itself, between thirty and fifty beasts must be kept. A herd of fifty cattle would require something of the order of 70 ha of open grassland in order to ensure adequate grazing, yet pollen analysis in the Limburg indicates a largely closed forest canopy, with very small patches of cultivated land, and meadow in the valley bottoms. This picture is corroborated by assemblages of charred plant remains dominated by shade-loving weeds, suggesting garden plots of cereals surrounded by forest. While clearance in the Belgian Hesbaye may have been more extensive (Keeley 1992, 86), it is clear that the Dutch LBK sites could not have functioned as self-contained cattle-producing centres. Without even needing to invoke the obvious philosophical objections to territorial hypotheses in prehistory, we can dispense with the image of LBK farmsteads set at the centre of infield/outfield systems. Two conclusions follow from this: herds of cattle were probably not held as the exclusive property of individual households, and animals were probably not grazed in the immediate vicinity of the settlements for all of the year.

In this connection, it is relevant to note that not all LBK occupations are distinguished by the presence of large timber houses. Across the North European Plain, in lowland areas beyond the loess belt (such as the Dutch

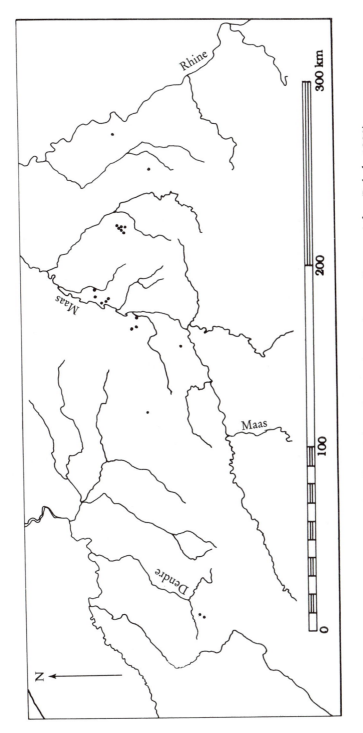

Figure 5.3 *Linnearbandkeramik* settlement in north-west Europe (after Bakels 1982)

sandy soils), small sites with no house plans are comparatively well-known (Wansleben and Verhart 1990, 398; Bogucki and Grygiel 1993a, 413). These are often conjectured to have been temporary settlements. Structural remains are restricted to shallow pits, while the faunal assemblages from these sites are dominated by cattle bones, and traces of domesticated cereals are very scarce (Milisauskas and Kruk 1989, 409). Bogucki and Grygiel (1993a, 414) have suggested that these sites may represent a specialised LBK adaptation to lowland conditions, but it might be more plausible to see them as complementary to the loess settlements. If all or part of the upland LBK communities were to herd their cattle into the lowlands on a seasonal basis, these occupations might be the consequence: temporary camps without evidence of horticulture. Graves are also absent from the lowlands, and it may have been that anyone who died in the transhumant season was brought back to the more permanent occupational focus for burial.

This evidence appears to support Whittle's 'mobile LBK' hypothesis, and argues that we should reconsider the character of the longhouse settlements. Since the excavations of Köln-Lindenthal and Bylany, the image of dozens of massive posthole structures, aligned on a common axis, has dominated our understanding of the European early Neolithic. Perhaps too often, any discussion of what people did in these places has been restricted to the identification of activity areas and room functions. A reconsideration might begin by asking why the houses themselves were so massively constructed, by comparison with the domestic structures of later prehistory and protohistory in northern Europe. The impression of architectural homogeneity can largely be attributed to the modular structure of the longhouses. Each house is composed of some combination of three structural units: a 'north-west' part which was generally surrounded by plank rather than wattle walling; a central part in which the upright posts were relatively distantly spaced; a 'south-east' part in which the posts were often paired, suggesting an upper floor (Modderman 1975, 268). Most often, these are described as functionally distinct elements: a sleeping area, a living area with hearths, and a storage area with a raised granary (Modderman 1988, 96). Rather than argue for this hermetic separation of functions, we might suggest that everyday activities are likely to have been dispersed or stretched across the internal spaces of the house. Hodder (1990, 119) argues that since the houses were probably entered from the south-east end, their internal space was effectively graded in a linear fashion, between the 'public' front and the more secluded back. If this is so, it seems unlikely that the most public part of the house would have been a storage area, through which one would have had to have passed in order to gain access to the living space. An alternative might have been that the front space had a raised floor which served as a focus for semi-public activities within the house. These might have ranged from eating, receiving visitors, and exchanging to laying out the dead and conducting ritual performances. This much is supported

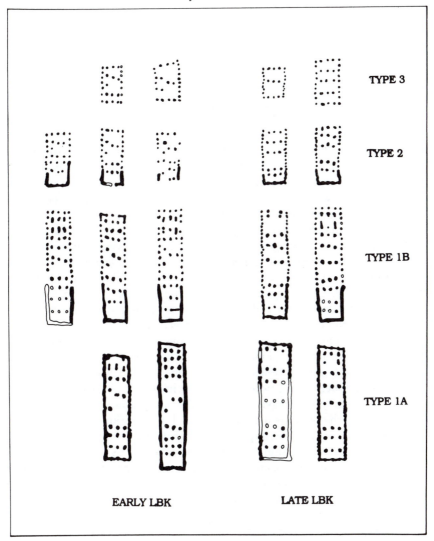

Figure 5.4 *Linnearbandkeramik* house plans (after Modderman 1988)

by the concentration of finds of pottery around the entrances of houses (Lüning 1982a, 18).

Three basic house types can be defined according to which of the structural elements are present. The largest (*Grossbauten*) are composed of all three parts, the medium-sized houses (*Bauten*) lack the 'south-eastern' raised unit, while the smallest (*Kleinbauten*) have only the central part (figure 5.4). While there is always a large house on any excavated settlement, the numbers of the smaller structures appear to have increased through time (Modderman 1988, 99). Thus amongst the Aldenhovener Platte sites, the medium-sized houses are later in date, while at Bylany there are more small houses in the later phases of occupation (Lüning 1982a, 15; Soudský 1962, 192). This indicates that whatever the purpose of the 'south-east' part of the house, at some sites it was confined to a smaller number of houses as time went on. Following the suggestion that this space was used for semi-public activities which gathered people together, we could argue that these activities were increasingly concentrated in fewer houses. Where both large and smaller houses are present in the same settlement, the artefactual assemblages from each are often quite distinct. The large houses at Langweiler 8 were surrounded by a larger number of pits containing arte-factual material, while amongst the Limburg sites adzes were preferentially associated with such houses (Lüning 1982a, 17; van der Velde 1990, 32). At Cuiry-les-Chaudardes, the large house number 380 had over 50 per cent of the flaked stone debitage from the entire site, but very few tools (Illett *et al.* 1982, 58; Keeley and Cahen 1989, 158). Longhouse 6 at Olszanica was a focus for finds of axes, adzes and chisels (Milisauskas 1972, 72). Another particularly interesting contrast was evident at Langweiler 8, where, despite clean grain and quernstones being found in the immediate area of all of the houses, more chaff and weed remains were found in the large houses (Lüning 1982a, 17). While van der Velde (1990) uses this infor-mation to construct an argument in which the large houses are connected with more highly ranked households, this kind of social stratification is not necessarily implied. The gradual restriction in the numbers of 'south-east' house elements might have involved the concentration of communal activities like the winnowing of grain and flintworking into a smaller number of spaces. Yet this might indicate that in these often larger settle-ments, only one such communal area was required by a kin group who occupied a number of separate houses. Whichever the case, the variations in the ratio of large:medium:small houses between different parts of Europe (2 per cent of structures at Köln-Lindenthal were large houses, as opposed to 14 per cent in the Limburg: van der Velde 1990, 25) provides an indication that social relations were not identical in all LBK communities.

As constructed spaces, LBK longhouses were symbolic forms as much as they were shelters, even if we can argue that the meanings attributed to them were not fixed within or between communities. Several aspects of their design imply that their construction was conventional and set in tradi-tion. The north-west/south-east orientation does not correlate with patterns of prevailing winds in all areas (Modderman 1988, 90), and is more likely a solar orientation. Any communal space around the house entrance would face into the morning sunlight. Oak was used almost exclusively for the building of houses, although it did not always dominate the forest surrounding the settlements. Other woods were used for other purposes: pine was preferred for fuel, for instance (Modderman 1988, 93; Kreutz 1990,

251). This suggests an acute awareness of the materials which were being used, and a recognition that in reconfiguring one's material surroundings, a repertoire of material symbols is being brought into play. The establishment of an LBK settlement would have involved the felling of trees and their re-erection as posts, and the digging of holes in the ground, revealing earth and subsoil and providing material for daub. These acts will have had the effect of making these materials show up in a conspicuous way, so that dwellings were created which were at once clearly human products and yet still connected to the earth. Such a project of construction will have forged a community's relationship with a place, and will have done so by drawing upon earthly materials in both a symbolic and a quotidian way. Dwelling within these structures, people would effectively have been bound into the substance of the place. The individual houses were monumental structures, far more substantial than would be required for the mere provision of shelter. The number of load-bearing posts within each house is far greater than is strictly required (Coudart 1987, 4), and the effect of this will have been to impede movement and restrict lines of sight within the structure. LBK buildings were intended to last, and to represent an enduring presence in the landscape: as Whittle suggests, a significant place to come back to. Inside, they would constitute an impressive volume of dark, enclosed space. However, the total scale of this space would only have been appreciable from certain points within the house. For the most part, the houses would have been experienced as vaulting spaces subdivided by upright trunks, not unlike the forest spaces familiar to their inhabitants.

The orientation, layout and constituent materials of LBK longhouses were such that dwelling in them and moving around them would have generated a rich fabric of meaning. The same could be said of the actual process of construction. As Startin (1978) implies, more people may have been involved in building the houses than would have lived in them, so that the provision of labour would have been a means through which alliances were expressed and indebtedness negotiated. Once built, the house would become a testament to the pooled labour of households or kin groups. Amongst the most characteristic structural features of the buildings are the pits which run outside and parallel to their side walls. Milisauskas (1972, 70) has demonstrated that the volume of these pits would have been adequate to provide sufficient clay for use as daub on the wattle walls. However, in areas like the Aisne valley where houses were built on a gravel subsoil, the pits are still present. Illett *et al.* (1982, 55) suggest that in these circumstances the pits may have served primarily as mixing basins, where different substances were brought together and melded into a material to smear onto the hurdlework. In many places where cob walls are constructed today, materials which would have been available to LBK communities are used as binding agents: chaff, cereal stalks, animal dung and cattle blood. It is perhaps not too much to claim that the longhouses were not simply built from the substance of these materials, but from their meanings as well. The act of construction would thus have fixed, spatially, a set of relationships between households and their labour, the forest, livestock, earth and plants. The house became an embodiment of those relations that structured these people's world. As in many contemporary societies, the house is a microcosm of the world at large, objectifying the order of the cosmos at a scale in which human beings can intervene decisively (Hugh-Jones 1979, 235; Bourdieu 1970, 160). However, houses are never merely a representation of a community's surroundings; they provide an orientation and an attunement to the world by establishing a frame for everyday activities (Moore 1986).

In discussing the Neolithic of south-east Europe, Ruth Tringham (1991, 123) has suggested that there is a connection between the life cycle of a household and that of the house itself. At Opovo, houses appear to have conventionally been burnt at the end of their use, and Tringham makes the suggestion that this burning may have taken place on the death of the head of the household. This provides an instructive contrast with LBK houses. These were rarely ever burned, and instead appear to have been allowed to slowly collapse and rot where they stood (Modderman 1988, 97). None the less, the abandonment of a particular house was generally followed by its replacement by a new structure close by, indicating a sense of continuity with a particular community occupying a certain space through the generations (Van der Velde 1979, 130). If a house were not continuously occupied by all of its household, and were to be conceived of as a place to which people returned at intervals, it might have a certain autonomy of identity, as opposed to the congruence of house and household which Tringham describes. LBK houses would have been places which had histories of their own, punctuated by the cycles of separation and return which structured the lives of their occupants. Individual buildings and settlements might then be said to have had narratives, made up of the processes of construction, dwelling and decay, and the rotting houses which would have formed a part of each settlement served as evidence of the continuing relationship between people and place (Bradley 1994). This is not to imply that housebuilding represented a kind of claim to territorial rights, so much as that the manifest history represented by occupied and decaying houses demonstrated a sense of coherence which the social group itself may have lacked. If we are to argue that the circulation of herds of cattle from place to place was a pivotal institution in LBK life, it may not be that all of the community was involved in this seasonal movement. Other people may have stayed at the settlements, tending cultivated plots, while others still may have gone in search of wild resources. We should not assume that the subsistence tasks undertaken by a prehistoric community were undifferentiated, and any division of labour will involve heterogeneous patterns of movement and experiences of the world. As places where these communities periodically reconstituted themselves, houses and settlements embodied the history of the group.

Thinking in these terms renders several aspects of LBK settlements and houses comprehensible. At Bylany, Soudský remarks that there was no trace of repair to the houses (1962, 199), and this may imply that rather than being routinely renovated, buildings were replaced comparatively often. House building was a conscious intervention through which communities created their relationship with their surroundings, and in the process reaffirmed their ties with each other. By building structures which were far more monumental than was required, these relationships were dramatised and enhanced, while the event of building itself became an opportunity for the performance of sociality. Furthermore, the buildings contained spaces within which communal activities could take place. The elaborate raised area immediately inside the entrance represented a 'stage' for performances which drew the household and its allies together. Because the houses were places in which activities such as meetings, corporate labour, feasting, the laying out of the dead, visiting, the exchange of gifts, marriages and so on will have occurred, they were places within which memories would cluster. In a sense, people would remain *close* to them even when physically distant. As the centre of a person's social world, the longhouse was a place which they would both carry with them and return to, and hence it was their relationship with that place which was instrumental in the maintenance of group identity.

These group identities were not given, but were reproduced by being performed, within the space of the longhouse and in the seasonal patterns of separation and reunion. Identity was thus a matter of practice, continually being brought into being. Consequently, although the house and its attendant material culture was the means through which communities were created, the performances in which they were caught up differed from place to place. At particular sites, details of artefact distribution and deposition reveal subtle variations in the ways in which houses and their immediate surroundings were used. At Olszanica, the east and west sides of the houses were associated with different tool assemblages: plain blades and endscrapers versus scrapers and cores respectively (Milisauskas and Kruk 1993, 75). At Langweiler 8, each house was surrounded by a characteristic pattern of pits, in addition to those flanking the house. Distinctive sets of artefacts were found in pits in specific locations (Lüning 1982a). At Cuiry-les-Chaudardes, two distinctive 'tool kits' (arrowheads and borers versus serrated flake tools) were found associated with different houses (Illett *et al.* 1982, 58). Some of these sets of artefacts may arise from particular activities having been concentrated in specific areas, while others might be the consequence of differentiated patterns of discard and deposition. The latter in turn might have been considered as overt symbolic statements, or might simply have been guided by criteria of the relative appropriateness of locations for disposing of particular materials. Whichever is the case, patterns of repeated activity in relation to the longhouses (whether everyday or 'ritual') appear to have given meaning to space in rather localised ways. LBK longhouses contextualised, framed and dramatised everyday activities within a monumental context, drawing attention to social interaction in such a way as to facilitate social integration. At the same time, by locating this process spatially, settlements fixed a particular place as being instrumental in founding a relationship between a group of people and their world. In all of these respects, the house was not a structure that possessed a positive meaning, so much as being a means by which the meanings of places and activities might be created.

In a similar way, the artefacts of the LBK demonstrate the common currency of a range of material forms amongst widely dispersed communities who need not necessarily have held much else in common. Stone tools, in particular, appear to have been exchanged over considerable distances. Materials for the manufacture of blade tools, like Polish and Limburg flint and Slovakian obsidian, were frequently moved over at least 20 km (Modderman 1988, 123; Kozlowski 1989, 391). Stone adzes were often made of materials which had to be brought over 100 km to their place of use (van der Velde 1990, 32). In the west, it has been recognised that each cluster of sites ('settlement cell') may have used adzes drawn from a particular distant source (Keeley and Cahen 1989, 174). These examples demonstrate the existence of mechanisms capable of circulating raw materials and finished goods over very long distances, and represent another argument that LBK groups formed parts of a higher-level entity. Yet what is striking is that these objects were often used in rather different ways by different groups. The stone adze is as much as any other artefact seen as en emblem of LBK unity, a symbol held in common by distant social units. However, in funerary contexts, this symbol appears not to have had an unequivocal meaning. At Sonderhausen, adzes were found exclusively with male burials, while at Aiterhofen adzes were only predominately in male graves. However, at Nitra adzes were found with a number of female burials (Bakels 1987, 77). While this begs a number of questions concerning the relationship between biologically sexed skeletons and gender identities in the past, it suggests that the ways in which artefacts were used to present the social identities of the dead were not uniform from one community to the next. In his study of the cemetery at Elsloo, van der Velde attempted to distinguish between male and female graves on the basis of artefact associations (1979, 84). However, there was a great deal of overlap between the artefact sets that he was able to define, many graves not being clearly 'male' or 'female'. While inhumations and cremations were rather distinct in their sets of associations, most of the grave goods found at Elsloo could be combined with each other. This suggests that rather than forming a rigid semiotic system for expressing rank or gender, the burial of artefacts with the dead was a flexible and strategic means of attributing meaning to the dead body.

On the periphery

Although the *Linnearbandkeramik* is presented as an homogeneous cultural phenomenon, an integrated package which introduced agriculture and pottery to the north and west of Europe, there are a number of less well known assemblages from around the peripheries of the LBK zone that require discussion. The first of these is the La Hoguette pottery, from the Rhine, Main, Neckar and Maas valleys, as well as scattered occurrences further west. This material appears to be as early in date as the earliest LBK (Bogucki and Grygiel 1993a, 406). It includes vessels which are deep and conical, with ridges and raised bands (Lüning *et al.* 1989) (figure 5.5).

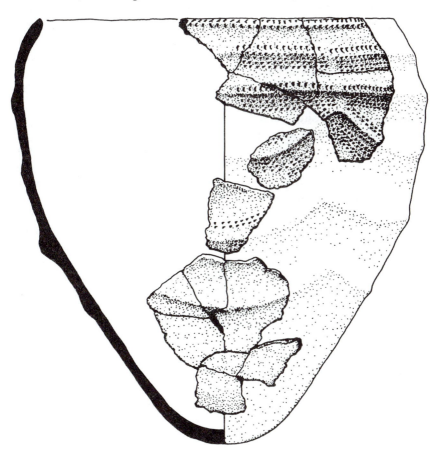

Figure 5.5 La Hoguette style pot (after Lüning *et al.* 1989)

A number of authors have pointed out that while these pots are dissimilar from LBK wares, they may have a generalised affinity with the Cardial pottery of the Mediterranean (Lüning *et al.* 1989). At Friedberg-Bruchenbrüken, an earliest LBK site from the Rhine-Main area, La Hoguette pottery was found in substantial quantities. On the same site, an appreciable proportion of the lithic assemblage was made up of Maas valley flint. At this time, the Maas was not occupied by LBK settlements, and it has been suggested that both the flint and the pottery were acquired through exchange with non-LBK people (Gronenborn 1990). At sites like Sweikhuizen near Geleen, La Hoguette assemblages unassociated with LBK material have been recovered (Louwe-Kooijmans 1993, 125). This presents the interesting possibility that on the western fringe of the LBK, from its earliest inception, groups of people existed who were in contact with LBK settlements, yet who were using a distinct material culture. Presumably, these people must have been indigenous, and formally Mesolithic, although little can be said concerning their subsistence economy. If so, these were communities which were able to adopt some aspects of Neolithic material culture (whether through contact with LBK or Cardial users or both), without becoming fully assimilated.

Rather later, contemporary with late LBK, the so-called Limburg pottery emerged, and is found in a similar geographical area. Limburg pottery is also found on LBK sites, as at Köln-Lindenthal and in the pits at Cuiry-les-Chaudardes, as well as in 'pure' assemblages in areas outside the LBK zone, as at Kesseleyk on the Limburg sands (Louwe-Kooijmans 1976, 238). In most respects, Limburg pottery is distinct from LBK ceramics: it has different forms and firing, and is heavily gritted with organic temper, including bone (Bogucki 1988, 109; Keeley 1992, 82). Its decoration with cross-hatched areas and incised lines is also distinctive (Bogucki and Grygiel 1993a, 406). Once again, connections with Cardial Ware have been invoked to explain this material (Keeley and Cahen 1989, 171; Louwe-Kooijmans 1993, 125). Finally, and still later, in the Belgian Hainault the Blicquy group pottery may represent a similar phenomenon to La Hoguette and Limburg. This pottery again occurs both in LBK contexts and alone (Modderman 1988, 125), although the possibility exists that it represents no more than a local style derived from the LBK tradition. Taken together, these assemblages may suggest that while the LBK constituted a closed cultural world, where a certain set of material forms were reproduced through many generations, other communities were able to appropriate aspects of the tradition and put them to new uses. If the connections with the Cardial zone are not too fanciful, it may be that these groups were engaged in a kind of *bricolage*, adopting elements of different traditions and mixing them together in novel ways. This is a pattern which we will later see to be more widespread, for in the period in which the LBK devolved into a series of localised material traditions, many Mesolithic groups in the surrounding areas seem to have adopted Neolithic innovations in quite varied ways. However, this raises a considerable problem. What was it about the La Hoguette, Limburg and other late Mesolithic groups which differentiated them from the LBK communities? Why were the former able to take up Neolithic traits piecemeal, while the latter maintained the integrity of a cultural assemblage for hundreds of years? We have suggested that in terms of social organisation there may have been great variability within the LBK, and it may not be necessary to argue that all LBK groups were colonists from the east. The main distinction between an LBK community and its neighbours may have been that one used an interconnected set of material culture as a medium for establishing its place in the world, while the other experimented with creating a new symbolic order. The difference, then, may be between a flexible pool of material resources and a *tradition*.

Post-Bandkeramik Developments

Throughout much of the area which had been occupied by the LBK communities, the period after 4800 BC (*c.* 4000 bc) was one of considerable change or reorganisation. Discontinuity can be recognised in material culture, funerary practice and settlement organisation. This is most obvious in pottery decoration. In the middle phase of the LBK, a broad division had emerged between eastern ceramic styles with *Notenkopf* punctuated decoration, and western assemblages with more complex unpunctuated motifs (Bogucki and Grygiel 1993a, 403). Later, quite distinct regional ceramic styles developed. In the Rhine/Maas area, *stich* filling was used within decorative bands; in the Rhine/Main region, fine hatching was employed; in the Main/Moselle district, bands were filled with herringbone (Louwe-Kooijmans 1976, 239). In the Aisne valley, vertical band motifs and pivoted comb decoration were employed, while in Moravia and Poland the Zeliezovce style involved angular incisions and lozenge-shaped punctuations, and in Silesia and Bohemia the Sarka style has ladder and herringbone motifs and stab-and-drag marks filled with white pigment (Illett *et al.* 1982, 47; Bogucki and Grygiel 1993a, 404). Gradually, this process of regionalisation gathered pace, resulting in the formation of what are recognised as distinct regional 'cultures': the Rubané Récent du Bassin Parisien, Villeneuve-Saint-Germain, the Omalian of Belgium, Grossgartach in the Rhineland, Hinkelstein in the Upper Rhine and the *Stichbandkeramik* of eastern Germany and Poland. These in turn would give way to yet more distinctive entities in the Cerny, Rössen, Bischeim and Lengyel. Bogucki (1988) defines all of these groups, together with the LBK, as elements of a 'primary Neolithic'. This is an important characterisation, for in a sense all of these changes in material culture can be seen as permutations derived from the range of possibilities made available by the original LBK material assemblage. Following the arguments developed earlier in this book, we could suggest that this diversification of material culture style was not merely a reflection of growing regionalisation, but that to some extent it was a means through which bounded identities were brought into being. This need not have involved any external influence from other societies or from changing environmental circumstances: it seems that those communities which were embedded in the LBK tradition were undergoing a series of transformations which were internally generated. In many areas, this was a period in which settlement contracted, and there was little sign of expansion onto the western part of the north European Plain (Starling 1985, 49; Louwe-Kooijmans 1987, 234). In the Rhineland, the number of settlements occupied appears to have declined in a process of nucleation, and on the Aldernhovener Platte abandoned sites were replaced by larger groupings of trapezoid houses (Bogucki 1988, 100; Louwe-Kooijmans 1976, 241). In central and southern Germany, *Stichbandkeramik*, Rössen and Gatersleben settlements are all considerably more nucleated than LBK sites had been (Starling 1985, 44; Hodgson 1988, 369).

The sequence on the loess country thus gives an impression of societies drawing back into themselves, while using the symbolic resources available to them in order to forge more distinct local identities. However, in two particular areas, changes were taking place which were somewhat at odds with this pattern of retrenchment. In the eastern part of the north European Plain, and in northern France, there is a clear picture of continued 'Neolithicisation', although there is every indication that this was quite different in character from the initial LBK expansion. The developments which took place in these regions help to illustrate the more general structural problems which were afflicting the post-LBK primary Neolithic communities, but at the same time they show new social and cultural forms beginning to emerge which drew as much from indigenous Mesolithic ways of life as from the LBK heritage. My suggestion is that it was in these areas of enhanced cultural *bricolage* that the foundations were laid for a quite different form of Neolithic – patterns which would only become more widespread much later.

In the eastern part of the north European plain, this sequence is one which culminates in the *Trichterbecherkultur* (TRB), a cultural entity whose geographical extent would eventually rival that of the LBK (Midgley 1992). As in the case of the LBK, the question of exactly what it means for people over such a vast area to be simultaneously making use of closely related forms of material culture is not one which has been satisfactorily answered. The first traces of substantial Neolithic settlement on the north European plain date to the Late Lengyel/Rössen phase (*c.* 3400 bc/4200 BC), by which time the character of primary Neolithic activity had diverged considerably from the LBK pattern. Rössen and Lengyel longhouses exhibit a great variability in size, Rössen houses in particular often being extremely large (Sherratt 1990, 157; Lüning 1982b). At Brześć Kujawski in the Polish lowlands and Inden I on the Aldenhovener Platte, arguments have been put forward to suggest that individual houses were developing a greater degree of autonomy. Grygiel (1984) writes of the 'household unit' as the fundamental atom of Lengyel and Rössen settlement: the house surrounded by its own pits and working areas. Nevertheless, sites like the Langweiler Rössen settlement represent nucleated groups of these households, in this case with nine trapezoidal structures occupied at a single time (Whittle 1985, 194). Bogucki (1987, 7) notes an increased use of wild resources at this time, and suggests that Lengyel communities would have had an extremely structured yearly round involving seasonal access to agricultural and wild foodstuffs. As much as with the LBK, then, domestic architecture may have formed a focus to which people returned on a habitual basis, rather than the continual habitation of an entire community.

The extensive excavation and detailed analysis of the Lengyel settlements of Brześć Kujawski over the past sixty years (Bogucki and Grygiel 1981; 1986; 1993b) has provided invaluable information regarding post-LBK activity beyond the loess zone (figure 5.6). There was occupation in the area over a considerable depth of time, the houses gradually becoming larger and more heavily-built, culminating in Phase II of the Brześć Kujawski group of late Lengyel (3450–3300 bc/4300–4000 BC) (Grygiel 1984, 253). In subtle ways, the life-histories of these houses contrast with those of *Bandkeramik* dwellings. Many of the houses had been repaired a number of times, and some like House 56 on Site 4 had been rebuilt on the same location, in this case having collapsed and been burnt (Grygiel 1984, 74). This enhanced emphasis on the longevity and continuity of the individual structure fixed in a particular location can perhaps be connected with changes in funerary practice. Rather than there being a defined cemetery which served a given settlement or group of settlements, burials were now deposited around the houses, often in pits containing domestic refuse. At Brześć Kujawski there were sixty burials scattered amongst the houses (Bogucki and Grygiel 1993b, 155). In the immediate vicinity of House 56 there were ten graves. Male burials were associated with antler mattocks, and females with ornaments made of shell, copper and animal bone and teeth (figure 5.7). Significantly, all of these materials were worked within the sites in the Brześć Kujawski group, but always in what appear to have been conditions of relative seclusion. Copper was smelted on Site 3, and antler, bone and shell working was restricted within sunken hollows surrounding House 56 (Grygiel 1984, 219). This seems to suggest that the production of goods required for essential rites of passage had become a form of cultural knowledge which was restricted to particular household groups.

Altogether, this evidence implies that societies in the Rössen and Lengyel areas had developed in such a way that the household had become a more bounded unit, monopolising the production of goods and the disposal of

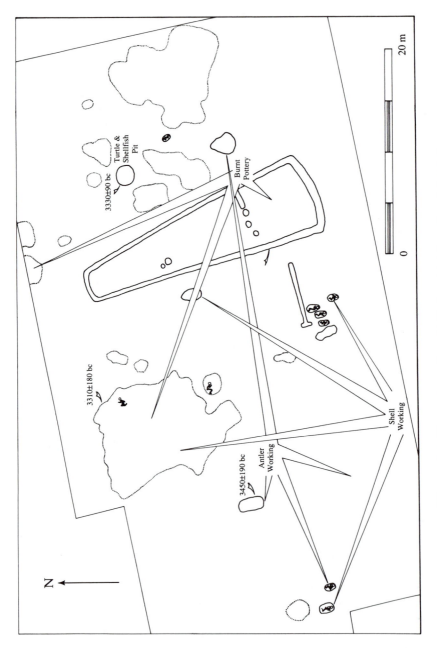

Figure 5.6 House 56 at Brześć Kujawski (after Grygiel 1984)

N ←

Turtle &
Shellfish
Pit

3330±90 bc

Burnt
Pottery

3310±180 bc

3450±190 bc

Antler
Working

Shell
Working

0   20 m

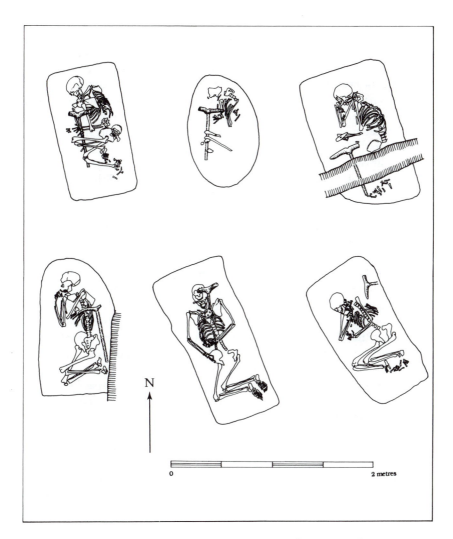

Figure 5.7 Burials at Brześć Kujawski (after Grygiel 1984)

its own dead. These dead might by now be conceived of as household or lineage ancestors. Just as long-distance contacts and alliances were being curtailed with the emergence of defined local cultural identities, so individual settlements, although increasingly nucleated, were composed of a series of separate communities of self-interest. This suggests that networks of co-operation which extended beyond the household were beginning to fail, and societies were becoming more and more atomised, thrown back upon themselves. While people living in LBK times may have considered themselves as part of a wider community, the indications are that by now the household, turned inwards upon itself, had become the dominant identity. If the shared material traditions of the LBK had been a means by which contacts between communities had been maintained over both space and time, the way in which material culture was being used as a means of defining separate identities may now have become a part of a self-amplifying process in which each household, each settlement and each settlement cluster became more distinct from each other, and possibly more hostile to outsiders.

In a climate of increasingly bounded social relationships, the gradual development of ditched enclosures associated with Neolithic societies is comprehensible (figure 5.8). From the late LBK onwards, enclosed sites of a variety of forms became increasingly numerous (Whittle 1977). In some cases the LBK ditches surround groups of houses (Bogucki 1988, 69), although in the case of Köln-Lindenthal Bradley (1994) argues that each successive enclosure contains a recently abandoned group of dwellings. At Langweiler 8, however, there was no habitation (Modderman 1988, 103), and Meindling and Straubing-Lerchenhaid in Bavaria are peripheral to house groups (Hodgson 1988, 373). Keeley and Cahen (1989) point out that enclosures emerge at the peripheries of the LBK zone, and it may follow that they are connected with the practice of defining social groups in relation to outsiders. In the case of the Belgian Upper Geer enclosures (ibid., 160) the argument for a defensive function can be made, but this is perhaps subsidiary to a broader pattern of defining areas of space in distinction to the surrounding world, defining 'special' activities which took place there, and defining those people who could enter in distinction from strangers. As with pottery decoration, this would not have been merely a side-effect of social segregation, but a means through which division and separation were achieved. In the post-LBK period, many of the enclosures were clearly used for symbolically significant activities involving the deliberate deposition of artefacts in the ditches, as in the cases of the *Stichbandkeramik* and Lengyel 'rondels' of Bylany and Těšetice-Kyovice (Midgley *et al.* 1993, 95; Behrens 1981). The use of enclosed spaces for ritual suggests a context in which emerging identities could be performed and thus enhanced.

While the earliest Neolithic groups on the north European plain may have been following a similar trajectory to that on the loess, it was in their immediate vicinity that a rather different pattern was emerging. Although in some areas there is a straight succession between Lengyel and TRB (Louwe-Kooijmans 1987, 17), it seems that the earliest TRB assemblages (3600–3500 bc/4500 BC) are found around the fringes of Rössen and Lengyel settlement, between the Vistula and the Elbe (Midgley 1992, 47).

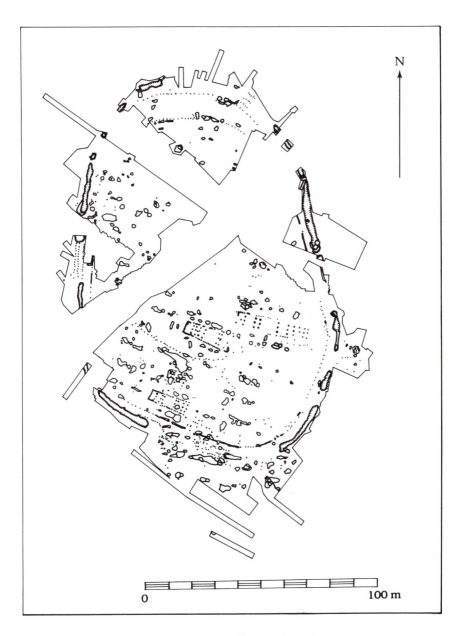

Figure 5.8 The late *Linnearbandkeramik* enclosure at Darton
in Belgium (after Keeley 1992)

These are the Rosenhof of north-west Germany and the Sarnowo of central Poland. Some degree of chronological overlap between the two traditions is indicated by the presence at the early TRB sites of Pikutkowo and Wiórek of shell beads very similar to those from Brześć Kujawski (Grygiel 1984, 259). Bogucki (1987, 11) obviously imagines that the TRB was an indigenous phenomenon, involving 'a selective incorporation of cultigens and domestic animals into an essentially Mesolithic way of life'. If so, it was clearly those Mesolithic groups who were most deeply involved in interaction with Rössen and Lengyel communities who were responsible. In discussing TRB origins, Midgley (1992, 7) is unwilling to cite any one tradition as a progenitor, suggesting instead that the TRB involves a fusion of Mesolithic, LBK and other elements. If we wish to move beyond a straight culture-historic interpretation at this point we must consider that a series of cultural 'streams' were not simply flowing into each other, but that for some reason particular people were drawing upon a number of different traditions in order to create something new and distinct from any of them. This was not simply the development of a new economic strategy, as Bogucki implies, but the construction of a 'bridge' between two ways of life that had remained irreconcilable throughout the previous millennium. In discussing the La Hoguette and Limburg pottery we have suggested that peripheral social groups who were not embedded in the LBK tradition may have been in a position to draw upon both the LBK and Cardial cultural repertoires in order to construct a distinct identity. With the emergence of the TRB a much clearer example of the same kind of process is evident. However, as we will see below, this period of cultural *bricolage* was the ultimate outcome of a lengthy period during which the Mesolithic populations of the Baltic, Scandinavia and the north European plain had been experimenting with Neolithic material culture in a range of creative ways. Midgley's (1992, 51) observation that the *Dümmerkeramik* from the site at Hüde could be seen as having similarities with the Ellerbeck point-based pots which precede it on the site, or Rössen, or Bischeim, or the early TRB which succeeds it, demonstrates very effectively the extent to which at a certain point, in a band running across Holland, north Germany and central Poland, a great deal of interaction and exchange of cultural knowledge was going on. It was from this zone of intense interaction that the TRB pattern was to expand outwards, into Pomerania, Little Poland, central Germany, southern Scandinavia and Holland.

It is instructive to compare the sequence on the north European plain with that in north-west France. Here again, the end of the LBK involved the emergence of regional traditions, like the Rubané Récent and Villeneuve-Saint-Germain. While the former of these has a material assemblage which is clearly derived from the LBK, the latter involves alien elements such as schist bracelets and pottery with bone tempering alongside house forms which are certainly similar to those of the LBK (Ilett 1983, 15; Constantin and Demoule

1982). The situation in western France is further complicated by the presence of Impressed Ware seemingly of Cardial heritage on sites in the coast of the centre-west, sometimes associated with Mesolithic flint artefacts (Scarre 1992, 124). As Patton (1994, 282) argues, this means that in the period after 5000 BC (4100 bc), two entirely different *kinds* of Neolithic would have been active in France. Indeed, after 4600 BC (5750 bc), Cassen (1993a) suggests that the Cardial and post-LBK Cerny 'areas of influence' would have overlapped geographically. The contrast between the LBK settlement of central Europe and the Cardial presence in the west Mediterranean is distinct: while LBK sites generally contain the whole range of cultural forms from houses and pottery to ground and chipped stone artefacts, Cardial pottery can turn up in a range of different associations. This has led to the suggestion that Cardial pottery circulated in an exchange network which also facilitated the exchange of domesticated plants and animals amongst indigenous populations in the western Mediterranean basin (Lewthwaite 1981, 296). Indeed, it remains a possibility that Cardial pottery was introduced into an existing Mesolithic exchange network (Scarre 1983, 226; 1992, 127). It follows from this that the north-west part of France would have been an area in which a series of different cultural heritages may have been available to the indigenous population, and that this may have facilitated the emergence of a series of quite new cultural forms (Kinnes 1982). It seems possible that, just as the TRB was the outcome of indigenous populations drawing on their own cultural heritage and that of their neighbours, so traditions like Cerny, Chambon, Castellic and Sardun were pieced together from the materials made available by the Rubané Récent, Villeneuve-Saint-Germain, the Cardial Atlantique and the Breton Mesolithic (Cassen 1993b; Scarre 1992, 132; Sherratt 1990, 152). Consequently, the early TRB of the north European plain and the 'Cerny horizon' represent two parallel contexts: both were the outcome of active processes of hybridisation carried out by Mesolithic communities, who were able to appropriate a series of separate cultural traditions, rather than simply reproduce any one. It was to be in these two highly fluid cultural milieux that a 'new Neolithic' was pioneered. Most significantly, it would be in these two geographical areas that the first monumental tombs of Europe were built. However, before we address monumental architecture it is essential to consider the place of the late Mesolithic communities in these processes.

MESOLITHIC TRANSFORMATIONS

If western France and the Polish lowlands demonstrate novel cultural developments in the period after 4800 BC (3950 bc), this does not simply represent a renewed expansion of Neolithic settlement. On the contrary, it is most likely that these areas saw a fusion of elements from both Neolithic and Mesolithic cultural traditions, assembled predominantly by indigenous population groups. It is comparatively well known that the introduction of the LBK onto the loess country of central Europe was followed by a significant period of relative stasis, during which time upland agriculturalists and lowland hunter-fisher-gatherers must have existed in some proximity to each other (Zvelebil and Rowley-Conwy 1986). Given the very specific locational preferences which characterise LBK settlements, it is even possible that Mesolithic communities continued to use some parts of the loess country, if only seasonally (Scarre 1983). Thus the central problem is that of why Mesolithic communities should finally have been induced to 'become Neolithic'. It is widely accepted that in economic terms the Mesolithic way of life was both reliable and sustainable (Zvelebil and Rowley-Conwy 1984, 110). Yet, while it is no longer thought likely that Neolithic agriculture rolled across Europe as a great, inorexible 'wave of advance' (Ammerman and Cavalli-Sforza 1973), it is still conventional wisdom that the end of hunting and gathering was signalled by some form of resource crisis which rendered foraging unworkable. If the period is seen as characterised by competition between two incompatible ways of life (Zvelebil and Rowley-Conwy 1984, 105), it seems that the only possible outcome was the eventual adoption of agriculture by the foragers. The question is not presented as one of *whether* this would take place, but of *how long* it might have been delayed. This seems to imply that the Mesolithic economy was inherently more fragile than the Neolithic one, or that as a way of life the Mesolithic was inherently inferior. It is curiously never speculated whether loessland agriculture might have collapsed in famine, leaving the farmers to revert to hunting and gathering. Yet if we avoid reducing the Mesolithic to being exclusively a productive economic system, and recognise that Atlantic Mesolithic groups had cultural traditions and distinctive forms of social organisation of their own, it becomes possible to argue that the Mesolithic/Neolithic transition was not a one-way process. More was involved than the passing on of subsistence skills and cultural innovations from one set of peoples to another.

As we have seen, the decline of the LBK and its aftermath was characterised by increasing structural pressures amongst the loessland agricultural groups. This suggests that the Neolithic can scarcely be presented as an ideal way of life which might recommend itself to hunters and gatherers. What seems more likely is that the experimental hybridisations of cultural knowledge created in the encounters between farmers and foragers in western France and northern Poland had a transformative impact on both Mesolithic *and* Neolithic communities. However, since we are accustomed to thinking of this period in terms of a series of arrows denoting cultural influence moving northward and westward across the map of Europe, the changes affecting established primary Neolithic groups seem to be considered of less import. Gordon Childe (1926) recognised long ago that the kind of Neolithic which is found in the Atlantic zone is in some way different from the 'Danubian' way of life in central Europe. However, his 'Western Neolithic' was conceived of as a separate set of peoples. In seeking to establish the notion of a *different kind* of Neolithic which emerged from interactions between the LBK and the Atlantic Mesolithic traditions, I imagine instead a new and different form of organisation. This did not consist in a single set of social relations or an ideology which was homogeneous across the whole of Atlantic and Baltic Europe. Instead, what these widespread social groups shared was a set of material forms which allowed communities with diverse economic strategies to build a sustainable set of relationships amongst themselves and with their landscape. As I will hope to demonstrate, this was achieved by drawing together elements of both Mesolithic and Neolithic cultural heritages.

We have seen already that both the TRB and Cerny material traditions can be interpreted as having been created out of diverse cultural repertoires. These processes are best understood as parts of a wider set of interactions across the boundary between Neolithic and Mesolithic populations. The effects of this contact were initially more evident amongst the hunter-gatherer groups. Best-known are entities like the Ertebølle of Scandinavia, people who appear to have kept domesticated animals as one element of a 'broad spectrum' subsistence pattern, and to have made their own pottery. However, these examples can readily be added to, to such an extent that we can argue that from the later LBK period onward the agriculturalists of the loess were surrounded by a 'penumbra' of Mesolithic groups all of whom were able to assimilate some aspects of the Neolithic way of life. Not all of these experiments with the exotic would have been under way at the same time: we have suggested that they may date back as far as the appearance of the Limburg pottery, and it is to be presumed that innovations would have been discarded as often as they were adopted. What remains unclear is the extent to which the availability of novel cultural and economic resources facilitated the emergence of larger and more sedentary social units along the Atlantic fringe (Rowley-Conwy 1983, 115). The possibility is that exotic goods and species acquired from Neolithic groups to the south served to amplify tendencies already surfacing amongst the Atlantic foragers. Thus domesticated cattle and pigs, and stone shafthole adzes might have represented prestigious feasting foods and exchange goods, enabling social differences to be enhanced and alliances to be forged (Fischer 1982, 7).

The Ertebølle and Ellerbeck communities of Denmark and Sweden and Schleswig-Holstein are closely comparable with traditions like the Boburg/Nollheide groups in lower Saxony (Midgley 1992, 13). While in some ways the point-butted pots of these groups can be compared with Rössen ceramics (Fischer 1982, 11; Larsson 1990, 294; Louwe-Kooijmans 1976, 244), the sparse decoration and quite distinct vessel forms indicate that more was involved than a simple copying of Neolithic forms. We can suggest that while pottery manufacture may have been introduced to the Atlantic Mesolithic groups from outside, the significance of ceramics was transformed by its acceptance into this context. Similarly, it may be that domesticated animals, or the cereals documented by seed impressions in Ertebølle pots from Löddesbord (Nielsen 1986, 241), had a range of different significances to hunter-gatherer groups than to Rössen/Lengyel populations. Consequently, it would have been this recontextualisation *outside* the Danubian tradition within which they originated which allowed aspects of Neolithic culture to be recombined in new ways. So the contrasts between Rössen and Ertebølle-Ellerbeck artefacts may be at least as significant as the similarities. By appropriating Neolithic technologies and yet transforming them in the process, Mesolithic groups may have been able to create new identities which clearly differentiated them from the loessland agriculturalists. Using distinctive forms of ceramics, and eating the meat of domestic animals in specific contexts (such as funerary rituals) may have served to distinguish groups of people as different from the Rössen and Lengyel communities with whom they may have had routine social interactions. This suggests a situation very like that described by Homi Bhabha in the context of the contemporary post-colonial world (1994, 4; 219), in which the emergence of cultural hybridity is to be expected at the interstices of more solid cultural formations. Bhabha emphasises that the social articulation of difference through cultural media is neither essential nor given, but is performed and played out through the recontextualisation and hybridisation of existing traditions. He argues that new community identities will often begin to emerge within the interstitial spaces between existing cultural formations. This emergence may have a subversive or insurgent character. Hybridity is not the passive consequence of a kind of 'cross-pollination' of cultures, as culture-historic archaeology might have assumed. It is the outcome of a deliberate construction of the foreign out of the familiar, which 'brings newness into the world'.

As we have noted, the pattern of hunters and gatherers at least having access to Neolithic artefacts, and beyond this of having incorporated domesticates and pottery production into their way of life, was widespread. In the Dutch wetlands, the site of Swifterbant has provided rich evidence of a semi-mobile way of life involving the seasonal use of wild species and the herding of domesticated animals. Barley seems to have been grown on the levees, and point-butted pottery similar to Ertebølle was in use (de Roever 1979; Louwe-Kooijmans 1987, 237). Further inland, in the Maas valley, Mesolithic sites containing elements of LBK material culture have been found at Weelde-Paarsdonk and Merlo (Wansleben and Verhardt 1990, 398). In Belgium, further point-butted pots have been recovered from the sites of Oleye and Mesele (Keeley 1992, 87–8). In the Polish lowlands, and particularly the Oder basin, the so-called 'Wistka culture' assemblages involve pottery associated with Janislawice-style microliths (Cyrek *et al.* 1986, 102). Similar 'Pit Comb' style pottery was used by foraging communities further east in the Baltic with the Narva, Sarnate and Serovo groups (Midgley 1992, 15). The interchangeability of formally Mesolithic and Neolithic traits in the Polish lowlands is demonstrated by sites like Deby 29, where a Janislawice flint assemblage was associated with pig and sheep bones, Podgaj 32, where LBK pottery was found with flints of the Kolankowo group, and Łacko, where earliest TRB pots occurred with Kolankowo style lithics (Domańska 1989, 450). Seemingly, the emergence of the TRB is simply the final stage in a continuous process of native experimentation with Neolithic material culture. Here again, it may be legitimate to invoke the notion of a separate identity being created out of diverse raw materials.

None the less, we should not give the impression that the native communities of Atlantic Europe were in the process of forming themselves into a uniform and integrated ethnic entity in opposition to the Neolithic groups to the south. It might be more appropriate to think of a series of diverse and parallel histories, only some of which were meshed into each other by exchange, interaction and alliance. In the Alpine foreland of Switzerland, the pattern of piecemeal adoption of Neolithic innovations is recognisable in the latest Mesolithic of the Alps, the Notched Blade Horizon, where cereal and plantain pollen occur at Birsmatten, and domestic cattle and pig from a number of sites (Sakellaridis 1979, 183). Finally, in the north-west of France, the emergence of the Cerny group is prefigured by the circulation of Danubian shoe-last axes amongst Mesolithic groups (Patton 1994, 286).

What is striking about the final Mesolithic of north-west Europe is that many of the innovations of the period which owe nothing to the LBK tradition are none the less reminiscent of cultural phenomena which would later be characteristic of the Atlantic Neolithic. This is particularly the case with ritual, ceremonial and funerary activities, many of which were later to be incorporated into Neolithic practice. For example, the Breton midden sites of Téviec and Hoëdic have frequently been cited as precursors for megalithic funerary practices (e.g. Renfrew 1976). Within these two substantial mounds of shell debris, burials were laid out, sometimes in cists and sometimes as multiple inhumations (figure 5.9). At Téviec, the covering slabs over the graves had fires lit on them, and the jawbones of pig and deer were deliberately placed there before cairns were built up over the whole (Bender 1985, 22). Two of the burials were surrounded by clusters of deer antlers, and other bodies had been re-arranged *post-mortem*. At Hoëdic, a paved area near to the graves may have served as a focus for performances venerating the dead (Péquart and Péquart 1954). Together, the two sites suggest repeated and prolonged observances, involving feasting, complex body treatment and the establishment of particular prominent locations as being connected with the dead. However, the Breton

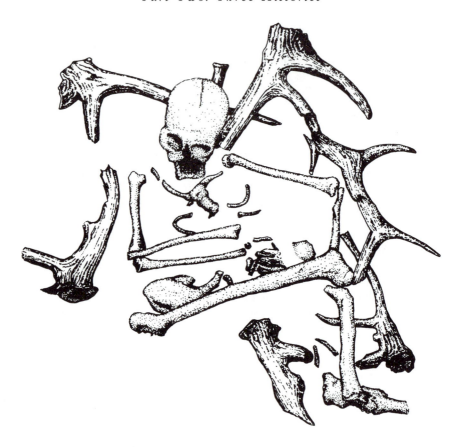

Figure 5.9 Late Mesolithic burial at Hoëdic in Brittany
(after Péquart and Péquart 1954)

material does not stand in isolation. The Mesolithic cemeteries at Skateholm in Scania have produced striking evidence for pre-Neolithic complex funerary activities. Grave 26 at Skateholm I was covered by a trapezoid wooden structure which had been deliberately burnt down, and the excavator explicitly compares this with later, TRB wooden structures which were constructed beneath earthen long mounds (Larsson 1988, 14). Even more striking is the timber structure found within the Skateholm II cemetery, consisting of a large sunken area containing wooden uprights. Within this area were clusters of deliberately deposited flints, burnt material, and large quantities of red ochre (Larsson 1988, 9). Given that burials in the many graves on the site were also associated with red ochre, it seems most likely that this structure was the location for pre-burial treatment of the bodies of the dead. The impression that the dead were not simply disposed of in the most efficient manner is enhanced by the evidence from sites like Ageröd I, also in Scania, where isolated skeletal elements from human beings were found with Mesolithic assemblages. The strong possibility is that this relates to the circulation of human bones, a practice which appears to have been common in the Neolithic of north-west Europe. While we have already noted that primary Neolithic enclosures sometimes contain deliberately deposited artefacts in their ditches, the practice of placing objects in pits located at significant places in the landscape may have a Mesolithic background. At Beg-er-Vil in Brittany, animal bones, antler, and decorated shell and bone objects were found in a pit deposit of Mesolithic date (Kirk 1991, 123). Similarly, in southern Britain, a series of enigmatic pits containing Mesolithic artefacts have been found (Clark and Rankine 1939; Leakey 1951). Consequently, while we are familiar with funerary monuments, human bone deposits and placed materials in pits from the British, French and Scandinavian Neolithics, it may be that these ultimately represent the incorporation of Neolithic artefacts into a set of practices which have a greater antiquity. This introduction of new media into old practices is a good example of the kind of cultural hybridisation which distinguishes the change from Mesolithic to Neolithic on the Atlantic fringe of Europe.

THE EARLIEST FUNERARY MONUMENTS

In a recent contribution, Andrew Sherratt (1990) has drawn attention to the first appearance of mortuary monuments in areas peripheral to the loess, most notably north-west France and the north European plain. Sherratt's interpretation involves the introduction into these areas of the 'longhouse' model of sociality, transformed into the earthen long mound, thus enabling the integration of more dispersed social groups. In time, the megalithic tomb in a round stone cairn emerged as an indigenous response to this alien imposition. While acknowledging that Sherratt has identified the geographical context within which monumentality emerged, I should like to diverge from this argument in three ways. First, rather than placing the impetus for this development with the continued expansion of agricultural settlement, I would suggest that it forms an extension of the process by which indigenous populations appropriated and transformed Neolithic material culture. Second, I will argue that the emergence of tombs and barrows should not be seen in isolation, but must be understood as *one element* in a new repertoire of material culture which was constructed in the encounter between loessland agriculturalists and Atlantic fringe hunter-gatherers (Kinnes 1984). Third, I should like to emphasise the role which monuments played in transforming landscapes. The primary Neolithic LBK settlements were probably established by incoming groups of people, who had considerable liberty in the way in which they might interpret their new surroundings. Or, more precisely, they would have understood the loesslands through a matrix of cultural perceptions of their own, which had been generated in a different context (Mugerauer 1985). But if we accept that in the Atlantic zone there was a continuity of personnel across the Mesolithic/Neolithic boundary, these people would have been heirs to deeply sedimented traditions of place. Having habitually moved from one location to another for hundreds of years as hunters and gatherers, these communities would doubtless have had an intimate knowledge of land-marks which would certainly have been integrated into systems of meaning, myth and cosmology. In this context, the construction of funerary and other monuments represented a physical intervention into the mythic fabric of the land, a 're-writing' of places which enabled the relationship between people and landscape to be recast (Thomas 1993). As with the raising of primary Neolithic longhouses, it is the status of monuments as *buildings* that I will emphasise: acts of construction which involve a physical engage-ment with the materials of which the land is made up – earth, clay, wood, chalk and stone (Bender 1992). Through the labour of building on the earth, people re-founded their dwelling on the earth.

It follows from the above that funerary monuments were not merely a *product* of the contact between Neolithic and Mesolithic groups. Tombs and barrows were integral parts of a new technology of the social. These structures existed to introduce the ancestral dead into the habitual space of the living, so that tradition and the social past were constantly referenced in everyday practice. However, there is considerable evidence that the relationships between the living and the dead which were being created and affirmed through the building of tombs may have varied from one commu-nity to another. The architecture of these early monuments reveals a basic contrast between closed cists or graves beneath or within a mound or cairn, and open chambers, often accessed by means of a passage. In that the former implies a single event of deposition and sealing, while the latter involves continued access to the mortuary deposit for a prolonged period, the status of the remains of the dead is clearly different in each case. The two struc-tural arrangements imply considerable differences of practice, and hence of the role of the ancestral dead within society. This contrast may be more significant than the distinction between round and long mounds, which some have chosen to link to Mesolithic and Neolithic domestic architecture respectively. Hodder (1984) suggested that in some senses trapezoidal long mounds may derive from primary Neolithic longhouses. More recently, Bradley (1994) has argued that in areas like the Polish lowlands, the two structural forms overlap chronologically. Like primary Neolithic long-houses, the Kujavian long barrows and the Passy enclosures of northern France occur in clusters. According to Bradley, such a group of low, long mounds would resemble nothing so much as an abandoned and derelict settlement, the houses collapsed into mounds of debris and wall daub. Literally, this would represent a 'village of the dead'.

However, while longhouses and long mounds can be fitted into the same chronological horizon, it is striking that they *cannot* be found in the same cultural context. Although the Kujavian mounds and the Brześć Kujawski group settlements may have stood within a few kilometres of each other, the former are associated with the early TRB, and the latter with late Lengyel (Midgley 1985). Similarly, in northern France longhouses are found in Rubané Récent and Villeneuve-Saint-Germain contexts, and early funerary monuments are Cerny-associated. This suggests that the *idea* of a monumental location devoted to the dead was one which was created by groups of people in the process of *becoming Neolithic*, rather than those who were enmeshed in the primary Neolithic 'Danubian' tradition. We could go so far as to say that the emergence of monumental funerary architecture was a part of this process of transformation. Once again, it involved an appropriation and recontextualisation of Neolithic elements, which might be given new significance outside of their tradition of inception.

In the French context, recent debate has concentrated on the relative chronological priority of earthen long mounds and enclosures (of eastern, primary Neolithic origin) and passage tombs (connected with Iberia, the Cardial zone, the indigenous Mesolithic and the west in general) (e.g. Boujot and Cassen 1992; 1993; Cassen 1993a; Scarre 1992; Patton 1994). These arguments only continue to make sense if we see material forms as directly representative of groups of people. As Patton (1994) implies, it is quite possible that chambered tombs and long mounds emerged contemporaneously, in a milieu characterised by intensive social interaction and a widespread circulation of cultural knowledge. Given extensive networks of exchange and contact, native communities in Normandy and Brittany may have evolved several different forms of monumental architecture by drawing selectively on a range of different sources. In the Paris basin and Normandy, the Cerny phase saw the construction of numerous very large linear enclosures, as at Passy-sur-Yonne and Rots (Kirk 1995; Chancerel *et al.* 1992) (figure 5.10). These often contain axially set pit graves, and, as Hodder (1990, 222) suggests, this may reasonably be said to represent the introduction into the funerary context of the principle of linear movement in graded space, hitherto associated with Neolithic longhouses. However, the linear graves and stone *coffres* involved suggest Mesolithic funerary practices rather than the crouched burials in pit-graves generally associated with the LBK tradition. Similarly, in the Morbihan several of the low long mounds or *tertre tumulaires*, including Mané Ty Ec, Mané Pochat er Ieu and Lann Vras have produced Cerny material or appropriately early radiocarbon dates (c. 3550 BC/4350 BC) (Hibbs 1983, 280; Cassen 1993a, 200). As with the Passy enclosures, the *tertre tumulaires* display connections with

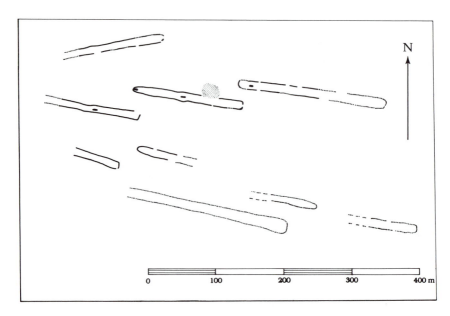

Figure 5.10 Long enclosures at Rots in Normandy
(after Chancerel *et al.* 1992)

the central European primary Neolithic, in the linear structure of the mounds and artefactual associations including schist bracelets and stone rings (Boujot and Cassen 1993, 479; 483). But again, the closed cists inside these mounds are more easily compared to the structures at Téviec and Hoëdic than anything of Neolithic ancestry. These mounds were often constructed after lengthy sequences of events had taken place on the site (Kirk 1993, 210), and at Manio I, Carnac, the complex arrangement of stone settings, hearths and cists beneath the mound is very reminiscent of the midden sites (Le Rouzic *et al.* 1923; Thomas and Tilley 1993, 239). Where Mesolithic practice had involved the gradual creation of a shell mound by groups of people returning seasonally to a set location and placing their dead there, a series of events was now marked and commemorated by incorporating their traces into a linear mound.

While Boujot and Cassen argue that all Breton and Norman passage tombs are a feature of their Middle Neolithic II, the Chasséen/Carn/Cous/ Bougon horizon after 4100 BC (3300 bc) (1993, 485), this may be stretching a point too far. Cassen's (1993a) argument for the late date of the Carn pottery from Barnenez and Ile Carn is convincing, but the early dates of sites like Roc'h Avel, Les Fouillages, Colombiers sur Seulles and La Hoguette seem secure, and several of these too have Cerny associations. As Patton (1994, 286) points out, these early chambered tombs are all found in the north and west of Armorica, geographically distinct from the long mounds. Thus, while Boujot and Cassen are correct in pointing out that passage tombs are always intrusive into the *tertre tumulaires* and Carnac mounds of the Morbihan (1993, 485), this is because megalithic tombs were introduced into this area from the north and west. As we will see, the expansion of material forms out from restricted areas of inception is a widespread and important phenomenon. Whether the round form of some passage tombs can really be attributed to Mesolithic domestic architecture (Sherratt 1990, 151) is arguable, and indeed the shapes of early megalithic tombs are quite variable: from the trapezoidal mound of Les Fouillages (Kinnes 1982) to the oblong of La Hoguette (Caillaud and Lagnel 1972). In general, it is perhaps best to see the emergence of megalithic tombs in Armorica as part of the broad pattern of cultural reconstruction in the Atlantic fringe, whereby individual communities and regional networks might produce quite different artefact styles from the same background of available materials. The crucial difference between the chambered tombs and the long mounds is one of practice rather than cultural origin: the distinction between a place set aside for continued encounters with the remains of the dead, and one which commemorates a series of past events. None the less, the likelihood that some of the Iberian passage tombs are as early as those of Armorica must be taken into account in developing a picture of a broad geographical expanse over which parallel and interlinked processes were taking place.

On the eastern north European plain, a rather similar pattern can be discerned. The TRB long mounds were eventually to be found in western Pomerania, lower Saxony, north Germany and Denmark, largely dating to a period after 4000 BC (Midgley 1985, 205; 1992, 52). However, the earliest of the mounds, in Kujavia, may date back to the Sarnowo phase, roughly contemporary with the later part of Cerny. As Midgley (1985, 197) has remarked, the burials beneath these earlier mounds are exclusively extended inhumations, which appear to follow Mesolithic traditions in the area. By contrast, the LBK, Rössen and Baalberg burials to the south and west take the form of crouched inhumations. As in the west, it is difficult to account for the emergence of funerary monuments here in terms of the cultural knowledge available exclusively to any one population group.

A NEW NEOLITHIC

We have seen that the period between roughly 4600 and 4100 BC (*c.* 3800–3250 bc) was one of considerable cultural diversity across northwest Europe. The increasingly regionalised primary Neolithic groups of the loess were building larger houses and ditched enclosures, and making elaborate forms of decorated pottery which facilitated the emergence of more distinct regional identities. Simultaneously, many of the Mesolithic communities of the Atlantic zone were becoming more sedentary, adopting new economic strategies and more elaborate ritual practices. With Cerny and the early TRB, cultural assemblages were beginning to develop which were not exclusively drawn from the existing Neolithic or the Mesolithic traditions. In these contexts, entirely new phenomena, such as funerary monuments, began to be brought into existence. In the south of France, the Chasséen assemblage had begun to emerge, amongst groups whose background lay in the Cardial tradition (Phillips 1982, 55). This was a phase characterised by extremely regionalised developments, and yet it was followed by one in which many of the localised innovations became much more widespread in their distribution. As we have mentioned already, Childe (1926, 304) saw this horizon as one characterised by a new influx of migrants, distinct from the 'Danubians' and issuing out of Provence and the Pyrenees. Here, local hunters and gatherers had adopted Neolithic ways from Cardial people, forming the Cortaillod and Lagozza cultures (ibid., 287). In this scenario, the spread of the 'Western Neolithic' can readily be understood as the dispersal of a separate population group and their distinctive material products. However, as we have seen, it is difficult to imagine all of the innovations of the period emanating from a single source. Yet what remains difficult to understand is how this 'new Neolithic' gradually took on a coherent form which is recognisable across much of north-west Europe. Without wishing to give an impression of absolute cultural homogeneity, it is clear that such phenomena as megalithic tombs, earthen long mounds, causewayed ditched enclosures, polished stone axes, plain carinated pots and hemispherical bowls have extremely broad and overlapping geographical distributions. While not arguing that material culture suddenly became uniform over a vast area, it is possible to suggest that a particular repertoire of material forms had become generally available, which was drawn on and used in highly regionalised and idiosyncratic ways. What this implies is an opening out of social relationships and an enhancement of exchange and the circulation of information.

Looked at from a perspective fixated with economic change and the spread of agriculture, this period is primarily notable as that in which the Neolithic spread into Scandinavia, Britain, Ireland, the Alpine foreland and the western north European plain. Such a view reduces all of the variability involved in 'the Neolithic' down to a single trait-complex, and simply charts its rate of advance across space (Ammerman and Cavalli-Sforza 1971; 1973). In exactly the same way as Childe looked for a migration of people and objects northward from the west Mediterranean, it expects the expansion of farming to be a uniform and unidirectional transfer. The argument presented here suggests the opposite. While we might agree that the people of the Atlantic fringe effectively ceased being Mesolithic and 'became Neolithic' at this point, in the loess country of central Europe the advent of the Michelsberg and the TRB involved a decline in substantial domestic architecture, an increase in mobility, an increase in the importance of exchange and a lessening of material culture differentiation between communities (Midgley 1992, 322; Nielsen 1986, 242; Wansleben and Verhardt 1990). Thus, in a sense, these established Neolithic groups were becoming more 'Mesolithic'. This was an era in which a quite different landscape began to take shape in the north-west of Europe. Tombs, barrows and enclosures became the fixed points around which human movements cohered, and with the increased importance of exchange the locations of production of exchange goods took on an increased significance. This was the period in which large subterranean flint mines began to be dug, at Rijkholt, Spiennes, Mesvin and St Geertruid in the low countries (Louwe-Kooijmans 1976; de Grooth 1991), as well as in Sussex (Clark and Piggott 1933). While the maps of culture groups which can be drawn for the period after 4100 BC are quite as complex as those of the preceding era, it is clearly the case that the boundaries between regional assemblages are much less pronounced than before. In France, Cous, Rocquefort and Cortaillod can all be seen as closely related to Chasséen pottery styles (Scarre 1983, 337). The Chasséen in turn merges into the Belgian Michelsberg or Chasséo-Michelsberg (Louwe-Kooijmans 1976, 249; Schollar 1959, 55). This, again, is similar to the Hazendonk pottery from the Dutch coastal lands, and the British Grimston series (Louwe-Kooijmans 1980, 204; Herne 1988).

What I wish to suggest is that in this phase of rapid change in the forms of material culture which were in use, the whole role of artefacts had been transformed. Out of the lengthy period of co-existence between hunters and farmers in the fifth millennium BC had come a new attunement to the material world. Neolithic material culture had been introduced to Europe north of the Alps as a closely integrated tradition that enabled people to create a place in the world for themselves. Now, after a considerable period of 'unpicking', the contents of a series of separate traditions (LBK, Cardial, Mesolithic) had been opened up and rendered manipulable, equally available to be drawn upon in the construction of localised systems of meaning. This 'new Neolithic' was one which could be assimilated equally by communities of quite different cultural backgrounds and practising quite different economic regimes. It is for this reason that what *appears* as the geographical expansion of the Neolithic took place at this point: this set of material media was as appropriate to Mesolithic as to Neolithic groups. This 'Neolithic' did not inhere in a uniform productive technology, or a set of social relations of production, or an ideology (*contra* Thomas 1988a). All that was shared by groups of people in different parts of Europe was a 'material vocabulary', a range of legitimate artefactual forms which were combined and rendered meaningful in day-to-day practice. Individual social groups might build tombs, make and use pots and hold ritual obser-vances in ways whose meanings were quite specific to themselves. But the compatibility of the things themselves with those used by distant and far-flung communities meant that exchanges, alliances and shared meanings might at least be negotiated between them. The effect of material culture's emergence as a 'technology of the social', a set of resources which enabled social relationships to be constructed and maintained, was twofold. Between social entities, relationships might now be re-created, and the atomisation and regionalisation of the previous era might be reversed. Yet within communities the same material culture might have the effect of segregation, grading and regulation. As a means of classification, Neolithic material culture served to draw distinctions between classes of persons (younger, older and ancestors; genders), places and activities. In some cases, the outcome of this would have been more internally differentiated social groups. However, it makes little sense to discuss these processes at such a level of generality. The point is that they were effected at the level of everyday practice.

PERFORMING THE NEOLITHIC: DYFFRYN ARDUDWY

When Stuart Piggott wrote his great synthetic work, *The Neolithic Cultures of the British Isles* (1954), one of the central problems that he found in applying the culture-historic framework to the inception of the British Neolithic was the absence of a clear place of origin on the continent (ibid., 17). Piggott's 'Windmill Hill culture' consisted of a range of monument and artefact types which all showed some affinity with continental styles (earthen long barrows, causewayed enclosures, flint mines, round-based pottery and a range of chipped stone tools including leaf-shaped arrowheads), yet there was no single geographical area from which these might all be derived. Piggott's immediate answer was that such an origin might eventually be found in the area between Belgium and Brittany, where at that time archaeological fieldwork was relatively underdeveloped. In addressing the same problem, Case (1969) was to remark that the British Neolithic in its archaeological manifestation was mature and non-experimental. If no single continental source could be located, this was because a Neolithic economy had been established in Britain for many decades before it became archaeologically visible. Only when conditions of stable equilibrium had been generated, and an economic surplus had been generated, would pottery, polished stone tools and field monuments have been produced, and by then cultural 'drift' would have ensured that these took on idiosyncratic forms specific to Britain and Ireland. However, recent work has demonstrated that these cultural forms are integral to the earliest Neolithic presence in these islands (Kinnes 1988, 5). The argument that has been rehearsed in this chapter would imply that the indigenous inhabitants of Britain and Ireland were not merely the recipients of a complex of cultural traits which originated on the European mainland. As much as any of the continental groups, these people were actively involved in creating for themselves a new material culture which drew on both their own and a series of alien traditions. Consequently, there is no reason to assume that the earliest appearance of some of the cultural innovations of the period should not have happened in Britain. The merging or blending of cultural traditions did not take place at an abstract or cognitive level, but in practice. In drawing together different elements in acts of manufacture and construction, people created a new world for themselves. The Neolithic of Atlantic Europe was not first a set of ideas which were later acted out; it existed in and through its own performance. The cultural knowledge from which it was crafted had no positive meaning outside of performance: it was in making and using things that people rendered both them and their world meaningful. Since this took place at the level of practice, it is best understood through an example.

Six thousand years ago, on the slopes of Moelfre, a low eminence over-looking the sea in north Wales, a small chambered tomb was constructed. This monument, Dyffryn Ardudwy, was of a type now known as a portal dolmen. The hillside was strewn with large stone slabs, and one of these was selected as a floorstone about which the structure would be erected (Powell 1973, 8). The box-like chamber involved a septal slab flanked by two portal stones, forming a false entrance. Side-stones and back-stone were clustered around the floor-slab, and the whole was topped by a slanting capstone of tabular grit. According to the excavator, 'the general aspect of the chamber is that of a tomb effectively shut in after the capstone had been placed in position' (Powell 1973, 9). While initially it might have been possible to gain access to the chamber over the south side-slab, the presence of a small ovoid cairn of stones around the chamber would have rendered this less practicable, if not obstructing entry entirely. This cairn initially surrounded three sides of the chamber, leaving a small concave forecourt, spreading out to either side of the chamber portal (figure 5.11). Within the forecourt, and directly in front of the portal, a shallow, wide pit was dug, and into this pit were placed a number of rounded stones, and many sherds of broken pottery, in a matrix of soil and charcoal. The pottery came from three or four pots, all of a smooth, hard fabric, and all being undecorated, carinated bowls (figure 5.12). The sherds had all been selected from the upper parts of the vessels, and were often nested together in groups, some-times sticking up vertically amongst the stones (Lynch 1976, 66). Soon, and perhaps immediately after the filling of the pit, the forecourt was filled up with further cairn material, completing the ovoid shape of the mound.

This series of actions appears to have been carried out in a rather careful and formal manner. They involve highly symbolic materials, placed together

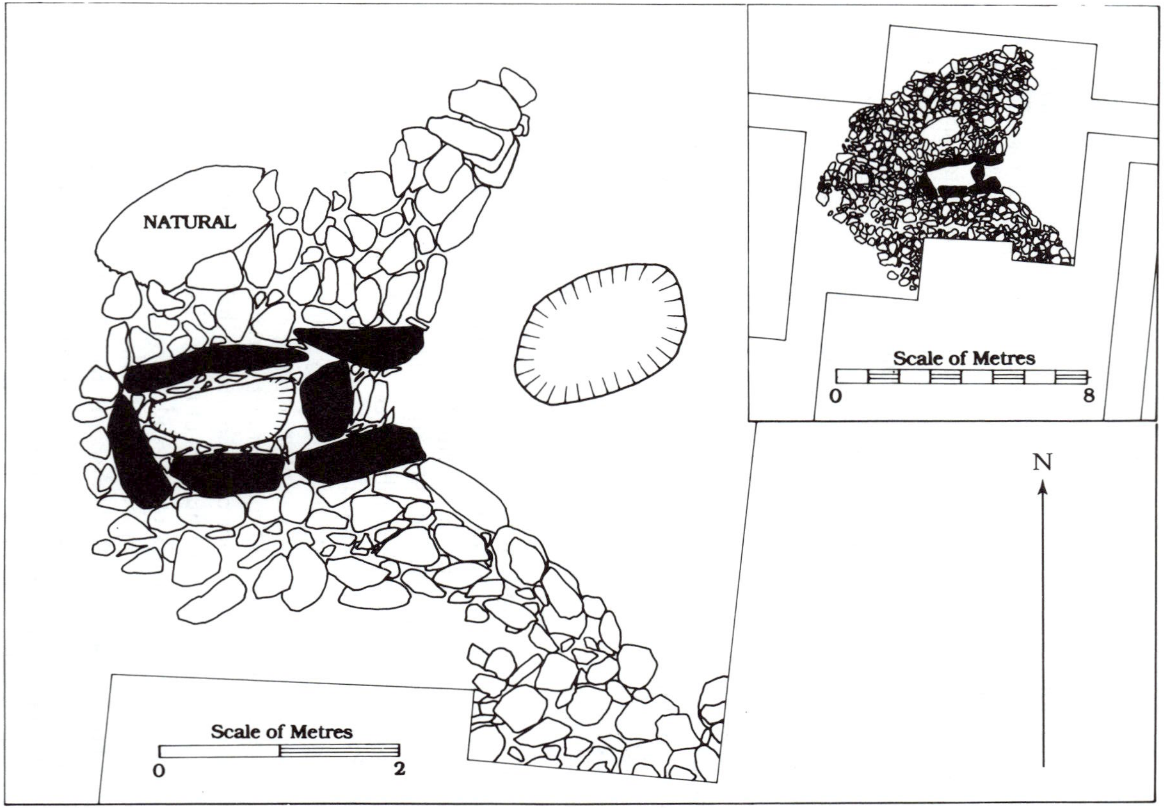

Figure 5.11 The megalithic tomb of Dyffryn Ardudwy, showing the western chamber and the pit (after Powell 1973)

Figure 5.12 The ceramic vessels from Dyffryn Ardudwy
(after Powell 1973)

in a prominent location, in a very deliberate sequence. A space for the remains of the dead was constructed, and rendered inaccessible. In relation to that place of the dead, a space for performance was defined, and objects and materials were deposited there. Since only parts of each vessel were present, and there was no trace of burning in the forecourt, these materials were in some way representative of activities which had taken place somewhere else. At least one of the pots had been drilled with holes to allow it to be suspended (Lynch 1969, 150), either over a fire or in some way on display. The performance at the tomb involved living people bringing these traces of past actions, carrying with them connotations of food, eating, cooking and burning, and placing them in juxtaposition with the bodies of the dead. Following this performance within the bounded space of the forecourt, that space itself was blocked and rendered inaccessible. Just as the chamber contained and commemorated the dead, so the monument as a whole now fixed and drew attention to the event of their veneration. These acts and the substances associated with them brought together a series of associations (human bone; stone; earth; fire; pottery sherds made of earth, transformed by fire and containing the traces of fire in their charcoal gritting), which together established a matrix of potential meanings. In their sequencing, the separate elements of the performance constructed a narrative of place. Yet for all of the formality which this implies, there is no sense in which these actions were merely the enactment of an empty formula, a fixed set of rules and codes. This kind of ritual action is an active creation of significance which transforms whatever resources are employed (Barth 1987).

Dyffryn Ardudwy as it now exists is the outcome of a series of meaningful events, not the imposition of an abstract template onto the Welsh coastline. It is a unique structure, which embodies a unique history. Yet at the same time, its eventual form was only possible because of the thousands of years of cultural change which this chapter has discussed. The closed chamber set inside a mound is a concept which developed in southern Brittany some hundreds of years before Dyffryn Ardudwy was constructed. The portal dolmen chamber has a linear structure, differentiating between a 'front' made conspicuous by the false portal and a 'back' hidden away within the cairn. The use of such a graded chamber as the focus for a mounded monument has close connections with the timber linear chambers of the earthen long barrows of eastern Britain and Denmark, and the Clyde tombs of Scotland (Kinnes 1992, 122). The forecourt structure defining a semi-enclosed space in front of the chamber can be linked with the façades of long barrows in Yorkshire, Wessex and Denmark (Madsen 1979, 311). The architecture of the small chambered tomb at Dyffryn Ardudwy thus cannot be derived from any one tradition, but involves elements from both east and west. The pots from the forecourt pit have a local significance which derives from their use and the materials from which they were made, but they are also part of a very extensive grouping of plain carinated bowls which extends around the Irish Sea to Ireland, Devon and Cornwall, Yorkshire and Scotland (Herne 1988, 17). Beyond this, extremely similar vessels are parts of the Michelsberg, Classéo-Michelsberg and Hazendonk assemblages on the continent. Without any of the participants in the sequence of activities which took place at Dyffryn Ardudwy necessarily having any awareness of it, the presence of those pots was entirely contingent upon a deep and complex history.

CHAPTER SIX

LATER NEOLITHIC BRITAIN: ARTEFACTS WITH PERSONALITIES

——— .◆. ———

INTRODUCTION

The intention of this chapter is to reconsider the social role of material culture in the British later Neolithic, making use of the framework offered in the earlier part of this book. Arguably, our understanding of the later Neolithic period is a product of the series of conceptualisations of material things that have characterised archaeology through the past century. As I will hope to show, these ways of thinking about objects tend to bring with them implicit social models. Thus, by introducing a new way of thinking about artefacts, it will be possible to offer a reinterpretation of later Neolithic society. The core of the argument will be found in the observation that artefacts are not a mere reflection or product of society, but are integral to social relationships. In this sense, we might agree with Kopytoff that the 'conceptual polarity of individualized persons and commodified things is recent and, culturally speaking, exceptional' (1986, 64). As we have already argued, it may be the case in non-capitalist societies that human beings and artefacts have 'lives' which are rather similar to each other. Thus the ways in which the identities of persons and things are constructed may be rather similar. Depending upon the emphasis which we wished to place on the issue, we might wish to say either that artefacts may have a social life similar to that of persons, or that persons may represent no more than one particular type of artefact. Of course, it is not the aim here to present a picture of artefacts as being endowed with intentionality. We might say that while material culture is active, it does not act. But at the same time, we should also guard against the other extreme: a voluntarist position in which persons are seen as context-free rational decision-makers, endowed with the ability to act just as they desire. Consequently, we might not wish to consider agency in terms of discontinuous bursts of will emerging from out of the internal mental life of subjects. Social action will always be relational in character, involving persons and things operating within a world.

In Stuart Piggott's *Neolithic Cultures of the British Isles* (1954) a synthesis of the material traces relating to the Neolithic period in Britain then available was carried out under the rubric of culture history. Thus it was expected that the evidence should resolve itself into a series of spatially and temporally bounded assemblages, each representative of a distinct group of people. Piggott himself advocated a quite strict adherence to culture-historic principles:

> The use of the word 'culture', in its accepted archaeological meaning, should be confined to an aggregate of associated elements of material culture recognisable in the archaeological record.
>
> (1954, 302)

In the case of the earlier Neolithic in southern Britain, it proved possible to define just such an entity, the 'Windmill Hill culture', on the basis of the recurrent association of particular types of monuments, flint mines, pottery and stone tools (ibid., 17). However, the later Neolithic presented a rather more intractible problem. Piggott argued that as time had progressed a series of distinctive 'secondary Neolithic cultures' had emerged. These were the outcome of interactions and fusions between a number of different populations: the Windmill Hill folk who had migrated to Britain from northern France at the start of the Neolithic, the indigenous Mesolithic groups, and a new influx of migrants from Scandinavia. These latter were representatives of the 'circumpolar stone age' peoples, distinguished by their use of impressed and pitted pottery. Elsewhere, Gordon Childe was to argue that it was the migratory habits of these folk which allowed them to emerge as middle-man traders, circulating goods between sedentary communities and opening up the remote stone axe sources (Childe 1940). On the basis of this framework, Piggott was able to distinguish five of these secondary Neolithic cultures: the Peterborough culture, the Bann and

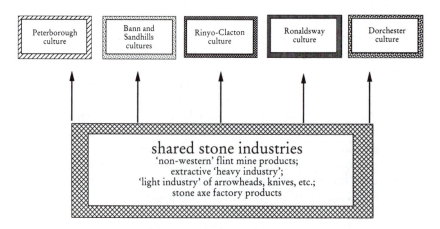

Figure 6.1 Piggott's secondary Neolithic cultures

Sandhills culture, the Rinyo-Clacton culture, the Ronaldsway culture and the Dorchester culture (Piggott 1954, 302) (figure 6.1). However, for the most part these cultural entities were defined on the basis of a single material type: styles of pottery. So, while each culture group could be identified by its ceramic assemblage, they shared in common a range of lithic types.

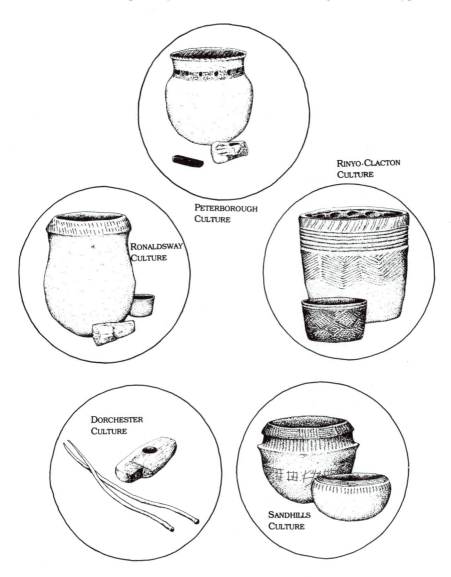

Figure 6.2 The relationship between lithics and other artefact types in the constitution of the 'secondary Neolithic cultures'

Consequently, Piggott suggested that the distinct ceramic traditions overlay a more fundamental cultural unity (ibid., 277). The picture which thus emerges is one of ceramic variability superimposed upon a substrate of lithic homogeneity (figure 6.2). The arbitrary nature of this division of the material is underlined by the case of the Dorchester culture, which lacked even a distinctive pottery style, and represented 'a residuum of cultures known from south and east Britain with no distinctive pottery but sharing other characteristics, including certain bone and stone types ... cremation cemeteries; ritual monuments of henge type; certain individual burials' (ibid., 281).

The stone tools shared by all of these groups were held to represent four related industries. These consisted of, first, types which had been absent from the 'western' assemblages of the earlier Neolithic; second a 'heavy industry' of extractive character; third an associated 'light industry' of more delicate tools which share technological features with the industrial implements (*petit-tranchet* derivative arrowheads, polished discoidal knives, etc.); and finally the products of the stone axe factories (ibid., 279). A processualist might object that this classification conflates style and function, establishing types associated with particular activities (picks) as cultural markers equivalent to arrowhead styles. Conceivably, Piggott might argue in response that these activities themselves were diagnostic of the way of life of a definable group of people. His own evident disquiet arose instead from having to use a single artefact type in order to define a cultural group. However, while he expressed his reservations in print, and acknowledged that to some extent all of the secondary Neolithic cultures 'interpenetrated' each other, he concluded that they remained 'convenient labels' for the groupings revealed by the artefacts (ibid., 373).

Another attempt to divide later Neolithic artefacts up on culture-historic lines is evident in Fiona Roe's study of stone maceheads (1968), published appropriately enough in a *festschrift* to Stuart Piggott (figure 6.3). Roe noted a broad distinction between those artefacts which were recurrently found in association with Peterborough Ware, and those connected with Grooved Ware. However, it seemed that this pattern broke down when Fengate Ware (arguably the latest style of Peterborough Ware) was considered (Roe 1968, 158). Working from a concern with a particular class of artefacts, Roe suggested that a number of distinctive late Neolithic material forms could be grouped together into an entity which she defined as the 'Macehead complex'. What is perhaps most illuminating about Roe's approach is the way in which it demonstrated that the same set of artefacts could be categorised in a range of different ways. By starting from the perspective that maceheads were a singularly significant type of object, she was able to establish a rather different classification from Piggott's. This suggests that later Neolithic artefacts do not naturally fall into clear and bounded assemblages which are valid across geographical areas and contexts of occurrence.

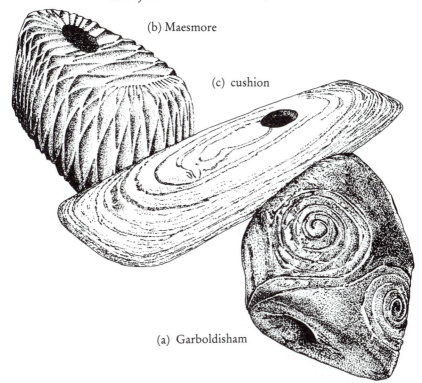

(b) Maesmore

(c) cushion

(a) Garboldisham

Figure 6.3 Three maceheads: the Garboldisham antler mace, a Maesmore decorated macehead and a cushion macehead

Implicitly, both Piggott and Roe appear to have recognised the absence of sharp boundaries, and the way that any classificatory entity created out of this material will tend to shade off at its edges, merging into other groupings. Pessimistically, this might lead us to believe that this material is entirely chaotic and unstructured, and that any attempt to sort it into groupings tells us far more about the preconceptions of the analyst than about the nature of the British later Neolithic. Alternatively, we could argue that the evidence simply fails to live up to the requirements of an approach which seeks to demonstrate the presence of distinct quasi-ethnic groups in the past through their identification with bounded and mutually exclusive artefactual assemblages.

If culture-historians wished to see these artefacts as a reflection of ethnic groupings in the past, the processual archaeology of the 1970s also sought to correlate the visible structure of the evidence with the hidden structure of past social groups. It was in this spirit, for instance, that Peebles and Kus (1977) attempted to define the 'archaeological correlates' of ranked society. A similar notion of *correlation* underwrote Colin Renfrew's (1973) investigation of Neolithic society in Wessex, where the gradual centralisation and increase in scale of monuments was held to represent the emergence of ranked societies out of a number of egalitarian communities. Renfrew was able to define a series of diagnostic traits of chiefdom societies, and suggested that 'using this notion, the size and distribution of the observed field monuments becomes intelligible, and they are seen as the natural counterpart of other features of the society' (1973, 556). Thus the clusters of large monuments in north Wiltshire, Salisbury Plain, Cranborne Chase and south Dorset represent these developing polities (figure 6.4). As will be clear from the arguments expressed in Chapter Three above, the disadvantage of this approach is that it views the material evidence (in this case the monuments) as a product or outcome of social processes, which thereby mirrors social form, rather than as a medium through which social activies and social change were enacted. Yet while this is a social model which has been imposed onto the evidence rather than in any sense derived from it, it none the less continues to enjoy the position of dominating our thought concerning the period. The role of portable artefacts within such a neo-evolutionary framework was explicitly considered by Stephen Pierpoint (1980). In hypothesising the rise of a ranked society in Neolithic eastern Yorkshire, Pierpoint drew on theoretical frameworks developed in advertising and animal ethology. For him, the elaborate artefacts found in the graves of his 'developmental' stage were a means by which individuals were able to signal their social identity (ibid., 216). This signalling behaviour served as an efficient means of ensuring group affiliation, social solidarity, and the acceptance of positions of authority within an increasingly internally differentiated society. This in turn increased the adaptive fitness of the group as a whole.

When we consider Renfrew and Pierpoint together as examples of a processual and neo-evolutionary approach, it is clear that societies were being conceptualised as adaptive or managerial wholes. While these units were recognised as being internally differentiated, this differentiation took the form of a hierarchical nesting of statuses, prerogatives and roles, such that progressively more of the functions of society were restricted within the higher orders of the community. Moreover, this distribution of functions was implicitly or explicitly regarded as beneficial to the group as a whole. It is in this latter respect that some of the accounts of the later Neolithic published in the earlier 1980s differ from this framework. Increasingly, the different strata of Neolithic societies came to be seen as mutually antagonistic, distinguished by separate sets of interests and objectives (e.g. Shennan 1982; Bradley 1984). However, while the functionalism of Renfrew's approach had been thoroughly rejected, the chiefdom or ranked society remained the main alternative to the ethnic group as the entity responsible for generating the material traces of the later Neolithic. Thus Kinnes (1985, 43), for example, refers to 'a fundamental shift in the mid-later third millennium ... to a more familiar

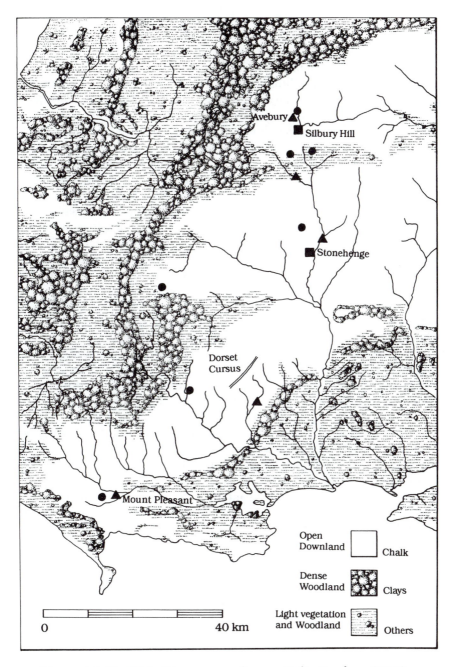

Figure 6.4 Neolithic Wessex according to Colin Renfrew (1973)

pyramidal structure'. Perhaps by now the ranked society has grown too familiar by half.

To some extent, the ranked society idea is implicit in Bradley's (1982; 1984) studies of assemblage variation in the Neolithic. Placing the nail in the coffin of later Neolithic assemblages as separate 'cultures', Bradley pointed out the lack of spatial integrity of these groupings (1982, 28). While the Ronaldsway culture, and even to a degree the Sandhills culture had clear regional identities, Peterborough Ware, Grooved Ware and the burials of the Dorchester series all had overlapping distributions. Other authors, implicitly recognising that these assemblages could not represent the equivalent of tribal groups, had already begun to experiment with hypotheses of cult packages (Burgess 1980) or priestly classes (MacKie 1977). In search of an alternative, Bradley turned to social anthropology. In societies where the circulation of goods is dominated not by money or barter but by the giving of gifts, it is often the case that different kinds of items will move in *ranked spheres of exchange* (Sahlins 1974, 277). Thus food, tools, prestige valuables and gifts of human beings may not be mutually exchangeable, standing as they do in a moral hierarchy in respect of each other. Instead, they circulate in separate networks of exchange contacts, and it may be the case that a more restricted stratum of society will have access to the more highly ranked items. In this way, goods may be less important in and for themselves than as tokens of one's prerogative to engage in particular kinds of social contact.

Bradley noted that one of the distinctive features of the British later Neolithic was the development of a range of complex artefacts: he was able to define twenty-four 'special items' whose currency became more diverse as time progressed (Bradley 1984, 48). These included maceheads, Duggleby and Seamer style flint axes, jet belt sliders, carved stone balls, fine arrowhead types and so on. These objects were not evenly distributed, but tended to be recovered in distinctive patterns of association: in particular, with Grooved Ware and with individual burials. Such artefacts, then, might have served as 'weapons of exclusion', restricted in their circulation and both reflecting and promoting status differences within society. Thus the distinct material assemblages of the late Neolithic could be associated with social position rather than ethnic affiliation. In the case of Grooved Ware, where pottery and other materials had been found distributed from Orkney to Wessex and from East Anglia to Wales, Bradley's suggestion was that this state of affairs documents the establishment of contacts between spatially distinct elite groups in different parts of the country. In this way, the artefact traditions had served to 'build bridges' between increasingly diversified regional systems (1984, 38). The appearance on Grooved Ware of motifs which were shared with the passage tomb art of Ireland and Brittany thus demonstrated a process of symbolic entrainment, a sharing of significant symbols by socially pre-eminent groups.

Bradley's argument presents a picture in which some degree of antagonism or struggle existed between the different levels of the social formation. This argument was elaborated by Thorpe and Richards (1984), whose account of later Neolithic Wessex is one in which access to different artefactual assemblages (associated respectively with Grooved Ware and Peterborough Ware) denoted not merely position within a social hierarchy, but engagement with rather different networks of exchange and sources of authority. In this way, the relationship between social factions is presented as a dynamic one. Shifts in the character of goods in circulation over time are connected with a continuous diversification in order to maintain the exclusivity of prestige objects (Thorpe and Richards 1984, 71). This evokes the notion of material emulation proposed by Miller (1982), in which the most highly-ranked members of a community must constantly acquire new material forms, since each in time will 'trickle down' the social hierarchy, dispersing their exclusivity. Something rather similar is presented by Bradley and Edmonds (1993, 198) in their vivid description of fluid and unstable exchange spheres, and continuous competition over access to goods directing the movements of stone axes. In each case, the accent is on control and competition for access, such that social power is vested in the ability to manipulate the disposition of material resources.

At the risk of seeming overly critical, it could still be suggested that, for all their vibrancy, all of these interpretations presume a social formation which is unitary and hierarchical. Moreover, while they present societies in which material culture was being strategically manipulated in the creation of social position, it is none the less the case that 'people with access to Grooved Ware' or 'Grooved Ware users' are only one step removed from 'Rinyo-Clacton folk'. That is to say, although we have moved away from a one-to-one correspondence between pots and people, the expectation is still clearly that the presence of particular artefact types on an archaeological site should alert us to the presence (in the past) of a particular kind of person. Ethnographic observations might lead us to question whether communities are ever so sutured and self-contained. Both the ethnic unit and the ranked formation are effectively ideal types, which may correspond more closely with the political aspirations, values or ideologies of particular interest groups than with their actual political experiences (Peterson 1993, 337).

ARTEFACTS WITH PERSONALITIES

A first step towards a reconsideration of later Neolithic material culture involves some reflection on the character of the artefacts themselves. A number of the authors whose work has already been mentioned have singled out Grooved Ware as diagnostic of an elite material assemblage. This has often been because this ceramic is found in a range of 'special' contexts: large henge monuments in Wessex (Wainwright and Longworth 1971), chambered tombs in Orkney (Renfrew 1979), formal pit deposits in southern Britain (e.g. Manby 1974) and cellular houses – supposedly the abodes of priestly astronomers – in Orkney (MacKie 1977). These, then, attest to the socially restricted character of the Grooved Ware 'package', in turn promoting their recognition as prestige goods. However, one of the defining characteristics of a prestige goods system lies in the scarcity of the objects in circulation (Dupré and Rey 1978; Friedman and Rowlands 1977). Indeed, in the case of the classic prestige goods-based kingdoms of central Africa, it was the penetration of western goods in large numbers, and their saturation of contexts in which they ranked as valuables, that brought about the collapse of the hierarchy (Ekholm 1972). Only so long as the supply of these items was maintained at a low level, monopolised by an elite group, did it contribute to the maintenance and promotion of social position. We have noted already that most of the objects which were in circulation in later Neolithic Britain were not confined to a particular cultural assemblage. None the less, it is instructive to consider those objects which are most closely associated with Grooved Ware as opposed to any other ceramic style. These include the carved chalk axes from Woodhenge (Cunnington 1929), decorated chalk plaques from Amesbury (Harding 1988) (figure 6.5) and chalk balls from Mount Pleasant and Maumbury Rings (Wainwright 1979; Bradley and Thomas 1984); marine shells from Woodlands (Stone and Young 1948) and Firtree Field (Barrett, *et al.* 1991, 80); fossils from the post holes at Woodhenge (Cunnington 1929); and oblique-shaped *petit tranchet* arrowheads from numerous sites (Green 1980) (figure 6.6). As with Grooved Ware itself, each of these objects involves raw materials whose supply could not readily be restricted. Marine shell and flint are certainly materials whose occurrence is far from ubiquitous, but it is arguable whether they are sufficiently scarce for their transfer from one place to another to serve as a basis for social domination. Chalk, clay and most sources of ceramic filler are comparatively easy to come by. While both potting and flint knapping involve a fair degree of skill, it is arguable how restricted this would have been within Neolithic society. Similarly, neither the manufacture of a Grooved Ware pot nor the knapping of an arrowhead would have involved the investment of huge quantities of effort (about 15 minutes' work in the latter case according to M. Edmonds, pers. comm.).

Thus while Grooved Ware, with its elaborate decoration, and those objects most intimately associated with it may have held considerable symbolic significance, they may not have constituted status markers as such. In developing an alternative perspective another strand of economic anthropology will be of help, concerned with the embeddedness of inalienable goods (Weiner 1992), which reintroduces the themes which were investigated in Chapter Three above. According to Weiner there is some

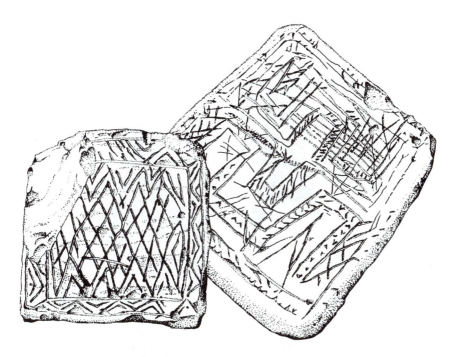

Figure 6.5 The chalk plaques from a Grooved Ware
pit near Stonehenge (after Harding 1988)

sense in which, even in western societies, particular possessions cannot be entirely divorced from the social context within which they have been fashioned and used. Thus until comparatively recently it was not acceptable for land to pass outside the family in many parts of Europe. It is commonly accepted in non-capitalist societies that things which have passed from one person to another as gifts still maintain some attachment to the previous owner. This is often explained in terms of debt: where different classes of object are not interchangeable, a social relationship will continue to exist between giver and receiver until another good of exactly the same type is used to cancel out the debt (Gosden 1989). Moreover, a complex etiquette may demand that such a return gift may not be made immediately. For a certain amount of time the recipient of the gift must endure the social disadvantage of indebtedness (Bourdieu 1977, 6).

However, this is only a part of the picture. Where a good can pass effortlessly from one owner to another in exchange for a universal equivalent (or even in barter), it may lose its embedded significance. The meanings which arise from the networked associations of things may be precisely what gives them their power. The embedding of a thing is the source of its authority (Weiner 1992, 102). Severed from a series of connections which

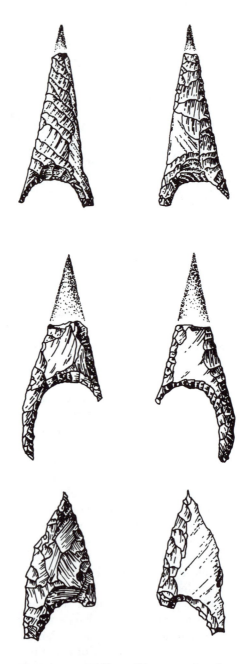

Figure 6.6 Oblique flint arrowheads
(after Wainwright and Longworth 1971)

render it intelligible in a particular way, the thing becomes a *mere thing*. In this sense, the gift is a thing which is engaged in a 'worlding' of a particular kind, whereas the commodity has been rendered unworlded, as an isolated and alienated focus of the analysis which affords it monetary value. As Weiner points out, what makes embedded goods so important is 'that their authentication is dependent upon the histories of ancestors, divine rulers, and God' (1992, 34). It follows that objects which pass from hand to hand have an ambivalent or duplicitous character: it is their engagement in a network of relationships with people, deities and other things that renders them powerful and desireable, but it is also this very characteristic that means they can never be owned in an exclusive sense. One accepts the debt that the thing engenders because it allows one access to the authority of the gifted good. For not only are things authenticated by gods, ancestors and spirits: their use may allow one to invoke the support of those beings.

This implies something slightly different from the notion of 'material culture as symbol' which emerged within archaeology in the early 1980s (e.g. Hodder 1982; 1985; Wylie 1982). Rather than representing the world in a formal, arbitrary and language-like manner, things may be held to embody forces and qualities (Morphy 1991, 102). Thus the use of specific raw materials for the manufacture of artefacts is an attempt to draw directly on the abstract qualities of the substance, the act of production itself invoking its latent power (Taçon 1991, 196). Similarly, objects may be considered to embody the force or substance of a person (Weiner 1992, 107). These observations add to the argument concerning the similarities between persons and things rehearsed in Chapter Three. What is significant is that in many non-capitalist societies, material things are considered as manifestations of more generalised qualities and properties, in very much the same way as people are not wholly unique in their characteristics. The similarity of artefacts and persons lies in the way in which, through their engagement in a web of relationships, they allow the richness of an intangible cosmology or history to become visible (Strathern 1988, 176). Because both things and people are 'eyewitnessable', they serve as evidence, exemplars and reminders of the interconnected nature of the world (Battaglia 1990, 6). What this suggests is that in societies other than our own there exist ways of thinking about the 'personalities' of objects that see them as manifesting qualities and associations rather than as maintaining their individual characteristics as a grounding essence. Obviously, this insight cannot be used as a direct analogy, which would involve the under-standing that all societies other than western capitalist ones possess very much the same kind of conceptual apparatus. This smacks of the notion of a 'savage mind' characterised by diagnostic modes of thought, and charac-teristic of all 'cold' societies (Lévi-Strauss 1966). However, it *is* suggested that working through the material traces of the later Neolithic within this kind of a logic may allow us a fresh perspective on the material.

To begin with, we might consider the kinds of connections which later Neolithic artefacts might have evoked. In the first place, the location of origin of many objects might itself have been significant. Bradley and Edmonds (1993, 42) point out that several of the stone sources exploited for the manufacture of stone axes and shafthole implements were spatially quite remote from everyday domestic activities. Some, like Graig Lwyd and Rathlin Island would probably have been approached from the sea, while others perched on mountaintops like Langdale or Killin would have involved actual physical danger in reaching them. The extent to which the users of artefacts would have been familiar with their geographical origins is difficult to assess, but it seems likely that at least verbal accounts of these sources would have circulated, contributing to the acknowledged histories of objects. In some cases, as with jet or amber from coastal sources, it might have been the locational specificity of the origin which was of principal importance. In other examples, as with mined flint or with bone, antler and other materials derived from animals, the means by which the material was acquired may have added more to its significance.

If it is difficult to document the importance attached to the sources of raw materials used for the manufacture of artefacts, the preferential choice of substances which have a striking visual appearance is much more obvious. As Coope (1979, 98) argues, thoughout the Neolithic period a rather selective range of materials was used in the production of stone axes, and Thorpe and Richards (1984, 71) were able to demonstrate the preferential use of exotic sources rather than local rocks within Yorkshire. This might mean no more than that the attempt was made to valorise those axes which were in more limited supply. None the less, it is remarkable how often visually distinctive raw materials have been chosen, and how often the working of the object serves to enhance its impact. In the case of stone axes, it is significant that two of the stone sources whose products are most widely distributed possess a very characteristic appearance: the blue-green volcanic tuff of the Lake District (Keiller *et al.* 1941, 58) and the dark porcel-lanite of northern Ireland (Francis *et al.* 1988, 137). In specific cases, much rarer materials have clearly been selected for their unique visual impact. Thus Oakley (1965, 120) mentions two axes from Troston, near Bury St. Edmonds which are made from a Jurassic serupid limestone containing marine worm tracks. Cushion maceheads were often produced from stones that contained natural streaks of serpentine or chlorite, which are made more impressive by the grinding and polishing of the implement (Gibson 1944, 19). Similarly, distinctive kinds of flint appear to have been used for particular types of artefacts, especially those which are recovered from 'special' contexts like burials, hoards, monuments and pit deposits. Duggleby adzes and Seamer axes, for instance, are for the most part made from flints of unusual colour (Manby 1974, 98), and this has generally been polished to a very glossy finish (Manby 1979, 69). A broad range of colours of flint were also used in the production of chisel-shaped *petit tranchet* derivative arrowheads (Stevenson 1947, 182). Conversely, the facetted mace-heads of the Maesmore group are universally made from light-coloured flint, suggesting that the specific character of the artefact type depended upon the material as well as the form into which it was fashioned (Roe 1968, 149) (figure 6.3).

In the case of any of these objects, the raw material was not merely attractive, but would have served to alert the onlooker or the user to its origin. By flaking, grinding and polishing the object, the artesan did not only fashion it into a useful or recognisable form. She or he also drew out something of the character of the material, allowing it to become more evident. Implicit in the manufacture of artefacts was a form of individuation which involved drawing attention to their origins. We might also suggest that the evidences of manufacture found on many Neolithic artefacts served to enhance the extent to which the object's history was immanent in its physical presence. These include the traces of flake removals still present on polished flint axes; thumb-prints on pottery vessels; the marks left by flint tools on jet belt sliders (McInnes 1968, 139); and the 'decorative' tooling and facetting noted on the preserved wooden hafts of some stone axes (Sheridan 1992). All of this suggests that the identities of later Neolithic artefacts were not the consequence of their uniqueness as a self-contained assemblage of traits and attributes. The individual identity of an object would have emerged from a background of materials, persons, practices and histories.

This argument allows us to return again to the issue of the connections between stylistically similar artefacts found in different regions of Britain and Ireland. These connections have principally been discussed in terms of the sharing of motifs between Irish passage tomb art and Grooved Ware (Bradley 1984, 52; Bradley and Chapman 1986, 132–4), although the wider representation of these motifs on stone plaques and other objects has also been noted. One interpretation of this phenomenon might be to invoke a process of 'symbolic entrainment' (Renfrew 1986, 8–9), whereby sets of symbols are held in common by elite groups in different areas. Such a symbolic repertoire might serve both as a means of elite communication (thereby enhancing solidarity) and as a form of restricted knowledge, whose significance would only be fully appreciated by the initiated. While this view has much to commend it, and must form an element of any inter-pretation, it does operate at a high level of generality. As Bradley and Chapman note (1986, 132) the production of these material media may actually be spread over some depth of time. This observation is bolstered by the recent suggestion that a distinct phase of activity associated with the use of Grooved Ware can be discerned in-between the building of the large passage tombs (*c.* 2500 bc/3200 BC) and the introduction of Beakers into the Boyne Valley (*c.* 2000 bc/2500 BC) (G. Eogan and H. Roche, pers.

comm.; Eogan 1991). Moreover, the instances of similar motifs associated with cist graves extend well into the Bronze Age (Simpson and Thawley 1972). What is involved here may be more than simply the synchronous utilisation of a set of symbols by groups of people in different parts of the British Isles. What is implied is a process of quotation and reference, in which connections were established both between different regions and between past and present.

This web of reference involves a number of different forms of artefacts. As Wainwright and Longworth pointed out (1971, 246), spiral and concentric circle motifs are shared by passage tomb art, Grooved Ware (figure 6.7), the Scottish carved stone balls (Marshall 1977), the chalk drums from Folkton in Yorkshire (Longworth and Kinnes 1985, 115–18) (figure 6.8) and the antler macehead from Garboldisham in Norfolk (Edwardson 1965). Another set of connections would link the lozenge-shaped facets of the Maesmore mace-heads and the lattice patterns on some crown antler maces (Roe 1968, 161) with the similar designs on some Grooved Ware (e.g. Wyke Down: Barrett *et al.* 1991, figure 3.23, 3), and in a more general sense with the lattice desgns of passage grave art (for instance Fourknocks: Shee Twohig 1981, 220–2), the Amesbury chalk plaques (Harding 1988), the Graig Lwyd stone plaque (Piggott 1954, 294) and from the houses at Skara Brae, and the filled lozenges of Clacton style Grooved Ware, the Folkton drums and later Beaker pottery (Clarke 1970). As Cleal (pers. comm.) has pointed out, these two sets of motifs are found together on both the Knowth macehead (Eogan 1983) and Grooved Ware sherds from a pit at Barrow Hills, Radley. Taking the argument further forward in time, one might note the appearance of similar filled geometric motifs on later Beaker pottery (Clarke 1970) and gold lunulae (Taylor 1980). Clearly, this range of material presents us with a continuum of degrees of connectedness between media, from direct quotation to more general cultural continuity. What is significant is that these various complex cultural expressions (Grooved Ware, carved stone balls, decorated mace-heads, chalk drums, passage grave art) are relatively seldom found in any direct association with each other. This argues against any notion of an homogeneous cultural 'package', as opposed to a series of overlapping and mutually referential artefact traditions. Certain objects, like the Folkton Drums, the Knowth Macehead and a Grooved Ware vessel from the Wyke Down henge which mixes styles of decoration, seem to deliberately fuse together different sets of references. That is to say, these objects may represent a means of asserting a connection with other forms of artefact which might not be locally available, or which might actually be inappropriate to a given context of use. The spread of forms of decoration from one medium to another would thus widen the range of contexts in which particular influences would be represented.

This perspective allows us to reconsider the notion of skeuomorphism, frequently in the past raised in relation to later Neolithic artefacts (e.g.

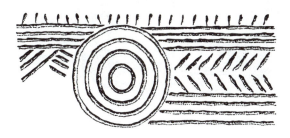

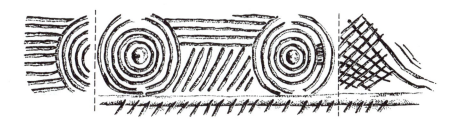

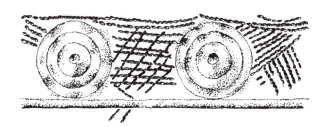

Figure 6.7 Spiral decorations on Grooved Ware
(after Wainwright and Longworth 1971)

Figure 6.8 The chalk drums from Folkton in Yorkshire

Smith 1956, 202; Wainwright and Longworth 1971, 246). Most often, this concept has been invoked with some form of evolutionary process in mind.

> For a basket to hold liquid easily it must be lined with clay, and if such a vessel chance to be burnt, the clay lining is seen transformed by the fire to a semblance of stone. It was only a matter of time before human adaptiveness was devising vessels made of baked clay alone ... and such novelties were naturally first made in the outward likeness of the familar basket, gourd, or leather bag.
>
> (Hawkes 1940, 74)

In these terms, the similarities between the cordons and parallel slashes of some Grooved Ware decoration prove comprehensible as an attempt to reproduce in ceramic form 'the familiar basket'. However, as Ray (1987) has demonstrated, skeuomorphism may involve a much more subtle intent on the part of the maker. In Ray's Igbo-Ukwu example, the role of basketry-styled pottery vessels was to make a covert reference to women's labour and women's baskets in an all-male social context. It is not necessary to draw any direct parallel between early historic central Africa and prehistoric Britain for the importance of this point to be appreciated. Evidently, the fashioning and decoration of several of the classes of artefacts with which we are concerned may have provided still another means by which objects brought embedded meanings with them to contexts of social interaction. In a strong sense it is quite impossible for us in the present to attribute particular meanings to these motifs. None the less, it is not too far fetched to imagine that the spirals, concentric circles, facets, lozenges, chevrons, zig-zags, parallel grooves and lattices of this decoration involved a series of references not merely to baskets, but to worldly phenomena like water (waves and ripples), rain, wind, clouds, vegetation, sun and moon and the human body (bones, scarification marks). This 'art' is not representational but geometric, and its ambiguity is a part of its stength. Much is alluded to, but it always requires explanation, and a series of parallel readings is always possible. Again, this implies that different aspects of an artefact's wealth of connotations might be foregrounded in different contexts and juxtapositions.

Each of the 'complex artefacts' of the later Neolithic, then, was a concrete manifestation of a series of networks of significance, involving places, the personal histories of people, substances, skills and symbolic references. The deep embedding of each object in these networks was such that it might give access to a complex world of meanings. However, these items never existed outside of a social world: they were constantly engaged. Artefacts were never abstracted things, but always part of a mobile set of social relationships maintained between persons and things. Consequently, their significance was always relative to the situation in which they were immersed. At the grand scale we can see this in the very different ways in which particular types of artefact were used in the different parts of the British Isles. Grooved Ware, for instance, may have originated in the north of Scotland, where a continuous sequence of development between round-based Unstan style vessels and true Grooved Ware may be distinguished at some sites (McSween 1992, 269). While in this 'home' region Grooved Ware pots may be found in both domestic and funerary contexts, in the south of Britain the ceramic is more often found in a more rarefied set of locations (figure 6.9). It may thus be that the exotic and alien quality of the pottery added something to its significance as it began to be used in more distant regions.

CIRCULATION AND LIFE-PATHS

So far, we have considered the embedded connections which artefacts may have brought with them. The next stage of the argument is to consider the temporal aspect of the emergence of object identities. Here, it may be helpful to return to the point with which we closed Chapter Three, the consideration of artefact histories as time-geographic life paths. Conventionally, when the process of circulation of goods is represented in archaeological discourse, a picture emerges of mobile objects 'hopping' between essentially static human groups (e.g. Hodder 1974; Renfrew 1975). Thus the archaeological distribution map comes to be considered as the

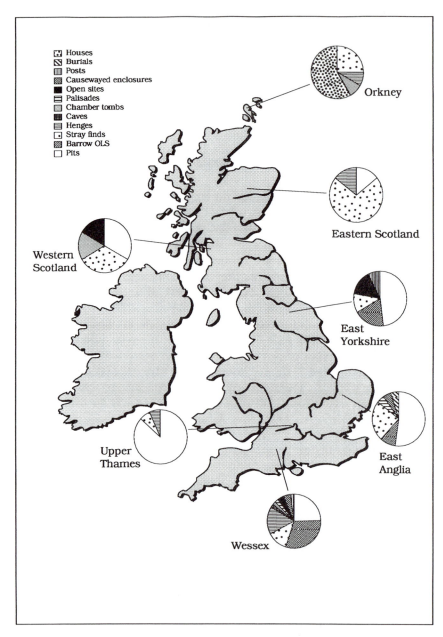

Figure 6.9 The representation of Grooved Ware in different types of context in various regions of Britain

PEOPLE AND ARTEFACTS

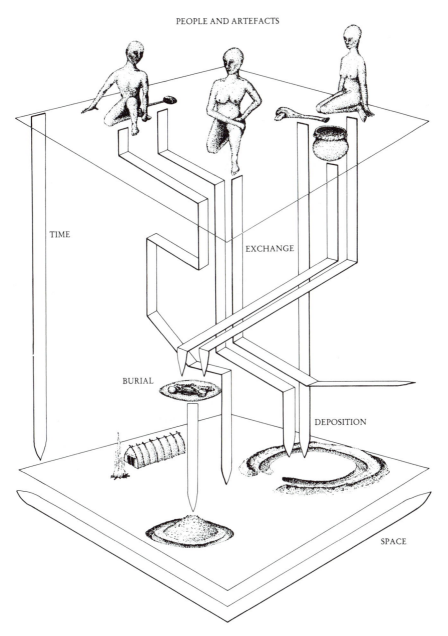

Figure 6.10 The interactions of artefacts, people and places in later Neolithic Britain

fossilised imprint of processes of exchange, each artefact coming to rest and registering archaeologically at the point at which it ceased to circulate. If instead we conceive of this process as one of syncronised encounters and separations involving persons and things, where both are imagined as having individual life histories, a rather different pattern emerges (figure 6.10). Each encounter can be thought of as a transaction involving a negotiation of the relationships between persons and things. Such a transaction has the effect of manifesting or objectifying the network of relationships in which those persons and things are embedded. Meetings and material transfers are thus a process through which people gain access to the worlds of meaning in which artefacts are engaged. It is also a process through which artefacts come to be bound up with the identities of individuals or groups of people (Weiner 1992, 33). It is the series of transactions in which both persons and things are involved which individuates them: through interactions which take place in specific locations, narratives of identity are constructed. Moreover, this same series of transactions may establish new forms of connectedness. Acquiring or using particular artefacts may create some form of relationship between the persons involved and absent manufacturers, ancestral generations, or far-away places (Battaglia 1990, 6; Helms 1979).

In the case of British later Neolithic artefacts, it does seem to be the case that different classes of object circulated in rather distinctive ways. It is in the nature of archaeology that we have relatively little information on the complex and lengthy histories of these items, since we only encounter them at the point at which they came to rest for one reason or another. However, the combination of the depositional context and the physical condition of artefacts is itself quite revealing, and does indicate major differences in their treatment. Some objects, like polished discoidal flint knives, Scottish carved stone balls and the stone axes found within Yorkshire are very seldom recovered from closed contexts, indicating that deliberate deposition was not considered appropriate (Manby 1974, 86; Marshall 1977; Manby 1979, 77). Thus the occurrence of an item as a 'stray' find may itself be significant. In the case of the stone balls, those examples which *do* come from closed contexts tend to be knobbed, but otherwise undecorated (Marshall 1977, 63). The highly decorated examples like that from Towie (Smith 1876) may thus have had a role which was independent of the formal settings of monumental structures and funerary ritual (figure 6.11). Despite the lack of defined depositional contexts for stone balls, however, they are rarely chipped or broken. Only 7.5 per cent of the known examples are damaged, by comparison with 16.7 per cent of battle-axes and 29.6 per cent of maceheads (Marshall 1977, 61; Roe 1968, 147). Particularly in the case of cushion maceheads, there is a clear pattern of these objects being broken across the shaft-hole (Gibson 1944, 17; Simpson and Ransom 1992, 222). Thus the 'lives' of these items may have conventionally been terminated in acts of deliberate destruction.

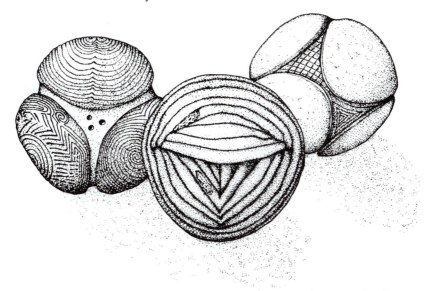

Figure 6.11 Later Neolithic carved stone balls from Scotland

The distinctive characters of the life histories of certain types of artefact may thus have been a major factor in maintaining their separate identities. This is particularly clear in the case of polished flint axes, which are frequently made of a different kind of flint from other artefacts found on the same site (Craddock *et al.* 1983, 135). By implication, it is the exotic or foriegn character of the flint which sustains the conceptual separation between the axe and the other stone implement types. It may be for similar reasons that certain types of artefacts were produced in quite restricted locations. We have already mentioned the remote and precarious sources of stone axes, but to this could be added the evidence that ripple-flaked oblique arrowheads may have been produced in a very few places in coastal Yorkshire, which may also have been responsible for the manufacture of Duggleby adzes (Stevenson 1947, 181; Manby 1974, 84; Kenworthy 1981, 191). Rather than seeing this exclusively in terms of some form of social control over production, we might hypothesise that the identity of these particular forms was bound up with their place of origin. Equally, the degree of evident wear or decay manifested by artefacts may have been of considerable significance. Thus jet sliders and cushion maceheads rarely show any sign of use or wear (McInnes 1968, 139; Gibson 1944, 17) and may have been purposefully deposited in a fresh condition, yet one can also cite the bone pin and boar's tusks associated with Burial 7 at Duggleby Howe, which were quite abraded (Kinnes *et al.* 1983, 98). It follows that in some cases it was the pristine character of the object and the disclosure of the raw material which was most valued, whereas in others it was the material manifestation of age, evidence of a long history of human involvement.

The qualities which distinguished particular objects and made them socially significant were thus never enclosed within the thing itself. The circulation of artefacts created histories which drew together places, materials and identities and made them available in specified locations. It has frequently been pointed out that concentrations of these 'fine goods' have been located inside or in the immediate vicinity of the major monuments of the period (Pierpoint 1980, 271; Bradley 1984, 57; Bradley and Edmonds 1993, 55). While at a descriptive level it is sufficient to note that these items are 'attracted' by the presence of the monuments, the specific processes which led to their deposition still remain to be fully understood. Obviously, the presence of high-ranking persons in a location is not sufficient reason in itself for the presence of clusters of artefacts of a particular sort. It may be that envisaging these events of deposition as the end points of life paths, the 'deaths' of artefacts, may be helpful in assessing their significance.

PATTERNS OF ASSOCIATION: AN ECONOMY OF SUBSTANCES

It is implicit in what has been suggested so far that the processes by which artefacts moved around the later Neolithic landscape were by no means random. Where a number of items were brought together in a particular location, the potential would exist for juxtaposition to result in new possibilities for the production of meaning on the part of the human observers. Consequently one might imagine that some form of etiquette would govern which objects, classes of person and types of places might be brought into mutual association. Just as in our own society it is not considered appropriate to enter a church carrying a lighted cigarette and an open can of beer, so the passage of things from place to place might be expected to be circumscribed to some degree. Objects might pass through a range of places in their life-time, and might be used alongside a range of other different artefacts. A given person might present themselves in public wearing particular dress fittings and carrying a number of tools and weapons, for instance. However, when an assemblage of items was placed in the ground together in an act of deliberate deposition, one might argue that a more forceful statement was being made. Rather than a temporary (or even playful) juxtaposition, this implies a fixing or fusion of the trajectories embodied in the objects concerned. At a time when domestic activity may have been transient and fleeting, leaving little in the way of an archaeological trace, this helps to explain why so much of the available evidence seems to be concerned with acts of deliberate deposition.

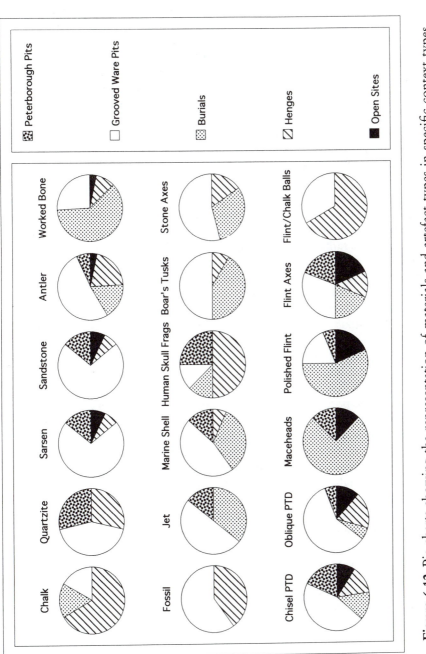

Figure 6.12 Pie charts showing the representation of materials and artefact types in specific context types

In order to investigate the structure of these located combinations of artefacts, the author undertook an analysis of the assemblages represented at 171 later Neolithic sites in Wessex, east Yorkshire and the upper Thames valley (figure 6.12). A range of different types of location were represented, although most were burials, henge monuments, scatters of material on ancient land surfaces ('open sites') or pits distinguished by the presence of Peterborough Ware or Grooved Ware. The argument for considering the latter as deliberate deposits rather than as the remnants of settlement or storage activity has been developed elsewhere (Thomas 1991a). Within this range of sites, the representaion of distinct artefact types (*petit tranchet* derivative arrowheads, stone axes, stone balls, flint axes) and of certain raw materials (chalk, quartzite, jet, sarsen, worked bone, etc.) was scrutinised. The initial expectation was that these might resolve themselves into distinct and bounded patterns of representation, such that particular substances might be repeatedly found in association with each other. This was not the case, and in retrospect the attempt to establish mutually exclusive assemblages is rather similar to Piggott's procedure in defining his Neolithic 'cultures'. Equally, when the contexts of these assemblages were taken into account, it was evident that particular kinds of places were not distinguished by unique sets of material culture. The pattern which emerged was rather more subtle (figure 6.13). Some kinds of objects and materials were relatively ubiquitous (various kinds of flint tools, for example). Others occurred in a rather restricted range of contexts (marine shell, carved chalk and fossils, found in Grooved Ware pits and henges; or boar's tusks, found in Grooved Ware pits and burials). These patterns of inclusion and exclusion tend to overlap, such that any pair of context types which can be defined seems to have some potential association in common (figure 6.14).

The artefacts and other materials in circulation in the later Neolithic thus do not appear to form cultural 'packages', any more than they are restricted to any one context type. So it may be inaccurate to talk of a 'Grooved Ware assemblage' or a 'Macehead complex'. What is found alongside any class of artefacts depends upon where it is encountered. Indeed, it is important to note that each artefact or substance itself forms a part of the context of each other object, such that the categorical distinction between object and context is muted (1). While quite clear patterns of exclusion occur (Peterborough Ware kept away from henges, ceramic traditions kept separate from each other), it seems to be the case that what distinguished different depositional locations was a diagnostic *combination* of objects and materials. If we imagine that any given artefact might have been used in a range of different contexts, and indeed may have had a different meaning in each, this becomes comprehensible. In the course of their 'lives', objects might move through a range of places, building up a history as they went. This history, a rich set of connotations, would be brought to bear on the place of deposition. The combinations in which things were deposited, however, would both reflect and construct

	Henges	Grooved Ware Pits	Burials	Peterborough Ware Pits
Marine shell	●	●		
Carved chalk	●	●		
Fossil	●	●		
Oblique arrowheads	●	●		
Grooved Ware	●	●		
Worked bone		●	●	
Boar's tusks		●	●	
Stone axes		●	●	
Polished flint tools		●	●	
Deer antler	●	●	●	
Quartzite	●	●		●
Jet		●	●	●
Human skull fragments	●			●
Maceheads			●	●
Chisel arrowheads	●	●	●	●
Flint axes	●	●	●	●

Figure 6.13 The representation of a series of materials and artefact types in specific contexts

the significance of the depositional location. These locations were thus distinct from each other, but at the same time always linked by some strand of similarity. At a certain level, then, the entire structure of people, places and artefacts could be said to be interlinked, forming something rather like a cosmology. However, this is likely to have taken the form of a series of simple principles of combination and exclusion which guided practice (and which

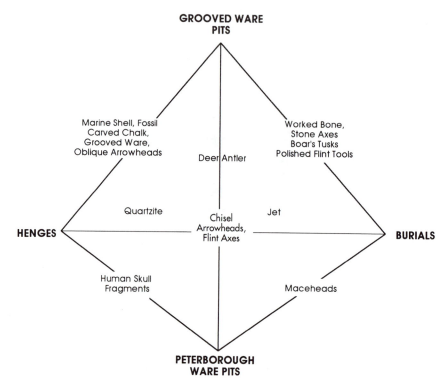

Figure 6.14 Combinations of materials and artefact specific to particular context types

quite possibly changed and were manipulated as time went on), rather than a complex fixed structure (Bourdieu 1977, 156). It would have been the process of the selection and combination of materials by skilled persons that served to reproduce the distinctive character of places. Some things were used alongside each other because they were similar or sympathetic, others because they clashed, bringing out different aspects of the place and the event. Perhaps the best way of describing this state of affairs is as involving an 'economy of substances', based upon the circulation of embedded values. We can deepen our understanding of these activities by looking in more detail at some of the kinds of locations of transaction and deposition involved.

THE PRODUCTION OF CONTEXT

The case of the round barrow at Whitegrounds, Burythorpe, Yorkshire (Brewster 1984) provides a clear example of the way in which a physical intervention can serve to 'fix' a set of relationships between artefacts in a given location. Here, an oval cairn of the earlier Neolithic, composed of sandstone cobbles over a core of gravel, surrounded a linear chamber. Inside were eight burials in various states of disarticulation and decapitation. Much later, in the late Neolithic, the crouched burial of an adult male was inserted through the top of the mound (figure 6.15). With the body were a jet belt slider and a Seamer-style polished-edge flint axe, placed against the small of his back. At the same time as the burial was inserted, the mound was reshaped into a round barrow, bounded by a stone kerb. What is implied here is a thoroughgoing transformation of a place: there was a physical reconfiguration, but also an act of deposition which fused together body, axe and slider, each with its own history and its own aura, its own matrix of association. Significantly, this happened in a place which was already important or meaningful, in that it was already a place of burial. That depth of meaning accrued from the past could now be both transformed and drawn on as sanction for present events.

As we have already argued, the bringing together of a group of artefacts has the effect of objectifying the relationships in which they are involved, while at the same time transforming those relationships. The physical proximity of things forges a relationship between them. This is particularly the case where the event in which this bringing together is achieved is some form of performance, an occasion where events and presences come to be accorded a particular significance. We might see these 'bundles' of activity which draw together persons and things as contexts in which identities (both human and object) are evaluated and negotiated. Moreover, since these kinds of events ('rituals', or whatever) frequently take place in locations of established significance, they will tend to be occasions for rememberance, in which place and artefacts serve as prompts for the recreation of memory. Given that some of these encounters of person and artefact involved quite small objects, or secluded spaces (the chambers of funerary monuments, remote parts of marshes, caves or forests), and that the potential range of meanings which might be evoked by things was immense and conditioned by the personal histories and knowledges of the participants, it follows that not all of the connections engendered were available to everyone. Indeed, one might suggest that some contexts of artefact use and deposition involved a degree of secrecy, and that the knowledge of which items were appropriate to which occasions was a major form of social power. The variability that we can discern in the evidence may thus involve the exclusion of particular classes of things and persons from certain contexts.

It has often been pointed out that context is essential to the meaning of any object (Hodder 1986, 139). If, however, we begin to think of context as more than a container or stage within which the thing shows itself, we might come to suggest that context is integral to social action. Things are

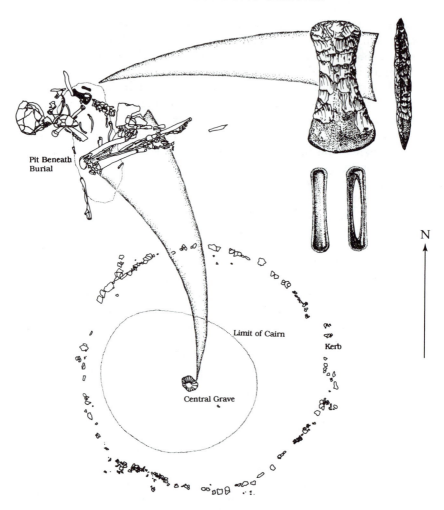

Figure 6.15 The Whitegrounds barrow,
Burythorpe, Yorkshire (after Brewster 1984)

thoroughly immersed in their settings, and reciprocally render one another
comprehensible. If this is so, then we could argue that in the later Neolithic,
the gathering of particular sets of artefacts in given locations implied more
than the appropriateness of certain items for the enactment of specific practices. Rather, as implicit in social action, these objects served to structure
the settings of interpersonal conduct. This suggests that it is not possible
to think of context as something stable, with fixed attributes and which
simply provides an unchanging backcloth for assemblages of artefacts.
The representation of particular things in a setting is actually a part of the

production of context. In the later Neolithic case, this means that the assemblages with which we are concerned had a role in establishing the forms of social interaction that took place at a given place and time. Particular social practices, then, were actually constituted through the bringing together of particular groupings of persons and artefacts. That both persons and things had life-paths which stretched between a number of different types of contexts would have been fundamental to this state of affairs. The same person, or the same artefact, might have been involved in quite different (and indeed mutually contradictory) practices at different times, and something of those other events would have clung to them still. Yet just as each artefact might be found in different patterns of association depending upon the context in which it was located, so too the mode of conduct elicited from a given person would vary according to location and event. In this sense, artefactual assemblages might be said to be constitutive of a person's 'mood': here solemn or respectful, here unruly or garrulous.

The archaeological literature which deals with the British later Neolithic is littered with examples of small numbers of artefacts which have been placed, seemingly inexplicably, in the ground. Consider, for example, the fresh and unused axe of Langdale rock which was buried blade down at the foot of the bank of Henge A at Llandegai in North Wales (Houlder 1968, 218). Yet the axe itself was not simply an isolated object, it was something deeply involved with particular sets of activities, each of which had its own proper place and time. Revealingly, while such axes are often found in the immediate vicinity of henges, they were very seldom deposited within the monuments themselves (Bradley and Edmonds 1993, 55). Consequently, the axe at Llangedai may represent the encroachment of one set of practices into the domain of another, a political act in which the significance and associations of a place are disrupted and reconfigured through physical intervention. This indicates another reason why the evidence resists easy categorisation into neat and mutually exclusive assemblages: whatever 'rules' were in operation were always capable of being bent or subverted. While one might never transgress the cardinal prescriptions surrounding places and performances, there would always have been room for the situation to be turned to personal advantage.

Just as the single axe at Llandegai may represent the introduction of a new sphere of activities into the place, thereby changing its meaning as a location, so a series of deposits inside chambered tombs of earlier origin may be seen as deliberate acts of redefinition. As Kinnes (1985, 42) notes, later Neolithic artefacts have in several cases been found in the blocking deposits closing off the chambers of Clyde tombs in western Scotland. These include a jet belt slider from Beacharra, Peterborough Ware sherds and a jet bead from Cairnholy, and Grooved Ware, two plano-convex flint knives, a polished-edge knife and a macehead from Tormore (Roe 1968, 154). As Simpson and Ransom (1992, 227) point out, the Tormore macehead, as well as those from Taversoe Tuick in Orkney and Knowth, County Meath, was not directly associated with human remains. This could indicate that these deposits should not be considered as 'grave goods' in the conventional sense. In each case, the introduction of the objects into the chamber may have taken place a considerable while after the last deposition of human bones. A similar pattern can be recognised in Caithness, where *petit tranchet* derivative arrowheads have come from the tombs of Ormiegill, Camster and Tulloch of Assery A, and fine polished-edge flint knives from Camster Round and Ormiegill (Clark 1934, 57; Davidson and Henshall 1991, 76).

Related to these deposits of artefacts in tomb chambers is the 'hoard' of objects from the plinth of the wall face at the large chambered cairn of Isbister in Orkney, comprising three axes, a macehead, a jet button, a jet ring and a limestone 'knife pendant' or preform (Davidson and Henshall 1991, 79). Here, the placement of a very rich set of objects at a point which must have been very late in the Neolithic sequence can perhaps be connected with a varied range of transfigurations which overtook some of the larger Orcadian chambered tombs at this time (Sharples 1985). Thus, the introduction of these objects, and the activities associated with the act of deposition itself, might be seen as similar in their impact to the digging of the surrounding ditch at Maes Howe (Richards 1988), or the construction of a platform over the flattened cairn at Pierowall Quarry (Sharples 1984). All of these events involve a physical transformation of a location, but we should not make the mistake of imagining that their contemporary impact was directly proportionate to their presently discernable archaeological trace. In that the Isbister deposit brought a series of artefactual life-paths and their broader connections to bear on a specific locale, the perceived and remembered transformation of the place might have been considerable.

The Isbister deposit can itself be compared with the celebrated collection of material from Ayton East Field, Seamer Moor, in Yorkshire (figure 6.16). This too had been buried in a funerary monument, a cairn within a long barrow, and was composed of four flint axes, five lozenge-shaped arrowheads, various other flints, boar's tusks and a few pieces of human bone (Smith 1921, 121). In this case, the presence of human remains has led to some debate as to whether the deposit represents a hoard or a burial. The same is true of a series of finds of Duggleby axes from Scotland, where the representation of a human body with what is taken as a funerary assemblage is either partial or questionable (Kenworthy 1977, 85–7; Sheridan 1992, 206). Indeed, it may be that these rather ambiguous deposits may be characteristic of this particular class of artefact. These instances might lead us to question the universal applicability of two rather artificial archaeological terms: either the material represents the last resting place of a particular person (a burial), or it is a store of artefacts of value (a hoard).

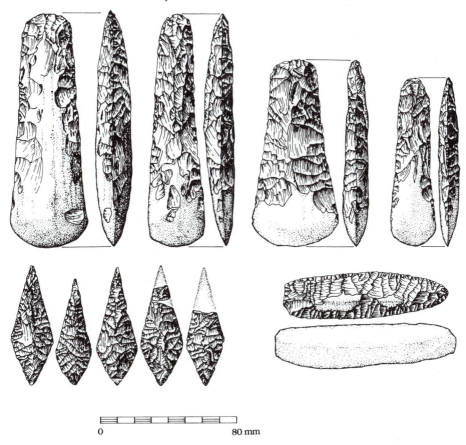

Figure 6.16 The Seamer Moor hoard of flint tools (after Smith 1921)

There is something to be said for blurring the boundary between these two categories. It need not be the case that when human bones are placed in the ground with artefacts the latter are always seen as a form of accessory, secondary in their importance to the human body. We might do well to consider 'hoards' as the 'burials' of artefacts which have come to the end of their social lives. This being the case, pieces of human skull might be included in the deposit as a means of referencing particular human qualities, rather than representing the identity of a specific deceased person. Ethnography demonstrates that the bones of ancestral persons can frequently take on the character of artefacts in any case, circulated between kin or kept in significant locations (Weiner 1992, 114). Moreover, as we have argued throughout this chapter, both hoards and burials should not be considered as isolated sets of objects. As meaningful things, both bodies and artefacts bring significance to place.

In this light, it is worth looking again at the 'hoards' of axes known from the Neolithic, considering them less as closed entities, and more as life histories 'fixed' in place. In several cases the information concerning these finds is minimal, and in some the axes concerned appear to have been fresh and unused (as at Bexley Heath: Smith 1921, 117). However, some of these axes have had more complex histories. One of the Group VI (Langdale) axes from Cottingham in east Yorkshire had been worked down from a larger implement, while the two axes from Kitching Farm, Wakefield appear to have been of Scandinavian origin (Sheppard 1926; Smith 1932, 450). Where descriptive information is available, it seems that the axe blades might have been placed in the ground in rather formal arrangements, as with the four axes arranged two above two, crossed, from Egmere in Norfolk (Smith 1921, 114). A particularly important piece of evidence comes from the York hoard, of fifteen axes, with scrapers, bifacial tools and other implements. Here, the artefacts were accompanied by a great many fresh and unused flint flakes, so many in number that they were taken away and used as ballast on the nearby railway line (Radley 1968, 131). This might suggest that some of the objects in the hoard were produced *in situ*, or at least that a considerable amount of knapping had taken place in or near the location of deposition. Similar collections of flint debitage have been reported from a number of types of sites, including the ditches of monuments (Edmonds and Thomas 1987, 196; Thomas 1991a, 68), and these may involve a deliberate intention to contextualise the act of working stone. This itself may be seen as a means by which the event of labour and the transformation of a raw material fixes a meaning to a place. 'Axe hoards', then, may be best understood as a form of meaning-producing activity, an event rather than a mere physical outcome, establishing a relationship between artefacts and place rather than just between artefact and artefact. None the less, this was an activity which was distinguished above all by the presence of a particular class of objects.

Yet if 'hoarding' was an activity which we can distinguish primarily through the presence of the artefacts themselves, it is also the case that some definable types of locations appear to have specific assemblages of artefacts associated with them. So while in some cases the combination of objects might have created a particular context, in others the pre-existing character of a place demanded the use of a specific set of items. Two context types where this seems to be indicated are caves and wet places, including rivers and bogs. In the case of caves, there is a particularly strong association between human bones and Peterborough Ware, something which is comparatively infrequent in other locations (Thomas 1991a, 92). Examples would include Fissure Cave in Derbyshire, Elbolton Cave and Sewell's Cave in Yorkshire and Sevenways Cave in Staffordshire (Gilks 1990; Gilks 1973, 44, 50; Raistrick 1936, 193). At Church Dale, Derbyshire (figure 6.17), Gop Cave in north Wales, and possibly Fox Holes in Yorkshire these

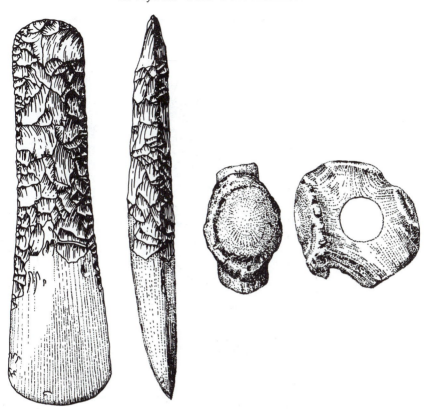

Figure 6.17 Duggleby Howe adze and macehead (after Kinnes *et al.* 1983)

deposits of human bones were found inside or around stone structures built inside the caves (Piggott 1953, 229; Boyd-Dawkins 1902, 170; Brodrick 1924). Other objects which might be found alongside either Peterborough sherds or human remains include the jet sliders and quartz pebbles from Gop, an oblique arrowhead from Church Dale, boar's tusks, a plano-convex knife and an amber bead from Raven Scar in Yorkshire (Gilks 1976, 96), and stone axes from Selside in Yorkshire and Rhos Ddigre in north Wales (Gilks and Lord 1985; inf. National Museum of Wales). Related deposits of human bones and later Neolithic artefacts have come from crevices on the Isle of Portland, at the Verne and Bumper's Lane (Mansell-Playdell 1892; Stopes *et al.* 1952). The relevance of all this detail lies in demonstrating the way in which a set of associations which would be difficult to parallel in other locations is repeatedly encountered in caves and fissures. Traditionally, caves have been regarded as a convenient location for the deposition of the dead, and on occasion it has been suggested that this

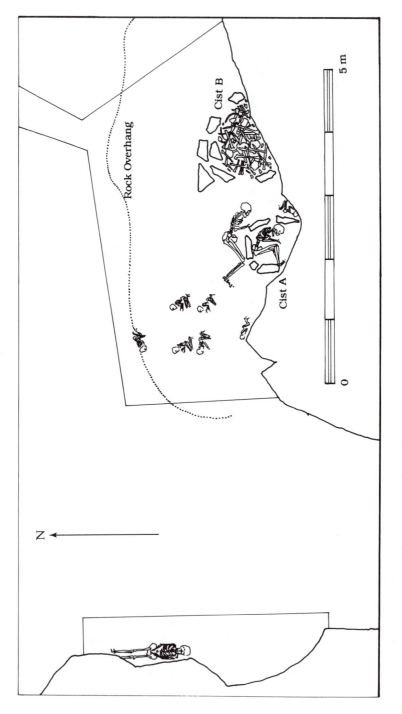

Figure 6.18 Plan of Church Dale rock shelter (after Piggott 1953)

sepulchral use bears out the proposition that megalithic tombs represent 'artificial caves'. The opposite may have been the case: by introducing a very distinct combination of materials into a cave, it may have been possible to transform it into a different sort of place. Bradley (1993, 26–9) has discussed the way in which 'natural' places can be translated into the human world through acts of deposition. Another way of putting this might be to say that caves are often significant topographical features (prominent in their location, yet containing a hidden interior), which might be incorporated into a broader understanding of the world though their use in a specific set of practices which deployed human bodies and material items in ways that were not sanctioned elsewhere. If we invoke the notion of an economy of substances, it may be significant that this took place *within* the rock itself. Moreover, such locations were secluded, and whatever form these activities took the details would not have been available to all.

In a similar way, rivers, bogs and other wet places received a distinctive set of deposits in the later Neolithic. Here again, Peterborough Ware vessels are encountered, but whole and unbroken, while Grooved Ware is totally absent (Thomas 1991a, 92). Axes, too, seem to have been introduced into rivers in large numbers and in unbroken condition (Adkins and Jackson 1976, 9). Especially large axes may be overrepresented in the sample recovered from the Thames (Chappell 1987, 339). The River Thames has also produced a large number of cushion maceheads (Ritchie 1992, 218), at least four antler maceheads (Piggott 1954, 360), and an unusually high proportion of the known maceheads fashioned from naturally perforated flint nodules (Roe 1968, 149). In this connection, both the Garboldisham antler mace, from the bed of the River Ouse (Edwardson 1965, 145) and the cushion macehead from beneath nearly two metres of peat at Knock in Lewis (Gibson 1944, 16) are also of relevance. Finally, three of the less than twenty known examples of jet belt sliders have come from peat deposits (McInnes 1968, 187). While one should not underestimate the particular taphonomic factors at work in rivers and bogs, the combination of Peterborough Ware, jet sliders, axes and maceheads suggests another distinct set of associations which serves to individuate wet contexts. When we compare this with caves, megalithic tomb chambers, burials, the upper levels of earthen long barrow and causewayed enclosure ditches, henge monuments, and pits associated with Peterborough Ware and Grooved Ware (for futher details see above and Thomas 1991a, Chapter 4) a strong case can be made for the production and reproduction of context through the web of associations formed by the circulation and deposition of artefacts. The wetness of a location may have been one more element in the general economy of substances.

IDENTITIES IN A HETEROGENEOUS SOCIETY

At the start of this chapter it was suggested that each way of conceptualising artefacts will tend to bring with it a particular understanding of society. Thus the aim of the argument developed here has not been simply to document the ways in which artefacts were used, but to consider their implications in terms of later Neolithic social organisation. If part of what has been presented has taken the form of a critique of the notion that artefactual assemblages provide evidence for the existence of ethnic groups or ranked societies, it is necessary to suggest some form of alternative. Implicit in this critique is the scepticism expressed elsewhere in this book of the extent to which 'societies' form self-contained and sutured entities. The picture which emerges from our analysis is one of a series of overlapping spheres of activity, in which different materials were made use of in different locations. Thus funerals, feasts, gatherings of secret societies or age-grades, exchange events, marriages, propitiatory offerings, sacrifices and so on may have been kept separate from each other both spatially and conceptually. It is hard to avoid the conclusion that this separated yet overlapping character might also affect the constituencies of these practices. That is to say, each activity which drew on a specific combination of artefacts and substances in order to establish its distinct character also attracted a specific grouping of persons. Some events – such as gatherings held within henge monuments – would seem likely to have involved large numbers of people. Recently, Barrett (1994, 29) has suggested that the construction of these very large monuments was involved in the creation of an elite group. The architectural spaces of henges, for instance, enable the establishment of locations from which authority can be exercised. However, we might ask to what extent this form of authority may have been specific to the context of the monument itself, and whether or not it extended beyond the enclosed space of the physical structure. We have seen that several of the other social activities in which later Neolithic people engaged involved smaller numbers of persons. It does not seem to be the case that all of these activities were hierarchically nested, so that a more and more rarefied stratum of the community was involved in small-group practices, as might be expected in a ranked or stratified society. Thus, for instance, activities in caves or in the chambers of redundant megalithic tombs do not necessarily seem to have used items which would have been restricted to (or diagnostic of) a pre-eminent group.

On the basis of the available evidence, it seems far more likely that the social groupings involved in these spatially segregated practices were defined by a series of cross-cutting criteria. Thus some activities may have been restricted on the basis of age sets, some according to gender (not necessarily a binary classification), some by membership of kin groups, some by agnation, and some by other sodalities such as hunting societies, sorcerers' lodges and so on. In all probability, many of these groupings crossed over the boundaries of any formal social units such as tribes, clans or lineages. In several cases an event might be expected to be organised or hosted by a small group of persons, yet witnessed by a larger group. A funeral or a communal feast, hosted by a kin group but attracting a wider attendance, would be examples. This is not to suggest that the later Neolithic should be characterised as egalitarian. Rather, it may have been a period in which power and authority were relative to the context in which they were exercised. So, as much as creating a kind of ambiance within which particular acts might be carried out, the presence of particular arte-facts at a particular time and place would have provided the preconditions for the wielding of certain forms of power. Thus, for instance, a rite held in the chamber of a crumbling megalithic tomb, or a feast held in the fore-court of an overgrown long barrow, might depend upon the sanction of a community of long-dead and quite possibly fictive ancestors. Equally, the deposition of a number of unbroken pots into a river or a bog may have been the prerogative of a specific kind of person (for instance a woman). Clearly, our problem in identifying precisely *who* was involved in using which artefacts and depositing them where is virtually intractible. For it is the objects which are visible to us in the present, not their users. Here lies the paradox: it is impossible to grasp the significance of the artefacts without hypothesising the people responsible for their disposition, yet any specific identification of social sub-units can only be hypothetical.

At a broader level of analysis, however, the form of social relations suggested for the later Neolithic bears at least some comparison with presently existing communities. Thus, for instance, in his study of the island of Pohnpei, Petersen describes the ways in which individual people are capable of operating in a series of overlapping spheres of practice, developing social strategies which are context-specific.

> Members of a community may engage in egalitarian activities in one space and hierachial activities in another; within a single sphere they may express egalitarian values at one moment and hierarchial values at another; and, of course, individual members of a single community may hold radically opposing views and engage in significantly different activities.
>
> (Petersen 1993, 338)

This recalls Geertz's (1973) observation that many Balinese find no contradiction in adhering to radically different understandings of tempo-rality and history in ritual and in everyday circumstances. This is not necessarily to suggest that in one context persons may follow convention, while in others they will 'say what they really believe'. Rather, it may be that particular beliefs and understandings are relative to context: hence the need to maintain their spatial separation. Since several of the sets of practices in which later Neolithic artefacts were used in Britain may have invoked mutually contradictory beliefs (communities of ancestors in the case of tombs, yet named ancestors in funerals (Barrett 1988b), beliefs concerning the character of materials and substances in various acts of deposition), it is quite plausible that people would have advocated separate understandings according to context.

Such a picture may tell us something about the character of personal identity in the later Neolithic. The ability to engage in some practices will have been a birthright (acquired according to kinship or gender, for instance), some will have been achieved at a certain age, and others may have involved some form of recruitment. This suggests that initiations of one kind of another may have been a significant feature of the period, and indeed some of the anonymous 'practices' to which we have been referring may have involved initiatory rites. Each person, then, might have been party to a specific set of events at particular times in their life. Since some at least of these events appear to have involved a degree of secrecy, the variation in experiences, knowledge and understandings which would have existed might have been considerable. Individual persons might have been present at quite different sets of events, and these would have contributed to quite different narratives of personal identity. Each person would have moved through a range of different contexts in the course of their life. Within each of these contexts, their ability to comprehend what was going on, and their ability to act, would itself have been quite variable. Thus in one context one might find oneself in a position of authority, and in another in one of ignorance and vulnerability.

There is a sense, then, in which we might suggest that in the later Neolithic persons were created by artefacts, rather than vice versa. For while people always have the ability to act, their action is always constrained by their social circumstances. While people always construct their own identities, they do so on the basis of a set of resources which is made available to them (Foucault 1988). In the later Neolithic, what was made available was a series of symbolically charged events whose character was established by the circulation of artefacts, an economy of substances. This general economy framed the conditions under which persons gained a knowledge of their social world, and thus of themselves. None the less, it also seems likely that if each event involved a different constituency, the artefacts used in any given performance would take on a particular meaning to those people present. Thus objects could not have a meaning which was absolute, and the same artefact might mean different things to different people. Hypothetically speaking, the entire Peterborough Ware bowl placed in a peat bog by an old woman might have had an entirely separate significance from that of the sherds of Peterborough Ware placed in a cave by a male initiate.

Later Neolithic society would thus have been extremely heterogeneous, composed of multiple overlapping communities whose loyalties may have fluctuated and required regular reinforcement. As much as anything, the ways in which people understood the world around them may have been quite varied. The authority commanded by particular persons may have been considerable, but limited to particular sets of circumstances, and never total. The ability to construct huge field monuments certainly suggests powerful social imperatives at work, yet the influence which they appear to reflect may have been temporary, relative or conditional. It is worth considering how this situation may have come about, historically speaking. In the earlier part of the Neolithic, the majority of the field monuments constructed appear to have had some role in the processing or deposition of the remains of the dead. This would include long barrows, chambered tombs and causewayed enclosures, used variously as sites of transformation or as conspicuous markers of the presence of the dead (Thomas 1991a; Thorpe 1984). Moreover, the material culture in circulation at this time was relatively homogeneous. Variation was considerable, yet the same basic repertoire of ceramic and lithic forms was drawn upon for use in a range of contexts. The monumental evidence implies a cardinal importance being attached to the remains of the ancestral dead by earlier Neolithic communities. In Weiner's (1992) terms, these bones were inalienable goods, completely bound up with the identity and the ancestry of the community. In these circumstances, it might arguably be the case that ancestry would represent the overriding criterion of authority within society. Certain artefacts, such as flint and stone axes and finely finished plain pottery bowls had an undeniable importance at this time, yet their circulation and use seems to have taken forms sanctioned by overarching social structures (Bradley and Edmonds 1993, 178).

One chronological coincidence which has seldom been commented upon directly is that of the synchroneity of the closure or abandonment of many communal funerary monuments and the sudden proliferation of material forms in the middle of the Neolithic (*c.* 2500 bc/3050 BC). Of course, this might be explained in part by the replacement of communal by individual burial, and the initiation of the deposition of grave goods with the body. However, this is only a part of a much broader pattern. What is suggested here is that the decline of a universal principal of ancestry, in which all forms of social authority devolved according to lines of kinship, was matched by the emergence of multiple sources of power and its authentication. As social units, which through the earlier Neolithic might indeed have consisted of quasi-ethnic 'tribes', began to fragment, pulled apart by a proliferation of interests, these new identities began to establish their own resources of authentication. Since the remains of the dead were connected with the identity of the corporate group, other aspects of the world's materiality were drawn upon: earth, stone, animals, plants, places. Thus the 'complex artefacts' of the later Neolithic can be seen as tokens of the way in which people were beginning to re-establish their relationship with the world that surrounded them. Instead of the ancestors representing the sole source of legitimate authority, multiple connections with the material world were now available to be referenced. Conceivably, these may have been rationalised in the form of spirits or deities embodied in raw materials, but more abstract forces are equally plausible. What is certain is that the emergence of antler and stone maceheads, jet belt sliders and the rest was not a consequence of the evolution of human technical abilities, or of a more stratified social system. Had circumstances been appropriate, there is no reason why these objects should not have been made from the start of the Neolithic, if not earlier. These kinds of items became important because the relationships between people and the world which they physically manifested had come to be of social significance. This would seem to imply that something of a realignment had taken place within the cosmology of the time.

CHAPTER SEVEN

TIME, PLACE AND TRADITION: MOUNT PLEASANT

——— •◆• ———

INTRODUCTION

Mount Pleasant, on the outskirts of modern Dorchester in the county of Dorset, was one of a number of extremely large embanked enclosures or 'henges' built at the end of the Neolithic period in Wessex (c. 2000 bc/ 2500 BC). It was partially excavated by Geoffrey Wainwright between 1970 and 1971, as part of a campaign of investigation which also included work at the henge monuments of Durrington Walls and Marden, both located in Wiltshire (Wainwright 1971, 1979; Wainwright and Longworth 1971). While the scale of the excavations undertaken at Mount Pleasant was somewhat more modest than that at Durrington, the results were remarkable for a number of reasons. First, although the bank and ditch of the henge were still vaguely discernible on the surface, excavation demonstrated the additional presence of a massive timber palisade, roughly concentric to and located within the earthworks. This palisade enclosure was subsequently dated to the years immediately after 1700 bc (c. 2000 BC), and its presence is related to the second unusual feature of the site, a rich pottery sequence running from the Neolithic into the Early Bronze Age. This in turn gave rise to some debate, since the ceramic assemblage appeared to demonstrate the contemporaneity of a number of different styles of Beaker pottery, and indeed of other traditions of Bronze Age artefacts, whose relationship had often been considered in exclusively developmental terms. This prefigured more recent concern over the dating of Beaker ceramics (Kinnes et al. 1991), and requires that some other relationship than a simple chest-of-drawers sequence be hypothesised to explain the coexistence of these styles. As Simpson (1968, 202) notes, it is easy to gain an impression of orderly succession in the funerary context: Beakers followed by Food Vessels, followed by Collared Urns and so on. The significance of the Mount Pleasant sequence is that it necessitates a reconsideration of a number of structures and patterns in the archaeological evidence which have hitherto been assumed to be chronological or developmental in character.

In terms of the objectives of this volume, Mount Pleasant presents an opportunity to investigate time and material tradition at the level of a single site, in the way in which it was transformed over a period of more than a millennium. The quality of the available evidence is such that the site can also sustain a rather more detailed investigation than is commonly attempted in synthetic works. This is important, since I should like to argue that the ideas developed in this book are as relevant to the close study of archaeological materials as to the development of macrosocial patterns. Mount Pleasant can be perceived as having had a dynamic and changing relationship with a surrounding landscape (and in particular with the south Dorset Ridgeway), which culminated in its becoming one of the two major monuments still in use in Wessex in the mature Early Bronze Age, the other being Stonehenge. Significantly, both of these sites are located amidst concentrations of the spectacular Early Bronze Age burials which have come to be known as the Wessex Series (Piggott 1938; Gerloff 1975). Over this period, both the structure of the site and the material culture which were in use there changed, and I hope to demonstrate that as a locus for the intersection of a number of material traditions, Mount Pleasant may have played a significant role in the reformulation of material order. In an earlier paper (Richards and Thomas 1984), the henges of Durrington Walls and Mount Pleasant were used to demonstrate the proposition that the disposition of archaeological evidence need not always represent the consequence of casual discard or day-to-day economic practice, but might be the outcome of deliberate actions which took advantage of the symbolic character of material culture. Here, it is hoped to expand this perspective by temporalising a concern with structured deposition, and thus considering the way in which these practices are engaged in the production and trans-formation of 'place'.

Elsewhere, I have suggested that henge monuments made use of architec-tural devices culled from a number of different monumental traditions which extended back into the earlier Neolithic (Thomas 1991a, 47). Arrangements of upright timbers, ditches, pits and enclosed areas might all be seen as parts of a Neolithic constructional repertoire. The combination of these elements was then structured in such a way as to establish a number of nested spaces which enabled distinctions to be drawn between objects, substances and persons arranged in spatial juxtaposition. Distinctions between inside and outside, or between above and below were enhanced by the deposition of different materials in distinct locations, yet at the same time helped to create an ordering of the world out of animal bodies, pottery vessels and stone tools (ibid., 72–3). Throughout the Neolithic in Britain, depositional practices served simultaneously to sanction the conceptual classification of the material world, while at the same time bringing meaning to particular chosen locations – frequently monuments of one kind or another. There was thus a reciprocal relationship between the making of place and the making of material order.

In the particular case of henge monuments, the argument has been made that this ordering took place in the context of ritual or ceremonial activities which involved the gathering together of large numbers of people, and feasting on a colossal scale (Richards and Thomas 1984; Wainwright 1989, 129). In this chapter, the intention is to consider the temporal significance of these practices, given the notion that henge monuments were axial to a renegotiation of meaning within which material culture played a central role. It has recently been suggested that some form of complementary relationship existed between the practices associated with round barrows and 'religious super-centres' (Garwood 1991, 19). Taking this proposition as a starting point, we can investigate the way in which depositional episodes at Mount Pleasant interrelate with changing material traditions in the surrounding landscape. As Barth (1987, 26) points out, tradition is not something which is automatically maintained: it may have to be reproduced. As we have seen, material items and structures may have a central place in this repro-duction, both as vehicles of memory and, through their deployment, as manifestations of a reconstituted order. The circulation of portable artefacts may allow individuals to 'remember' ties, obligations and relationships, and sometimes the gathering of a variety of kinds of materials and substances into a significant location may allow the fragments of a society to be drawn together, as well as the elements of a cosmology.

A monument like Mount Pleasant is a paradigm example of the way in which a human engagement with material things can serve to maintain order in social life. Building, the setting up of a structure, presupposes that future activities will take place which are to be given form by the space being configured. Even if the site is not continually occupied, and is frequented only on an occasional basis, conditions are laid down concerning the future use of that space. The construction of buildings is a production of memory, in that it establishes patterns of movement, congregation and interaction. The use (and deposition) of objects and substances within this context then serves to incorporate and manipulate elements of the world outside. These may have significance at a number of levels: directly representative of worldly materials or artefactual traditions, embodying abstract qualities, or making reference to absent classes of persons or beings (Ray 1987). In temporal terms, a location which is in some way central to the reproduction of the conceptual ordering of a world will not be a record of the endless restatement of a static structure, but will have been an arena for the evaluation and contestation of a symbolic order. Not simply the artefacts in use, but the site itself, will have been transformed and remade as part of an ongoing historical process. Across periods of hundreds of years, the incremental changes which may occur in symbolic orders may be consid-erable (Barth 1987, 31). What has perhaps been neglected in archaeological analysis is the recognition that the evidence which we study is frequently the outcome of these prolonged cycles of reordering and negotiation

(Barrett 1991). The ambiguous character of material culture is that its mere existence establishes the presence of the past in the present, yet its manipulation, modification and redefinition sanction the transformation of social and political relations. By focusing upon the reciprocal relationship between Mount Pleasant and its immediate environs, it may be possible to illuminate the ways in which long-term and large-scale cultural transformations are generated at the level of interpersonal social action.

CONTEXT: THE EARLIER NEOLITHIC

The henge monument at Mount Pleasant was constructed in the closing years of the third millennium bc (*c.* 2500 BC), that is, at the end of the Neolithic. However, it is important to recognise that the conditions which surrounded the building of the monument were the outcome of a lengthy sequence of historical development. As we have seen earlier in this volume (Chapter Five), the emergence of regional identities in Neolithic Britain can be seen as the consequence of localised social strategies which drew upon an originally more homogeneous cultural repertoire, causing incremental changes in the established norms and practices of local communities. By the time that the henges were being constructed, south Dorset had developed a quite distinctive regional character. Consequently it will be necessary to discuss the development of this local context before we turn to Mount Pleasant itself. Situated in the confluence of the rivers Frome and South Winterbourne (figure 7.1), Mount Pleasant is somewhat peripheral to a major focus of earlier Neolithic activity in the South Winterbourne valley (Woodward 1991, 31; Sharples 1991, 24). While pits containing sherds of earlier Neolithic pottery have been found at the Flagstones House site (Woodward 1991, 133), and concentrations of plain bowl ceramics were located beneath the bank at Mount Pleasant itself, these latter were associated with a radiocarbon determination in the latter part of the third millennium bc (*c.* 2500 BC) (Wainwright 1979, 7). Other evidence for activity in the earliest centuries of the Neolithic is scant.

In the earlier Neolithic, the most elaborate monumental centre in the Dorchester area was the causewayed enclosure at Maiden Castle, located peripherally to supposed areas of domestic activity on the Ridgeway and in the South Winterbourne valley (Evans *et al.* 1988, 82). In the present context, the main importance of Maiden Castle lies in the emergence of a series of variations in depositional practice which prefigure later developments, including activities carried out at Mount Pleasant. In a sense, this activity can be seen as establishing cultural traditions which were reworked into the later Neolithic and beyond. The Maiden Castle enclosure was not strongly defended, the banks attending the two concentric ditch circuits being minimal (Sharples 1991). Equally, cut features inside the enclosure

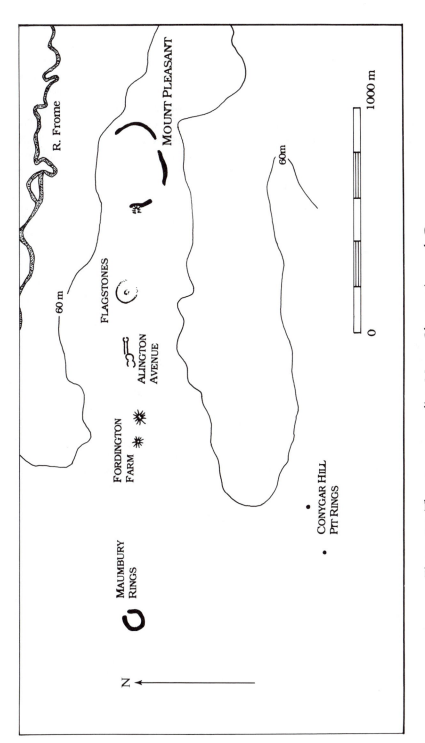

Figure 7.1 The area surrounding Mount Pleasant in south Dorset

were not numerous, and it may be that the site was used on a relatively sporadic basis. The evidence from the site certainly does not support a domestic interpretation. The butchery of cattle and pigs indicates that they were probably slaughtered onsite (Armor-Chelu 1991, 149), yet chaff fragments were largely absent from the carbonised plant remains, indicating that crop processing had taken place elsewhere (Sharples 1991, 254). The earlier Neolithic pottery was dominated by neutral uncarinated forms, with a number of large open vessels which might have constituted cookpots (Cleal 1991, 177). This contrasts with some local assemblages, like that from Rowden, which may contain closed and/or carinated vessels (ibid., 179), and conforms with a general pattern amongst the causewayed enclosures of southern England, that ceramic assemblages are better suited to the preparation and consumption of food than to its storage (Thomas 1991a, 89). The inner ditch of the enclosure was cut a little after 3000 bc (c. 3700 BC), and its primary fill was of relatively clean chalk rubble, containing a single human burial. Some two hundred years later, a series of 'intermixed loams and charcoal and artefact rich midden layers' (Sharples 1991, 51) were deliberately deposited in the ditch, although whether as a single event or a series of repeated actions is unclear. The outer ditch, which contained fewer artefacts, may have been dug at about this time. In Trench II of the recent excavations, the disarticulated skeletal remains of two juvenile and one adult persons were discovered, together with a scatter of flint flakes and a stone axe, while in his Trench R, Wheeler had found a young male adult skull (ibid., 52). Wheeler also excavated the skeletons of two young children, together with a small pottery bowl, in a shallow pit in the interior of the enclosure beneath the long mound (Wheeler 1943, 88). These probably relate to the use of the enclosure itself, rather than constituting a primary burial deposit for the long mound (Sharples 1991, 43). The long mound itself was probably constructed soon after the outer ditch, at around 2700 bc (3500 BC) (ibid., 102).

The significant point here is that the Maiden Castle enclosure underwent a continuous process of structural modification, in which the deposition of artefacts and other materials was instrumental. At some other causewayed enclosures, like Hambledon Hill in Dorset and Crickley Hill in Gloucestershire, such an elaboration involved an enhancement of the defensive aspect of the site (Mercer 1980; Dixon 1988). In all three cases, and also in the comparable example of the Abingdon causewayed enclosure (Avery 1982), the outcome was a more categorical definition of the enclosure, in both material and symbolic terms. A space which had in the first instance been marked out by a simple, discontinuous physical barrier was enhanced by the introduction of powerful symbolic media into the open ditch. While we can assume that these materials would have been swiftly buried, the knowledge of their presence may have been sufficient to draw attention to the barrier and to the distinction between the inside and outside of the enclosure. In the case of Maiden Castle, it is the use of human remains in this context which is most distinctive (even if it finds a more spectacular parallel in the north Dorset example of Hambledon). In the initial phase of use of the site, at least one burial was placed in the ditch, while with the later reorganisation it was the outer ditch which received further bones, despite the more extensive focus on deposition in the inner ditch. The addition of a second ditch circuit had had the effect that more complex distinctions could be drawn between materials deposited – not merely in separate yet equivalent ditch segments, but 'inner' and 'outer' ditches. The bodies of the dead came to define the outside. Both in the (perhaps quite early) interior pit grave and the outer ditch, the remains of the very young are prominent. Given the peripheral location (and perhaps function) of causewayed enclosures (Evans *et al.* 1988; Thomas 1991a, 35–6) and the boundary function of the ditch, this may be explicable in terms of the ambiguous role of the young in many traditional societies (LaFontaine 1978). Children, if they die young, may represent a conceptual anomaly, having been born and lived, yet never having undergone the initiations which define one as a full social being. The infant dead thus remain eternally on the boundary between identity and non-identity, and their physical remains might be expected to evoke liminality and 'inbetweenness'.

The construction of the Maiden Castle long mound, running across both ditch circuits and into the interior, can be seen as a further stage of structural elaboration. Just as the ditches had defined a more and more rigid distinction between inside and outside, the long mound lays down the way in which this distinction is to be experienced and understood, by establishing a linear axis of movement across the site (Thomas 1991a, 46). While the long mound was probably two metres in height, and while it is most unlikely that it was intended that persons would walk along the mound itself, Barrett (1988b, 34) has pointed out that in the case of Cotswold-Severn tombs at least, the presence of multiple chambers implies practices which involved movement around a long mound. The different spaces of the mound can only be integrated by passing along and around the perimeter of the cairn. This may suggest a broader pattern, in which the linear structure of funerary monuments was connected with particular forms of bodily movement. This much is indicated by the flanking ditches of long barrows, which determine that the monument cannot be directly approached from the sides. The development of longer mounds, bank barrows, and eventually cursus monuments in the earlier third millennium bc suggests the gradual emergence of ritual or ceremonial activities which required more closely defined patterns of linear movement, often between locations of some importance. In the case of the cursūs, this culminates in movement between two parallel banks rather than around a linear mound (Barrett *et al.* 1991, 47). At Maiden Castle, it is particularly significant that the structure of the monument is derived from the long mound tradition.

In the same way as the ditches use the remains of the dead to divide up space conceptually, a monument associated with the dead is used to define movement across that space. In both cases, changes in the way in which the landscape was to be understood were sanctioned by the evocation (or even invocation) of the dead. The long mound contained no burial, but efforts were made to establish its authenticity through acts of deposition. In the east terminal of the southern ditch of the mound, the skulls of five aurochsen were located (Armor-Chelu 1991, 139). Cattle bones, and especially skulls, have frequently been found associated with the burial deposits in earthen long barrows (e.g. Ashbee 1966), while at Beckhampton Road, a barrow which contained no burials held the skulls of three oxen (Ashbee *et al.* 1979), which have sometimes been interpreted as symbolic substitutes for human bodies (Thorpe 1984; Thomas 1988b). However, as we will see, the burial of cattle remains in significant contexts was a practice which came to be of particular importance in southern Dorset.

It is probable that the construction of the Maiden Castle long mound was roughly contemporary with that of a number of similar monuments in southern Dorset (Bradley 1983). Principal amongst these are the two bank barrows at Long Bredy and Broadmayne, located at opposite ends of the strip of upland to the south of Dorchester known as the Dorset Ridgeway. Woodward (1991, 131) interprets these structures as having had a territorial function, marking out separate zones of earlier Neolithic clearance and agricultural activity. An alternative interpretation might lie in considering further the way in which the bank barrows impose an orientation upon the landscape. The Maiden Castle mound, as we have seen, may have had a role in regulating access to and experience of the enclosure, and was moreover false-crested so as to be visible from the lower country to the north. Any activities associated with the mound would thus have been conspicuous at a distance. The Long Bredy mound runs at right angles to the Ridgeway, but it does so along a prominent ridge crest. Nearby, two small cursus monuments are so arranged as to lead in sequence toward the mound, and might thus be later additions, progressively constraining the way in which the barrow was to be approached (figure 7.2). At Broadmayne, the long mound is again false-crested, but runs east–west along the line of the Ridgeway, and like Maiden Castle is visible from the north, in the south Winterbourne valley. The two bank barrows between them define the ends of an area which was much later to represent one of the largest round barrow cemeteries (or more correctly groups of cemeteries) in Britain, and it is possible to see the construction of those mounds as being the precondition for that development. In much the same way as the construction of the Dorset Cursus transformed Cranborne Chase into a particular kind of cultural landscape, and set limits upon the way that it could be used for generations afterward (Barrett *et al.* 1991), these linear monuments oriented the Ridgeway and infused it with meaning.

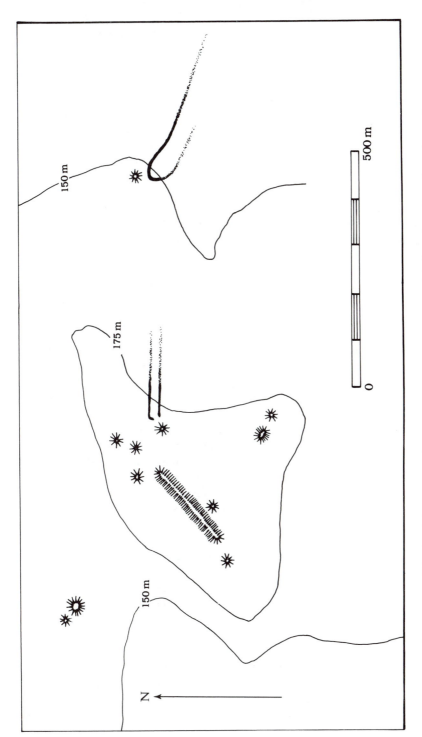

Figure 7.2 The bank barrow and cursus monuments at Long Bredy (after Woodward 1991)

This development is of significance to the Mount Pleasant sequence, not merely because it 'fixed' an area of landscape which was to prove complementary to the Frome/South Winterbourne interfluve, but because a similar monument seems to have played an analogous role in the latter zone. At Alington Avenue, a long mound was constructed, which has been dated to 2500 ± 80 bc (*c.* 3091 BC) (HAR-8579). Although the mound is only 75 m long, it has many similarities with the bank barrows: it was relatively slim in plan, and flanked by parallel linear ditches (Davis *et al.* 1985, 103). No trace was evident of any primary burial deposit, although cremation burials were present in an enclosed area added to the eastern end of the mound after the ditches had silted up (ibid., 104). On the base of the northern flanking ditch, a little way from the east terminal, the skull of an ox was located, in a position analogous to those in the Maiden Castle mound ditch. As with the bank barrows, the Alington mound was false-crested, so as to be visible from the south Winterbourne valley. As with the Ridgeway mounds, the Alington barrow later became the focus for a group of round barrows, but more importantly, the orientation which it established along the Alington ridge was one which drew together a number of contemporary and later monuments. A little to the east is the Flagstones House enclosure, late in date but distinguished by the presence of causewayed ditches, so that a parallel with the relationship between the Maiden Castle enclosure and long mound is germane. Further east again is Mount Pleasant itself, and the focal area of the henge, the timber circle of Site IV, is on the same linear alignment as Flagstones and the Alington mound (Woodward 1991, 136).

It thus seems likely that in the early part of the third millennium bc, a series of bank barrows and related mounds were constructed in southern Dorset which had as their primary role a reconfiguration of the landscape. From their first construction, they were associated with the deliberate deposition of various materials, most notably the bones of cattle. They were so related to landscape features and existing monuments as to establish a series of alignments and pathways which were to influence both the construction of later monuments and patterns of movement for more than a thousand years. The position of Mount Pleasant in relation to one of the long mounds suggests that the henge, although constructed at the end of the third millennium bc, was positioned in a setting whose significance had been instituted much earlier. It follows that the deposits of plain bowl (conventionally earlier Neolithic) pottery located under the bank were not purely fortuitous in character. The majority of the 355 sherds recovered from pre-enclosure contexts were from beneath the bank in the NNW sector of the monument (Wainwright 1979, 7). While the radiocarbon date of 2122 ± 73 bc (2583 BC) (BM-644) from charcoal associated with this pottery is rather late for this ceramic style, it is significant that the vessels are predominantly open and neutral in profile, as with the Maiden Castle assemblage (ibid., figure 45). This is hardly strong evidence, but in a general way it supports a suggestion that this was not a domestic settlement, and that in the period before the building of the henge the future site of Mount Pleasant had already been distinguished as a special place, an appropriate location for performances of some significance.

CONTEXT: LATER NEOLITHIC

At around the same time as activities resulting in the deposition of pottery, flint flakes and charcoal were taking place at Mount Pleasant, a small enclosure was constructed at Flagstones House, a little way beyond the east end of the Alington long barrow (figure 7.3). Antler from the ditch of this site has provided a radiocarbon date of 2130 ± 80 bc (c. 2586 BC) (HAR-8578). The Flagstones enclosure is composed of a single circuit of causewayed ditches, for the most part set closely together and with a circular rather than oval plan (Woodward 1988). The diameter of the enclosure is roughly 100 m. It both size and form, Flagstones stands out from the majority of British causewayed enclosures, yet in both particulars it resembles the earliest phase of construction at Stonehenge (Atkinson 1956, 22). Stonehenge, too, had a ditch which was originally dug in causewayed segments, and dates to the middle of the third millennium bc (Pitts 1982). Both of these sites draw on the established constructional tradition of the causewayed enclosures, but seem also to anticipate some of the characteristics of the later henges. These monuments seem to represent the emergence of new practices within the context of traditional activities. This tendency can be recognised not merely in constructional technique, but also in the character of deposition at Flagstones. The ditch segments themselves were swiftly backfilled, so that a number of pictograms, incised into the chalk of the sides of the ditch segments, were preserved (Woodward 1988, 271). As at Maiden Castle, human burials were present in the ditches. Three child burials were found in the ditch on the west of the site, on the principal axis defined by the Alington long mound, and a fourth on the north side of the enclosure (ibid., 268). Two of these burials were found covered by large stone slabs within the ditch, and another burial beneath a slab had been discovered in 1891.

Thus Flagstones shares with Maiden Castle the use of an interrupted ditch to enclose a special area, and the burial of children in that ditch in such a way as to draw attention to the significance of the boundary as a place of transition. Yet by locating the enclosure itself, and the burials within the enclosure, in relation to the Alington long mound, it builds upon these elements by adding a greater concern with orientation and position within the landscape. Also new is the practice of covering the dead with slabs of sarsen or Ridgeway limestone, which adds to the conspicuousness

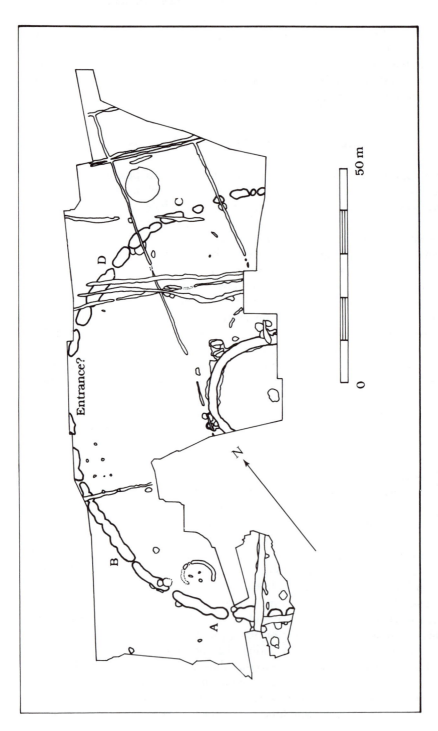

Figure 7.3 Plan of the Flagstones House enclosure (after Woodward 1988)

of the event of depositing the body in the ditch. It has been suggested that these stones might at one time have formed a setting of uprights, which would have stood in a series of vestigial sockets which were later cut by the ditch (Healy and Smith forthcoming). It is arguable to what extent the stones would have created a visible marker for the burial, but they would certainly have had the effect of introducing another worldly substance (stone) into the architecture of enclosures, alongside earth, chalk and timber. Stone is used here in association with the dead, and might echo the use of stones as orthostats and capstones in a small number of chambered long mounds, like the Grey Mare and her Colts, which lie on the western part of the Ridgeway (Piggott 1946). Thus a substance which already bears an association with the dead is introduced to a new monumental context, and underlines the production of a particular set of connotations for the ditch.

At Maiden Castle itself, the period after the construction of the long mound saw something of a decline of activity. While claims are made for later Neolithic use of the enclosure (Sharples 1991, 256), it is arguable that much of this dates to a time after the introduction of Beaker pottery to the site, at 2000 bc (*c.* 2500 BC) or later (see below). Some of the later Neolithic material at Maiden Castle may be earlier than the vestigial bank which at some point redefined the enclosure. The presence of Peterborough Ware inside the site, and of Grooved Ware restricted to pits outside the east side of the enclosure may represent a continued imperative to distinguish between the interior and exterior of the monument. It certainly seems that the later part of the third millennium bc in the Dorchester area saw the construction of a series of monuments which were not linear, but which enclosed an area of space. Unlike Maiden Castle, however, the new henges and pit circles had clear entrances, and thus in each case a principal axis can be defined, generally in some way linking the enclosure with other monuments or landscape features. Flagstones, for instance, seems to have had an entrance which faced north-west, down to the Frome valley. On the north side of Conygar Hill, two pit rings were recently excavated, in advance of the Dorchester bypass. The easternmost of these contained sherds of Peterborough Ware, that to the west had Grooved Ware (Woodward and Smith 1987, 84). In Dorchester itself, a massive post circle some 380 m in diameter has been located and dated to *c.* 2110 bc (*c.* 2577 BC), and appears to have Grooved Ware associations (Woodward *et al.* 1984). Finally, at Maumbury Rings, a henge monument was composed of a series of deep shafts which contained Grooved Ware, chalk balls, flints and animal and human bones deposited in complex patterns of association and segregation at different depths (Bradley 1975; Bradley and Thomas 1984; Thomas 1991a, 71). The site has provided radiocarbon dates of 2020 ± 70 bc and 1990 ± 130 bc (*c.* 2466 and 2459 BC) (BM-2282N and 2281R). Here again the entrance is directed towards the Frome basin (Barrett 1994,

100), adding to the impression that the valley represented an important axis of movement through the landscape.

All of this evidence together indicates a process of elaboration upon the established order of the earlier Neolithic. Earlier Neolithic monuments like Maiden Castle and the nearby long barrows had served largely to distinguish particular locations as special, sacred or associated with the activities of ancestors and divinities. The bank barrows had built upon this basis by knitting together significant locations, natural or artificial. From 2200 bc (c. 2860 BC) onwards, this orientation and alignment of the landscape was complemented by a renewed interest in enclosure and division. At a national level, this development is part of a general trend toward cultural diversification, in which a growing variety of artefacts and monuments served to sanction the increasing complexity (and mutual incompatibility) of social identities, statuses and practices (Thomas 1991a, 101; Chapter Six above). As contradictory tendencies emerged within society (between individual authority and that of the group; between individual burial and corporate ritual; between the roles of artefacts as bearers of symbolic messages and as gifts or wealth), separate spheres of practice and locations appropriate to their performance began to emerge. This process can also be looked upon as a proliferation of separate spheres of knowledge, which became increasingly exclusive in character. What we can see in the later Neolithic landscape of southern Dorset is the emergence of a series of enclosed spaces of various sizes and various degrees of permeability, each forming the context for a particular kind of performance, and the rehearsal of a particular knowledge. These recognisable divisions of space will have had a dynamic relationship with increasing divisions within society. As we argued in Chapter Six, later Neolithic British society may have been segmented in a variety of ways, in which access to spheres of contact and interaction, exchange and performance defined inclusion and exclusion. These divisions need not have been strictly hierarchical and nested, but may have formed complex overlapping patterns, in which the individual may have found himself or herself active in some spheres, but denied access to others. A monumental architecture which laid considerable stress upon the boundaries between included and excluded locations (often concentrically ordered) was well suited to the maintenance of these differentials of knowledge, particularly when this architecture involved banks and façades which could screen and restrict vision and movement. At the same time, it is of equal importance that an area which has been separated off artificially can become a bounded symbolic system, which enables a mimicking or reversing of the order of the outside world (Bourdieu 1970, 168). As we have already noted, a distinctive feature of henge monuments was the way in which the enclosed area allowed a system of material symbols to be manipulated as a bounded whole (Richards and Thomas 1984).

Mount Pleasant: Architecture and deposition in the later Neolithic

The significance of the construction of the Mount Pleasant henge can be understood in relation to both local and supra-regional processes. Its position astride the east end of the Alington ridge located it in relation to a series of earlier monuments, while at the same time it lay at the meeting point of the Frome and South Winterbourne valleys. Many of the earlier monuments had been placed in such a way as to be visible from the area around the south Winterbourne, yet with Mount Pleasant this is not strictly the case. The henge had four separate entrances through the bank and ditch of the earthwork enclosure. One each faced east and west, along the line of the ridge. A third faced south, and a fourth opened northwards, placed so as to allow access at a point where the slope is especially gentle (figure 7.4). Site IV, the timber post circle within a penannular bank and ditch which forms a focus for the monument as a whole, faces this entrance, giving the impression that this was the primary axis of the monument. If this were the case Mount Pleasant was similar to Flagstones and Maumbury in that it faced toward the Frome valley and the lower country beyond. The henge encloses a slight eminence at the end of the ridge, but Site IV is not placed centrally to this knoll. Rather, the entrance of the bank and ditch occupy roughly the highest point. The effect of this would have been that from the northern entrance to the embanked enclosure, the bank of Site IV and its entrance would be visible, but it would not be possible to see into the interior of the smaller enclosure. Performances taking place within the smaller enclosure would have been hidden from those viewing from a distance.

The layout of Mount Pleasant is thus by no means haphazard, but makes subtle use of the natural terrain in order to manipulate visibility of, and access to, particular spaces. While the large henges of Wessex are conventionally considered as a generic type of monument, in this respect they are quite different from each other. Durrington Walls, for instance, is constructed in a natural amphitheatre, which is enclosed by the bank and ditch (Wainwright and Longworth 1971). Inside, the free-standing circles and arrangements of timber uprights are unenclosed, so that activities taking place inside them would be comparatively open to the view of groups of persons gathered inside the henge. By contrast, the convex surface of Mount Pleasant, and the bank and ditch of Site IV suggest areas to which access was restricted, and whose contents were intended to be obscured. Beneath the superimposed Conquer Barrow, the outer bank presently survives to a height of 4 m (Wainwright 1979, 237), indicating the original massive scale of the feature. This would certainly have operated to hide much of what went on inside the enclosure from those denied access, but would in particular have rendered the ditch invisible. Throughout the Neolithic, ditches served as an important

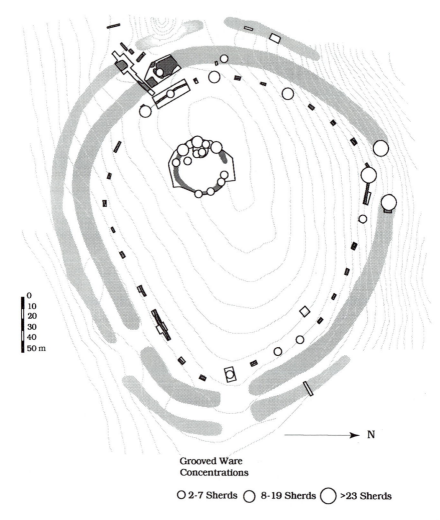

Grooved Ware
Concentrations

◯ 2-7 Sherds ◯ 8-19 Sherds ◯ >23 Sherds

Figure 7.4 Plan of Mount Pleasant, showing the
spatial distribution of Grooved Ware

locus for depositional practices, and it may be that the shift to *external* banks
with the emergence of the henge tradition was in part designed to ensure that
the character of these deposits would only be known to those granted access
to the interior of the monument. Mount Pleasant, with its two concentric
arrangements of bank and ditch, enabled the creation of a nested hierarchy of
access and of familiarity with deposited materials.

The penannular layout of Site IV is significant in defining a 'back' and
'front' to the enclosure, and also a single point of physical entry. The timber

settings take the general form of five concentric circles of posts, bisected by two aisles set at right angles to each other and oriented upon the cardinal points. In point of fact, these rings are not constructed as true circles, but as a series of separate arcs – a pattern paralleled at Wyke Down (Barrett *et al.* 1991). The southern aisle is effectively blocked by a single post at its northern end (164), so that it was probably not intended that one could pass from the entrance straight across the centre of the enclosed area. Pollard (1992) has recently argued convincingly that both at the Sanctuary (in north Wiltshire) and at Site IV the stone settings which post-date the timber rings must have been set up at a time when the posts were still standing. That is to say, the stones elaborate upon and clarify the pattern created by the timbers, forming part of a coherent structure. This being the case, we could argue that the purpose of the stones at Site IV was to emphasise and re-establish a 'correct' way of moving around the circle. This pattern of movement probably did not change, but was formalised by the erection of the stones. Thus while it was possible to look into the central open space of the circle along the north–south aisle, it may never have been accepted practice to walk directly to the centre. Eventually, Stone 177 was to close off the southern end of the northern aisle, while Stone 184 was placed just inside the entrance, and on the right-hand side, so as to encourage one to turn to the left, between the two outermost post rings (figure 7.5). In a similar way, Stones 178, 179 and 191 obstructed access to the centre of the circle from the east and west. Of course, none of these obstacles would have stopped a determined intruder. What is suggested is that these architectural devices served to remind and influence in their practice persons who had a broad acceptance of the legitimacy of the activities carried out within the circle. In a sense, much of the physical form of Mount Pleasant can be attributed to a materialisation of memory, since each successive phase of construction conformed more closely to an existing pattern of movement (Barrett 1994, 104). The addition of the stones to Site IV provided an enhancement of these cues for proper conduct, and as an element of the material evidence enable us to conjecture that there was an accepted way of moving within the circle. If this were indeed the case, the pattern of entering the circle and turning left, circling between the timber rings, is closely paralleled by the less regular post setting at the Southern Circle within Durrington Walls (Thomas 1991a, 48–51). Given the hypothesis that the activities which took place inside the circle involved relatively formal and prescribed ways of moving, it follows that the deposits which were placed in the ditch and elsewhere have to be considered in relation to the positioning of human bodies in the course of performance. In other words, it is highly likely that as well as being a practice which was in some sense rule-governed, deposition has to be envisaged as part of a broader set of observances which were both integrated and choreographed.

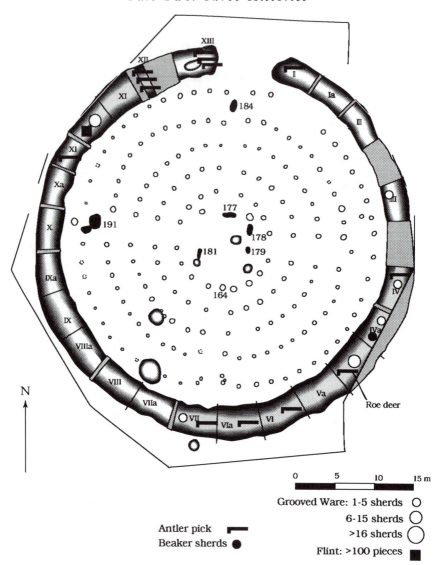

Figure 7.5 Mount Pleasant Site IV, the enclosed timber
circle, showing deposits in ditch layers 8, 9 and 10

Mount Pleasant was constructed in the century or so before 2000 bc
(*c.* 2500 BC), and the earliest activities within the monument were associated
with the use of Grooved Ware pottery. In the Grooved Ware levels of the site,
the detailed distribution of artefacts confirms the impression that deposition
was highly structured, and involved the manipulation of particular symbolic
principles. The pottery itself, for instance, shows a strong patterning

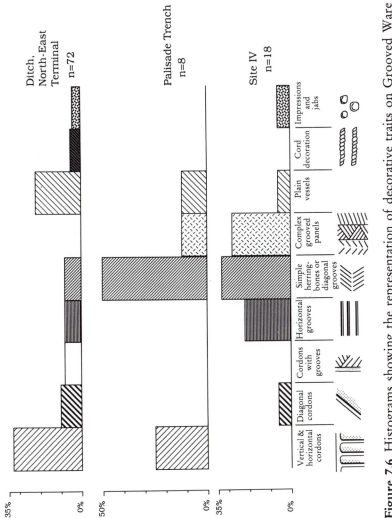

Figure 7.6 Histograms showing the representation of decorative traits on Grooved Ware from different contexts within Mount Pleasant

across the site according to decoration. The large assemblage of vessels from the east terminal of the ditch at the northern entrance is dominated by pots with simple, undecorated vertical and horizontal cordons, and a high proportion of undecorated vessels are also present (figure 7.6). Site IV, however, has a higher proportion of pots with incised diagonals and herringbone motifs, and of complex devices made up of panels of grooved and incised decoration. Plain cordons are entirely absent. Significantly, this variation does not appear to change through time – very much the same styles of vessels were deposited in subsequent ditch layers. Within Site IV there is further spatial variation, with the complex panel motifs restricted to the back right-hand side of the enclosure. What this suggests is twofold. Clearly, particular kinds of pottery vessel, decorated in particular ways, were appropriate for use in given parts of the site, or at least for deposition there. But in addition, the practice of deposition makes the link between location and object more emphatic and durable than the simple use of an item in a given place. It has frequently been pointed out that the decoration employed on Grooved Ware has affinities with the passage grave art of Ireland and Orkney (Bradley 1984; Richards and Thomas 1984, 192–3), while that art itself may have had a role in defining and drawing attention to the significance of particular locations within passage tombs (Thomas 1992). The episodic destruction of pots which bear markings of symbolic importance, and their deposition in significant locations can be seen as a way of fusing meaning and place, and thus of re-creating the connotations of specific points within the site. By creating an enduring link between a place and a style of artefact, it is thus possible to act out a process of remembering before a gathered group of people. Moreover, as we have already noted, this performance of memory often took place in locations which could only have been visible to restricted numbers of people, and thus these practices can be seen as a reproduction of sectional knowledge. In these terms, the kinds of performance which took place inside henge monuments represent a development upon some of the themes found in practices carried out in and around funerary monuments in the earlier Neolithic (Thomas 1990). While the presence of the dead was no longer of significance (or may purposefully have been avoided), the structure of performance remained one in which architectural devices intervened in order to restrict and graduate the awareness of different members of society of a focal set of activities. The artefacts used in these performances were often small, and the details of their decoration might have been obscure to those not directly involved in their use and deposition, although the general degree of ornateness might be more widely recognised. That different things were going on in different parts of the site, and that more elaborate forms of material culture were being taken into the enclosed area of Site IV, might have been understood by large numbers of people. The precise details of their use there would only have been known to a minority.

The location of the most elaborately decorated pottery within Site IV in ditch layers 8 to 10 is comprehensible within this understanding of the site (figure 7.5). If people were indeed entering the ditched enclosure surrounding the timber circles and then turning abruptly to the left, deposits of pottery might have been made when they had completed roughly half of a circuit, to the back of the enclosure. The great concentration of antler picks in ditch segments XII and XIII, however, are located at a point which one would only reach after walking around the entire circumference of the circle. Throughout the depositional history of Site IV, these locations of the back left and front right quadrants of the ditch appear to have been of importance, although the precise details of the deposits changed over time. The deposition of artefacts and substances in these places is best seen as part of a performative practice involving sequences of formal bodily movements, in which the meaning of place was evoked and recreated. In the relatively secluded space of the enclosed timber circle, combinations of symbolic media were brought together and fixed in space in ways which drew upon the existing significance of the monument, and yet transformed it in subtle ways, increasing the accumulated knowledge of those present. As we have suggested in Chapter Six, this kind of exegesis would have re-created and deepened the identity of the location, while strengthening the bonds of shared experience and shared knowledge which held the participants together. In this sense, monuments like Mount Pleasant may have been instrumental in the creation of specific interest groups within later Neolithic society.

This evidence suggests that a distinction was being drawn between the outer enclosure and Site IV, in terms of the activities taking place and the materials used. This pattern is also indicated by the faunal remains from the Grooved Ware levels. Unfortunately, the animal bones from Mount Pleasant cannot be spatially located with the same high degree of accuracy as the other artefacts, and are presently stored in boxes which identify only the broad archaeological context from which they were recovered. Despite this lack of precision, and the rather small number of bones, we can come to some conclusions regarding the deposition of animal remains, at a high level of generality. First, a distinction can be made between Site IV and the outer ditch in the representation of particular species. The assemblage from Site IV primary levels is dominated by bones of cattle, that from the outer ditch by pig (figure 7.7). This pattern is very similar to that at Durrington Walls, where certain focal areas of the site, like the Platform outside of the Southern Circle, had higher proportions of cattle bones relative to pig (Richards and Thomas 1984). Similarly, at Woodhenge, the ratio of cattle to pig bones increased with proximity to the centre of the site (Thomas 1991a, 71). These results are particularly interesting in the local context, as we have already seen that the remains of cattle were placed in pre-eminent locations within the south Dorset bank barrows. While cattle

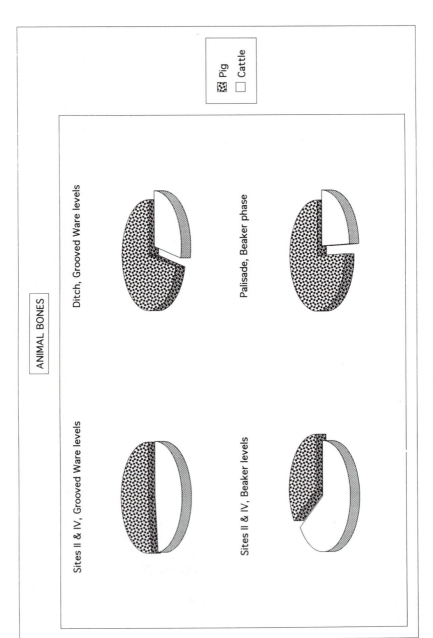

Figure 7.7 Mount Pleasant animal bones: species representation within different contexts

may have had a generalised importance within British Neolithic communities, it may be that in this particular region these remains gained a particular significance from a history of past practice. Another aspect of this evidence, however, concerns the relative proportions of animal body parts represented at Mount Pleasant. Although the bones were not in a condition to allow the collection of information on butchery marks, a simple count on the numbers of bones from particular parts of the animal (using the system introduced by Maltby, 1979) is informative. Amongst the cattle bones, there were high proportions of primary butchering waste from Site IV, as well as meat bones (figure 7.8). With the pigs, however, there was far less primary discard material, suggesting that the animals had been killed offsite and brought in at least partially butchered.

What this seems to indicate is that very different patterns of meat consumption took place in different areas of Mount Pleasant. Throughout the site, joints or sides of pork which had been prepared elsewhere were consumed, presumably in the course of communal feasting, and the bones deposited in both outer and inner ditches. Within Site IV, however, it is possible that cattle were slaughtered, butchered, cooked and eaten. This killing of animals which seem to have held a particular symbolic significance within the restricted space of the circle can perhaps be legitimately thought of as a form of sacrifice. This reinforces the impression that within the separate spaces of the henge monument, rather different performances and experiences were made available to different individuals. The henge was a huge space which could have held very large numbers of people, and while in this sense it can be considered a 'communal' structure, its use will have served as much to increase differentials of knowledge as it did to draw people together. Feasting and structured deposition were common to all areas of the site, but the precise details and the degree of complexity of these activities varied spatially.

CONTEXT: BEAKER PHASE

Some have suggested that the construction of the large henges of Wessex coincided chronologically, and may even be a consequence of, the introduction of Beaker pottery to the British Isles (Thorpe and Richards 1984). Certainly, the start of the third millennium bc was a period of considerable cultural change, in which the roles of artefacts and the practices for which they were deemed appropriate were radically redefined (Thomas 1991a, 98–102). In southern Dorset, this period of cultural *bricolage* saw both the emergence of new monumental traditions and the re-use of older sites. At Maiden Castle, the redefinition of the enclosure by the recutting of the ditch and the construction of a small bank may be of Beaker rather than late Neolithic date. The recut/terrace layers 537 and 541, which date this

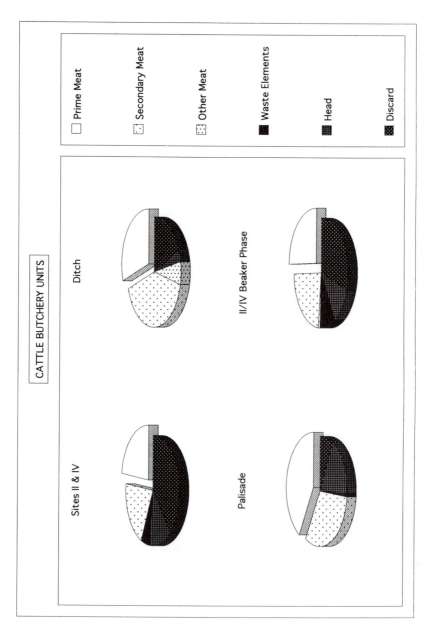

Figure 7.8 Mount Pleasant animal bones: 'butchery units' represented in different contexts

event, contain sherds of middle/late Beaker as well as Peterborough Ware, indicating that the recut may be as late as 1800 bc (*c.* 2140 Cal. BC) (Cleal 1991, 183). Large pits inside the enclosure contain both Beaker and Peterborough Ware, yet Grooved Ware is restricted to pit T1, outside the east end of the enclosure. In effect, the later activity at Maiden Castle reverses the cultural ordering found at the henges, where Grooved Ware is used inside the enclosure and Peterborough Ware excluded.

This seeming inversion may be connected with a growing contrast between the character of activities taking place in the Dorchester-Mount Pleasant area and that around the South Winterbourne and the Ridgeway. Amongst the large monuments around Dorchester there are relatively few round barrows which seem to be early in date. Of these only the barrow Dorchester 5 (Masonic Hall Site) has produced a Beaker burial on excavation (Grinsell 1959, 105). By contrast, there are a series of Beaker burials on the Ridgeway and to the west of Maiden Castle. These include barrow burials, like that containing a female skeleton inside a cist at Bincombe (Best 1965), and a flat grave at Broadmayne (Peers and Clarke 1967). The concentrations of Beaker burials thus appear to be broadly located in the areas of landscape which had been chosen as locations for the bank barrows. This may be no more than coincidence, given that the upper reaches of the South Winterbourne show signs of relatively dense occupation throughout the Neolithic and Early Bronze Age. Equally, it may be that the construction of the long mounds had had the effect of defining these areas as legitimate locations for the interment of the dead. Thus we might have a developing zonation of the landscape, with one area associated with large monuments and Grooved Ware, and another connected with funerary activities, Peterborough Ware, and the funerary use of Beakers. As I have suggested elsewhere, this pattern need not be interpreted in quasi-ethnic terms, characterised by distinct social groups with separate material assemblages and ritual practices (Thomas 1991a, 100–1). Instead, we might imagine that specific locations and artefacts were judged appropriate for particular forms of activity, conducted by defined but overlapping groups of people.

This division of the landscape between areas of funerary and monumental performance was to influence developments into the early Bronze Age. Despite this, Beaker pottery was eventually to be found in both areas, alongside Peterborough Ware at Maiden Castle and Grooved Ware in the secondary layers at Mount Pleasant. This demonstrates the way in which Beaker ceramics were able to circulate in a number of different spheres, employed in distinct ways in quite different practices (Thomas 1991a, 102). The consequence of this was that once Beaker pottery had begun to be used at Mount Pleasant, it began to be possible for activities there to reference or allude to activities which took place elsewhere. As we shall see, the more elaborate division of the landscape which emerged in the early

Bronze Age, and the use of different material items in these areas, increasingly produced a pattern which was drawn upon and replicated in microcosm at Mount Pleasant. Even more than had been the case in the late Neolithic, the architecture of the henge afforded the possibility of controlling and manipulating the material world of the early Bronze Age through ritual practice. It was at this time that the fabric of the site was transformed in a number of ways, and it is important to note one particular connection between these developments and activities outside the henge. As we have already mentioned, the principal modification to Site IV during the early second millennium bc was the addition of a number of upright stones to form a setting or cove. It was probably at around this time that a number of small stone circles were set up on the fringes of the Dorset Ridgeway: Rempstone (with two parallel stone rows) (Royal Commission on Historic Monuments 1970, 53); Hampton/Portesham (Wainwright 1967), Little Mayne, and the Nine Stones (Winterbourne Abbas). For the most part, these circles are located on the north side of the west end of the Ridgeway, on the periphery of the large barrow cemeteries (Burl 1976, 298). One of these monuments, the now-destroyed stone circle at Little Mayne, produced two Beaker vessels, now in Dorchester Museum. Thus at a time when the Ridgeway was coming to be used more regularly as a location for funerary practices, a series of monuments was constructed which defined the boundaries of the area. Given the association of large stones with mortuary activities which we have already noted, and the use of stones as cists within round mounds on the Ridgeway from Beaker times onwards, it may be that a set of associations between death, stones and boundaries was here being articulated. At Flagstones House, stones were used to accompany the dead in a boundary ditch, and now stones were used to create a bounded enclosure and a boundary around the dead in the landscape. The next stage was to introduce this complex of associations into Mount Pleasant itself.

Mount Pleasant: Beaker-associated activity

While the reconstruction of Mount Pleasant at a little after 1700 bc (c. 2000 BC) is clearly connected with the use of Beaker pottery, it is equally evident that Beaker ceramics had been in use on the site for some while before this. A glance at the distributions of pottery across the site shows a clear contrast between Beaker and Grooved Ware. Grooved Ware is comparatively widely spread, with major concentrations around the north entrance (figure 7.4), but Beaker sherds are far more focused upon Site IV, and in particular upon the west side of the ditch. The significance of this will soon become apparent. We have already noted that Grooved Ware bearing different forms of decoration was distributed in significantly different patterns across the site, and much the same is true of Beaker pottery, indicating that the importance of material culture as a means of creating and re-creating a significance for locations was maintained through time. Beaker pottery often bears rich, complex and highly variable decoration, and the consequence of this is that over the years archaeologists have chosen to classify it in a variety of different ways (e.g. Abercromby 1912; Piggott 1963; Clarke 1970; Lanting and Van der Waals 1972; Case 1977; Gibson 1982). What this means is that they have chosen different aspects of the variability of this material in order to split it into convenient sub-units. What the whole exercise of classification assumes, however, is that the significance of the form and decoration of material items is relatively fixed and bounded, and remains stable through time. However, it is increasingly clear that different aspects of an artefact's style and form may be drawn upon and foregrounded from moment to moment in social discourse, let alone from one decade to the next (e.g. Barrett 1988a; Tilley 1989). With an object as complex as a Beaker vessel, a whole series of planes of classification are made available, each of which may become relevant in different contexts of interaction. In consequence, aspects of a number of different classificatory schemes, when applied to the Mount Pleasant material appear to illuminate different aspects of the structure of the site.

A good example draws upon the recent reconsideration of Beaker form and decoration made by Mizoguchi (1995), which emphasises two aspects of variability: the slenderness or squatness of the vessel, and the number of horizontal bands of decoration. Together, these variables enable Mizoguchi to distinguish between the extremes of squat vessels with few bands of decoration, often of coarser fabric, and fine, slender vessels with multiple bands of decoration, frequently found in the context of elaborate burials. If this scheme is applied to Mount Pleasant, it seems that Beakers with multiple bands of decoration are concentrated in the ditch of Site IV, and in particular in layer 5 of segment XIII, the western terminal of the ditch. This context is of particular significance, containing a singularly rich deposit of 587 sherds of Beaker and other pottery, 1180 flints, and other items including antler spatulae, and supposedly being contemporary with the construction of the stone cove (Wainwright 1979, 12). One might easily suggest that these vessels mark out these contexts as being of particular significance, given their association elsewhere with persons of presumed social importance. But equally, if we consider those Beaker vessels which have incised decoration on their surface, the northern entrance and the palisade ditch appear to be emphasised (Longworth 1979, 88).

If Mizoguchi's scheme for classifying Beakers concentrates upon their 'quality' or 'fineness', that which was conceived by David Clarke (1970) was quite different in intent. Clarke obviously approved the notion that the users of Beakers were groups of people quite distinct from the indigenous population of Britain. Accordingly, Clarke used the results of his analyses on Beaker shape, decorative motif representation, and the organisation of decoration on the vessel surface in order to define a number of distinct styles which corresponded with different invading ethnic groups (Wessex/Middle Rhine, Northern/North Rhine, Northern/North Rhine, All-Over-Corded, etc.), which were eventually replaced by the emergence of native Beaker traditions (Northern and Southern). The geographical overlap of these different styles has always cast doubt upon the veracity of their representing distinct social groups. This doubt is compounded by the association of different styles in the same grave and by the occurrence of varieties of styles alongside each other at sites like Mount Pleasant (Barrett 1994, Chapter 4). At the same time, the recent series of radiocarbon dates from a range of British Beakers (Kinnes *et al.* 1991) seem to demolish any notion that these styles can be arranged in a neat chronological sequence, with the Northern and Southern traditions emerging at the end of a process of development leading from European Bell Beakers and All-Over-Corded vessels through the W/MR and N/NR styles. Despite this, it would seem that such categories as All-Over-Corded, Southern, Northern and Wessex/Middle Rhine do have some validity: they do represent ways of making and decorating a Beaker vessel which can be readily distinguished. While it remains a possibility that these distinctions are no more than the product of modern methods of classification, it remains an attractive notion that they genuinely relate to prehistoric cultural categories. Given that the vessels appear to be treated differently, and have distinct sets of material associations when found in the funerary context, the different styles of Beaker identified by Clarke would appear to be separate traditions of Beaker manufacture which were discriminated between by their makers. Since little functional difference is evident, it is reasonable to suggest that different styles of Beaker were understood as being different things, and were used in subtly different ways. Moreover, given that many of these styles were considerably long-lived, they might between them constitute a system of signification and classification, a material language used to construct messages about the dead in the funerary context, and to make other contextual statements in a site like Mount Pleasant.

The distributions of vessels attributable to Clarke's various groups are particularly distinctive (figure 7.9). All-Over-Corded vessels are concentrated in the ditch of Site IV, especially to the west of the entrance. Sherds of Wessex/Middle Rhine Beakers were also found at Site IV, but were plentiful in the palisade trench as well. Vessels of the Southern British tradition were found in most areas of the site, but were particularly numerous in the enclosure ditch, dominating the assemblage. Fingernail impressed Beakers were common in the palisade trench. At Site IV, an especially broad range of styles was present. Styles which might be mutually exclusive in their distribution elsewhere at Mount Pleasant are found in association at Site IV, which seems to draw together all of the traditions used on the site. This distinguishes Site IV as a location of unusual importance. In the funerary context, Beaker vessels are generally found in isolation from each

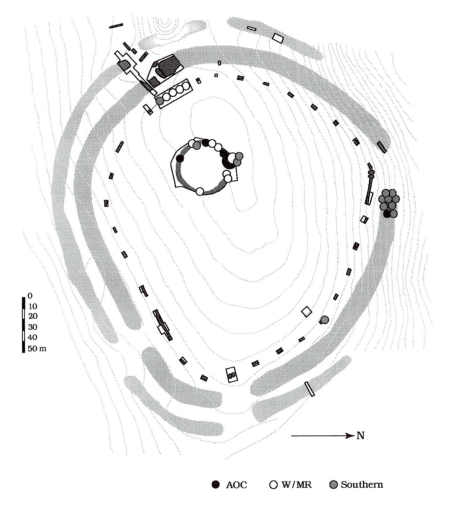

Figure 7.9 Mount Pleasant: spatial distribution of Beakers,
divided according to David Clarke's (1970) scheme

other. They appear to have been singularly important symbols, which played a decisive role in attaching meaning to a human body and other grave goods in the course of a funerary performance (Thomas 1991b). That different styles of Beakers may have brought different messages with them to the graveside is suggested by the different sets of material associations with which they are frequently connected: artisan's 'craft kits' with Northern Beakers, exotic goods with Wessex/Middle Rhine, and so on (Kinnes *et al.* 1991, 39). It follows that the Beaker pot had a part to play in the production of an image of personal identity in death. None the less, the precise connotations of the vessel were ones which must have been established in other contexts. The significance of Site IV, then, is that it would have been a location where Beaker traditions could have been evaluated in relation to each other in the course of performances which highlighted and referenced their symbolic content. Within Site IV, the symbolic power of vessels was negotiated through their mutual association in practice. This possibility is made all the more intriguing by the relative distribution of different Beaker styles around the circumference of the ditch (figure 7.10). In the eastern ditch terminal, on the left-hand side as one would have entered Site IV, only sherds of Wessex/Middle Rhine type were located. As one moves around the ditch toward the western terminal, more and more complex combinations of styles are to be found. In the west terminal itself lay the Segment XIII Layer 5 deposit, already mentioned, which contained no fewer than five styles of Beaker. This result has some significance in view of the claim which has already been made that the normal way of moving around the timber circle was to enter the ditched enclosure and turn left, then progressing clockwise. If this were the case, ditch deposits might be explicitly associated with the different stages of movement about the circle, the different combinations of Beaker styles ordered in terms of spatial and temporal sequence.

The restructuring of Mount Pleasant

Most of the patterns which relate to depositional activities associated with Beaker pottery which we have just discussed cover a considerable length of time. Within this period, though, a series of modifications were made to the fabric of the site which changed the way it could be used and the opportunities for deposition. Three main structural changes took place: the narrowing of the west entrance to the embanked enclosure, the construction of the timber palisade, and the construction of the stone cove. Of these, the extension of the west entrance ditch is the earliest episode, effectively dated by two radiocarbon determinations of 1784 ± 41 bc and 1778 ± 59 bc (*c.* 2136 and 2134 BC) (BM-645 and BM-646). The entrance causeway was reduced to 15 m in breadth, and this may be seen as the start of a gradual process of the restriction of access to the site (Barrett 1994, 104). At a later point, a bronze axe was deposited on a chalk scree in the north terminal of the ditch at the west entrance (Britton in Wainwright 1979). This would probably have happened at a time when the timber palisade had already been built. The palisade is unbroken at this point, having no west entrance, and it is notable that the ditch contains considerably fewer finds than that at the north entrance. It is thus possible that the deposition of this axe represents a statement concerning the cessation of activity at the west entrance: it is a deposit which signifies (or even brings about) the change of status of a location. Much the same might be said of the

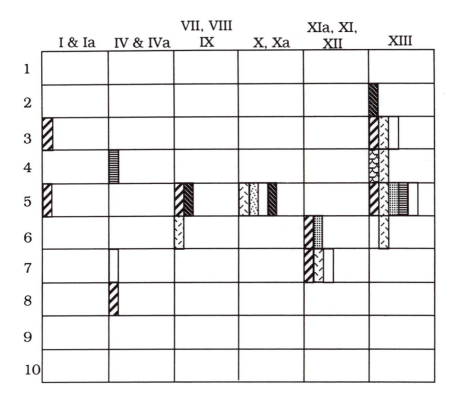

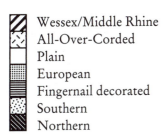

	Wessex/Middle Rhine
	All-Over-Corded
	Plain
	European
	Fingernail decorated
	Southern
	Northern

Figure 7.10 Mount Pleasant Site IV: styles of Beakers deposited
in the different segments of the ditch as excavated

rather similar bronze axe deposited outside the great passage tomb at
Newgrange (O'Kelly and Shell 1979), which relates to the end of the use
of that monument.

The next major remodelling of the site involved the construction of the
palisade itself, dated at 1687 ± 89 bc and 1695 ± 43 bc (c. 1975 and 2006

BC) (BM-662 and BM-665). It is assumed that the appearance of large quantities of sarsen flakes which appear in the Site IV ditch in layers dated to 1680 ± 60 bc (1972 BC) (BM-668) distinguish the construction of the stone cove as a contemporary event (Wainwright 1979, 28). Pollard (1992) has recently suggested another interpretation: that these stone flakes represent not construction but destruction. It is certainly the case that the supposed destruction deposit in the Iron Age layers of the ditch contains only 45 lbs as opposed to over 300 lbs of sarsen in the Beaker phase (Wainwright 1979, 163). Equally, all of the pottery associated with the cove is Grooved Ware rather than Beaker, supporting Pollard's suggestion that the stones are later Neolithic in date. Having said this, it also seems that Grooved Ware had continued to enter the ditch at Site IV long after the appearance of Beakers, in significant quantities and in relatively fresh condition. Moreover, the great majority of the pottery from the internal features of Site IV was Grooved Ware, and it may be that this is the consequence of custom and selection rather than chronology. It is thus hard to argue decisively for either Wainwright's notion of the cove as an Early Bronze Age replacement of the timber circle, or Pollard's picture of the stones as an integral element of a Neolithic structure. A middle course is to see the cove less as a replacement than an elaboration of the circle, which served to reinforce the spatial structure of the monument and its use. If this took place at the time suggested by the deposits of sarsen in the ditch as Wainwright suggests, it would require the timbers to have remained standing for some 300 years. This is somewhat longer than the order of time also suggested for the uprights at Durrington Walls (Wainwright and Longworth 1971, 225). However, the survival time of oak posts is not a constant, but is variable depending upon environmental conditions (Barker 1977, 85–7). What is clear is that the stoneholes and pits of the cove respect the postholes, and indicate a knowledge of the positions of the timbers. Whether they date to the same horizon as the palisade or an earlier phase, the stones indicate a further element of a more general pattern of the restriction of access and movement within the site.

The final and most distinctive element in this process of restriction was the construction of the palisade, a continuous timber structure set in a trench three metres deep (figure 7.11). As with the cove, it is perhaps better to see this structure as an elaboration of the existing enclosure than a replacement. The bank and ditch would still have represented substantial earthworks at this time, despite the accumulation of a coarse angular chalk primary fill in the latter (Wainwright 1979, 42). The effect of building a palisade of posts 6 m high within the existing enclosure was thus to establish a further level of hierarchically nested space, and to impede movement and vision into the centre. While the embanked enclosure had had four entrances, the palisade had only two. Since these were located to the east and the north, the site could now only be entered from below, rather than

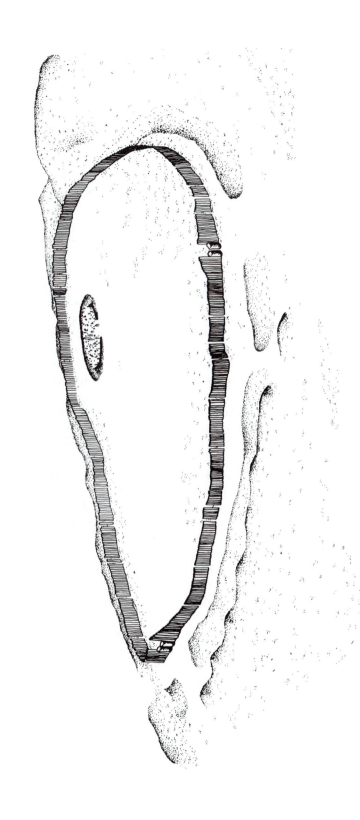

Figure 7.11 Reconstruction of Mount Pleasant in the palisade phase – ditches still visible as depressions

from along the Alington ridge. Events going on inside the enclosure would now have been totally obscure to those outside, looking up to the impressive structure from below. Rather than the broad gaps in the bank of the earlier phase, the entrances now comprised narrow openings between massive timbers, so closely set as to admit no more than one person at a time, and affording very little view of the interior. The closest parallel for the Mount Pleasant palisade can be found in the recently excavated enclosures at West Kennet, just outside Avebury (Whittle 1991). These two palisaded structures may indeed have formed the model for the Mount Pleasant example – what were at West Kennet free-standing structures being deployed as a means of adding to an existing enclosure. While Wainwright (1979, 241) claims that 'it is difficult to interpret this structure as anything other than defensive', the West Kennet examples suggest that other imperatives were at work. The individual posts were frequently surrounded in their sockets by deliberately placed deposits of animal bones and Grooved Ware sherds, for instance, while smaller associated palisade structures have close affinities with the clearly non-defensive enclosure at Street House, Cleveland (Vyner 1988). It is thus perfectly possible to place the Mount Pleasant palisade enclosure in the context of an indigenous tradition of timber structures of early second millennium bc date, rather than evoke chronologically diffuse parallels with defensive enclosures in central Europe (Wainwright 1979, 241–5).

The example of West Kennet alerts one immediately to the likelihood that practices involving the formal and structured deposition of material culture might continue into this phase of the site's use, and might indeed be transformed by the new spatial arrangement. The ditch, still open and still receiving cultural material, would now have been sandwiched between two physical barriers, the bank on the outside and the palisade on the inside. Interestingly, it does appear that its status as a depositional location changed subtly at this time, as if the addition of a further level of classification to the structure of the site allowed a still more complex material order to be addressed through depositional practice. This is particularly clear in the ditch deposits around the northern entrance. Here, layer 8 has a radiocarbon date of 1669 ± 55 bc (*c.* 1953 BC) (BM-790), statistically indistinguishable for the dates from the palisade trench and the enhanced activity at Site IV, and fitting in to a logical and ordered sequence of five other dates from the same location (Burleigh in Wainwright 1979, 186). This one location can thus be used as a secure control example to investigate the changing use of the ditch. The most immediately arresting change is the introduction of two crouched infant burials into the east terminal of the ditch, in shallow graves cut from layer 8 (Wainwright 1979, 45). Both of these had their heads aligned to the south-east, toward the centre of the enclosure. Prior to this time, the only example of human bone located anywhere at Mount Pleasant had been a single skull, again from the north entrance, in the west terminal. It is striking that, as at Maiden Castle and Flagstones, the bodies of children were being used in the redefinition of the boundary of an enclosure. Significantly, the bronze axe in the west entrance which has already been discussed was found in a position stratigraphically equivalent to that of the burials. Seemingly, the structure of Mount Pleasant needed to be renegotiated symbolically as well as transformed physically. Another hint that the character of the ditch had changed at this point is found in a cluster of stakeholes, also in the east terminal of the north entrance, and also cut from layer 8 (Wainwright 1979, 42). While these form no coherent structure, they are for the most part bracketed by the two graves. This lends support to the notion that the burials are not a casual means of disposing of a pair of infants, but that some different form of activity was being undertaken in the secluded space of the ditch bottom.

It is of some importance that this most profound reordering of the site took place at a time of considerable cultural change. This coincided not with the introduction of Beakers, but with the emergence of a number of new indigenous material forms: Food Vessels, Collared Urns and a series of associated artefacts which distinguish the full Early Bronze Age. Given that each of the ceramic styles now in circulation might be used in funerary practices as an accompaniment for a human body, it may be that a more complex system of classification had emerged than had been active in the Beaker phase. In round barrow graves, it is often the case that particular ceramics were associated with specific classes of person, Food Vessels frequently being buried with children in the south of England, Collared Urns generally with cremated bodies, daggers with males. If artefacts were being used in the mortuary context in order to establish a classification of persons, it appears that this structure was introduced to Mount Pleasant as a means of further distinguishing between locations. Thus a more complex architecture and a more elaborate material order emerged at Mount Pleasant at roughly the same time. This would seem to suggest that the social reality of the Early Bronze Age was one which required a more involved form of articulation.

These cultural changes, then, coincide with changes in the depositional status of the henge ditch. In the east terminal of the north ditch entrance, all carved chalk artefacts were found below layer 8. Their disappearance from the ditch is presumably contemporary with the deposition of large numbers of carved chalk objects in the palisade trench (figure 7.12). However, all objects of worked bone and antler in the east ditch terminal are from layer 8 or above. There is thus a radical break in the composition of material deposited in the henge ditch terminal, coincident with the construction of the palisade. At the same time, an equally drastic change overtook the deposition of ceramics at Mount Pleasant. The *quantities* of sherds which found their way into the ditch appear to have remained stable through time: the presence of the palisade had no impact in quantitative

Figure 7.12 Mount Pleasant chalk ball and phallus

terms. Rather, the character of assemblage composition appears to have changed (figure 7.13). From layer 8 onwards, sherds of Food Vessel, Collared Urn and Bucket Urn began to appear in the enclosure ditch, gradually replacing Grooved Ware. Collared Urn eventually became the dominant ceramic tradition. Beaker, although common in layers 9 and 8, gradually became scarcer in the outer ditch. However, in Site IV such a radical change is not apparent. The distinction between the enclosure ditch and Site IV was maintained, for in the latter area Beaker sherds continued to dominate, and while both Food Vessel and Collared Urn were present, Bucket Urn barely appeared at all. When one considers that these deposits must have accumulated over some hundreds of years, the impression is that the material used and deposited in Site IV remained remarkably stable over this period. New styles, as they were introduced, came to be used in activities which took place in the outer part of the monument, while the inner area remained somewhat conservative. In a sense, this may indicate that the site formed a kind of microcosm of the surrounding social landscape: a core of hidden and mystified traditional practice, maintaining a continuity with the past but at the same time drawing about itself a series of new cultural forms and integrating them into an established order.

If deposition in Site IV at this stage showed little change in terms of assemblage composition, it is none the less impressive in scale. We have already seen that layer 5 of the Site IV ditch, radiocarbon dated to *c.* 1680 bc (*c.* 1970 BC) and thus equivalent to layer 8 of the outer ditch and the construction of the palisade, contains a singularly rich deposit in ditch segment XIII, the west terminal (Wainwright 1979, 144). The pottery included All-Over-Corded, European Bell, Wessex/Middle Rhine, Northern/Middle Rhine and Final Southern Beakers, in association with

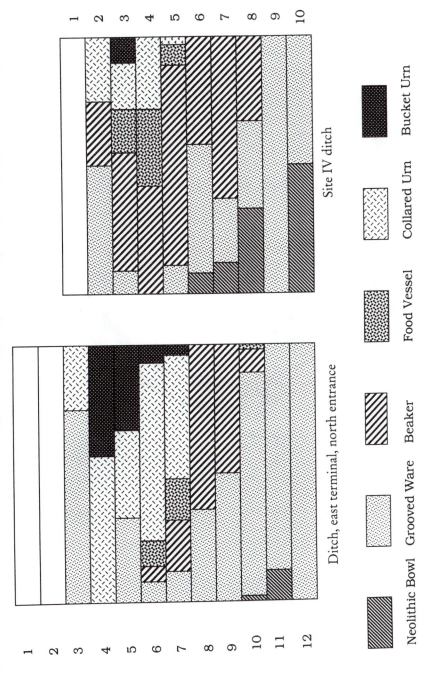

Figure 7.13 Mount Pleasant: composition of ceramic assemblages from the enclosure ditch and the timber circle (Site IV)

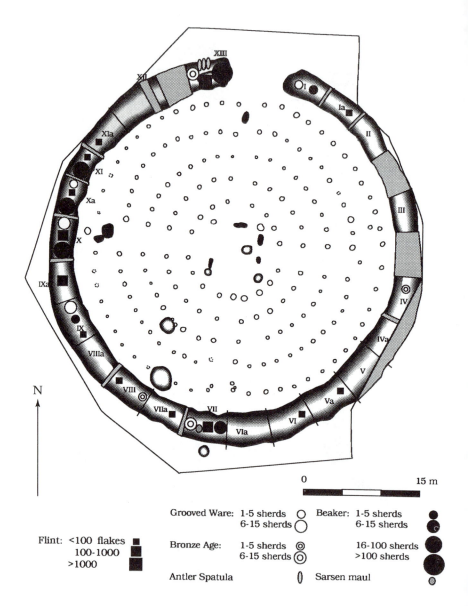

N

Grooved Ware: 1-5 sherds ○
6-15 sherds ◯

Beaker: 1-5 sherds ●
6-15 sherds ●

Flint: <100 flakes ■
100-1000 ■
>1000 ■

Bronze Age: 1-5 sherds ◎
6-15 sherds ◉

16-100 sherds ●
>100 sherds ●

Antler Spatula 〇

Sarsen maul

0   15 m

Figure 7.14 Mount Pleasant Site IV: distribution of
deposits in ditch layer 5

220

Food Vessel sherds, 1180 flint flakes and three antler spatulae. Diametrically opposite, in ditch segment VII, was another deposit of Beaker and Food Vessel sherds and flint, but with a sarsen maul, while more flint and pottery was deposited in the western part of the ditch (figure 7.14). This implies a continuation of the back left/front right duality indicated for the earlier phases of the monument, now enhanced by the construction of the setting of upright stones. As already suggested, Site IV appears to have been a location in which links with past practices were maintained. It is tempting to see the other materials deposited fitting into a now ancient performative structure, such that the sarsen stone (associated with death and transition) was placed halfway around the ditch circuit, and the antler spatulae (firmly connected with Beaker ceramics) marks the completed cycle at the point of the most elaborate deposit.

As in the case of the West Kennet enclosures already mentioned, the Mount Pleasant palisade trench itself served as a context for the deposition of cultural materials, presumably largely at the time of the erection of the uprights. This included a large number of clusters of lithic materials, including many flakes and cores. On the northern side of the enclosure, and especially around the northern entrance, were found concentrations of carved chalk balls (figure 7.15), clearly not artefacts which entered this context by casual discard. This pattern may partly be the consequence of the failure to bottom cuttings on the south side at the time of excavation. However, some were completely excavated, and most cuttings reached the layers which had contained the chalk objects on the north side (Wainwright 1979, 58–64). The conceptual division of the palisade circuit which this implies is elaborated by the distribution of other materials in the trench. Despite the relatively late date of the structure, the palisade contained major concentrations of Grooved Ware, especially in the north entrance, and in the western sector. In the west, opposite the west entrance to the henge ditch, a cluster of Beaker sherds was found. Antler artefacts, like chalk, clustered around the entrances, but in this case the east and (blocked) west rather than the north. In this context, it may be significant that antler objects were found in the interior of Mount Pleasant, while chalk artefacts were not, just as Beaker sherds had come to be more common in the interior (especially Site IV) and Grooved Ware around the edges of the site. This seems to indicate that from its construction onwards, the different parts of the palisade, and especially its different entrances, were treated differently. Different materials were deposited, bringing to each part a different set of associations, and thus indicating their appropriateness for different uses – perhaps use by different classes of person. This being the case it is interesting to note Wainwright's observation that different parts of the enclosure were destroyed in different ways (Wainwright 1979, 240–1). In the west entrance and the 'back' of the enclosure, the 'private' and more hidden part of the site, with its associations of Beaker pottery and antler, the timbers

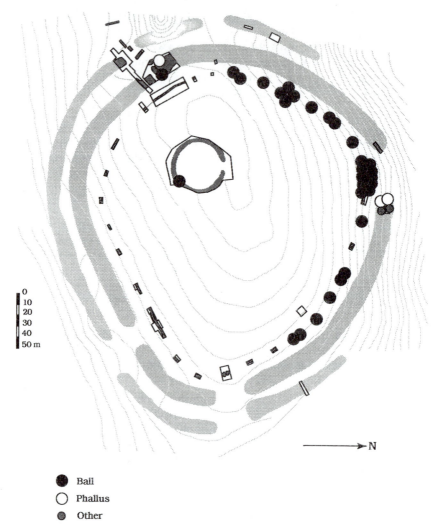

0
10
20
30
40
50 m

● Ball
○ Phallus
◐ Other

Figure 7.15 Mount Pleasant: distribution of carved chalk artefacts

were burnt while still standing in the palisade trench. This was presumably a costly enterprise, requiring the building of large fires, since 'some posts had smouldered to their bases' (ibid., 240). Along the more public 'front' of the palisade, around the north entrance, however, the posts were more likely to have been withdrawn, or simply left in place. Whatever the reason for the destruction of the palisade, it would appear that those engaged in the process respected a set of conceptual oppositions regarding the significance of the barrier which was established at its construction.

CONTEXT: THE EARLY BRONZE AGE

Having ventured into the Early Bronze Age, it is difficult to avoid some consideration of the relationship between Mount Pleasant and the large number of round mounds in its immediate vicinity. In particular, it has to be noted that one of the principal concentrations of the elaborate burials isolated by Stuart Piggott (1938) as the 'Wessex Culture' lies in this area. Fleming (1971), Renfrew (1973) and Burgess (1974, 166) have all drawn attention to the close relationship between major ceremonial centres and cemeteries of Early Bronze Age round mounds, largely in relation to the notion of the longevity of certain territorial units. However, since both types of site are ones which were frequented on a repeated basis for ritual activities which involved the manipulation and deposition of often identical items of material culture, a more detailed consideration of the relationships between them is required. If the identification of the Wessex graves as a discernible entity has any validity whatsoever, why do they appear to congregate around the two large monuments in Wessex which were still actively reconstructed in the Early Bronze Age? For Piggott, the Wessex Culture represented a temporal and spatial unit which filled an equivalent bracket to that occupied by the Food Vessel culture elsewhere (1938, 52). The diagnostic artefact types of the Wessex graves (daggers, cups, faience beads, gold, amber, battle axes, pins) were largely ones which possessed equivalents or parallels in relatively remote geographical areas (Brittany, Greece). Hence a degree of circularity is involved in an argument which distinguishes a group of burials on the criterion of the presence of exotic grave goods, and then claims that the entity thus defined resulted from an invasion from abroad. As Burgess (1976, 186) suggests, the Wessex phenomenon may not represent a 'culture at all, but a facet of a complex fabric of co-existent communities', separated out from the rest by a particular process of classification on the part of the archaeologist. None the less, this does not mean that the geographical location of these graves becomes meaningless. That items of material culture which derived from or bore the connotations of far-distant places were selected for use in particular funerary observances is itself of significance, as it is that this should take place preferentially in a number of 'core' areas.

Recently, Garwood (1991) has drawn a distinction between those rituals which were carried out at round mounds, which stressed 'the integrity of lines of descent', and those more communal arrangements associated with 'religious super-centres', which may have involved 'the ideological legitimation of the social order in terms of a timeless transcendental scheme' (ibid., 17). These two sets of activities, he suggests, would have involved different models of the sacred: a sanctification of the order of society in funerary practice, and a transcendence of social relations in communal ritual. Hence the construction of round barrows enshrined genealogical relationships in a material monument, a 'visible presence of "known history"'. Garwood's argument provides a good point of departure, although one could argue that the dichotomy which he sets up is overdrawn. Although round barrows and ceremonial centres represent quite separate spheres of practice, which might have attracted different (if overlapping) constituencies, they might not imply entirely separate cosmologies. It may be preferable to recognise them as being in some way linked and mutually influencing. Thus actions carried out in one context might alter the significance of the material items employed, in turn bringing new connotations to the other. Garwood is surely correct to point out that the 'ordered adjacency' involved in the structure of burial deposits in both individual mounds and barrow cemeteries is connected with relationships of descent and affiliation in life. Similarly, Barrett (in Barrett *et al.* 1991, 128) points to the way in which the enlargement or capping of mounds, and the production of above-ground and below-ground locations for burial within barrows, enabled a manipulation of the conceptual distance between individual burials. But while these events are certainly connected with communal history and personal memory, it may be wrong to conceive of them as being in any sense a presentation of objective social relations. Garwood acknowledges that funerary practice might be manipulated by individuals or sections of communities (1991, 17), yet this assumes that the raw material of mortuary ritual was in some way a true and undistorted image of kinship and descent. On the contrary, one might suggest that the performance of a funeral involves a *production* of history, which may have little connection with recorded events. A grounding in the past may be essential in traditional societies, but it may be a mistake to distinguish between 'true' history and 'false' myth. Rather, the truth value of any articulated past lies in its usefulness within strategies of power.

Given that round barrow burial was involved with 'fixing a new position within the landscape' (Barrett *et al.* 1991, 125) in relation to a particular deceased person, we might then question whether these actions did constitute a constant re-presentation of the past, or whether they were episodic and non-cyclical (perhaps in contrast to activities at communal centres). Garwood correctly indicates that round barrow practice would represent a context for cultural elaboration (1991, 25), in which each act of construction or deposition both referenced and transformed what had taken place before. Hence the event or performance would bring together persons, artefacts and places, transforming each in relation to the others. In this process, relationships would not be passively recorded so much as established, not necessarily ensuring the solidity of lines of descent but renegotiating genealogies. In all likelihood, this re-creation of the past might take place at a time of crisis, a juncture at which the transfer of authority between the dead and the living became problematic (Goody 1962). Where conflicts occur over the devolution of power, it is often the case that competing claims are substantiated through the telling of alternative stories about the past (Metcalf 1981), including the production of fictive kinships. By acting out the establishment of these relationships, round barrow burial becomes less a reflection than an intervention into social life.

These arguments indicate that what took place within barrow cemeteries was not simply haphazard, but that events of deposition and construction were engaged in the production of an increasingly complex material order, even if each act was immediately meaningful only in the context of a particular moment in local power strategies (e.g. Forde-Johnson 1958). The increasingly complex architecture of Mount Pleasant paralleled this process: the reorganisation of space within the henge was linked to the reorganisation of material culture in the Early Bronze Age. Mount Pleasant shadowed and thereby sanctioned depositional practice in the surrounding barrow landscape. The objects used at Mount Pleasant are predominantly ones which are more conventionally found in mortuary contexts, yet inside the henge they were used in rather different ways. Thus a reciprocal relationship can be suggested between the symbolic activities enacted within Mount Pleasant and those taking place in the wider landscape. Just as different parts of the henge were distinguished by the deposition of different cultural materials, so considerable variation can be detected in barrow deposits in various parts of the Ridgeway and the South Winterbourne and Frome valleys. This variation is noted by Woodward (1991, 145), who none the less explains it in terms of territoriality: three territories, originating in the Neolithic, retain their separate identities into the Bronze Age. Alternatively, we can suggest that the accrual of meanings by particular locations within the landscape (both cultural and natural) would have made them appropriate for different forms of practice in the Early Bronze Age, irrespective of any continued association with a particular group of people.

Collared Urns, we have noted, became the dominant ceramic style in the outer ditch at Mount Pleasant as the Bronze Age progressed. Collared Urns are found in barrows along the Ridgeway, especially in the south-east around Broadmayne, where they occur with both primary and secondary interments. Particularly noteworthy is the deposition of Collared Urns in pond barrows, structures used for multiple sequential burials, which are concentrated in the Stonehenge and South Dorset areas (Atkinson *et al.* 1951). In the area around the major monuments surrounding Dorchester, however, Collared Urns are more likely to accompany secondary burials. Beaker graves, and graves with Wessex I and II series goods, are split roughly equally between the Dorchester area and the part of the Ridgeway immediately to the south (figure 7.16). Food Vessels are relatively ubiquitous, yet Wessex Biconical Urns are not found in the vicinity of the large monuments, and Deverel-Rimbury Urns are densely concentrated on the south of the Ridgeway, especially the major cemetery groups (e.g. Thompson and Ashbee 1957). Even on the Ridgeway, it is interesting to note the presence of one Wessex I grave (Whitcombe 1) in the immediate

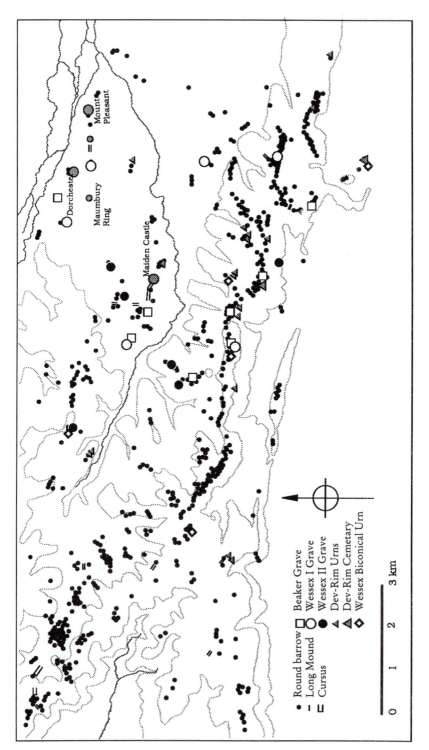

Figure 7.16 The Dorset Ridgeway and the Dorchester area, showing the representation of ceramic traditions associated with round barrow burials

vicinity of the Broadmayne bank barrow, yet the 'avoidance' of this location by Deverel-Rimbury interments, which form a 'halo' to the east, west and south of the long mound. The relative location of these funerary assemblages suggests some form of spatial grading according to proximity to major field monuments. Wessex graves and Beaker burials were deposited near to monuments, Deverel-Rimbury and Wessex Biconical cremations at a distance, with Collared Urns occupying an intermediary position, only valid with secondary interments in the vicinity of monuments. Given that the pattern holds for Wessex II graves, this does not appear to be a purely chronological consequence of a drift of activity away from the monumental focus. One need not suggest that these assemblages were necessarily 'ranked' in terms of relative social status, but it is argued that a social order existed which dictated respective positions for the dead in relation to those activities acted out at corporate monuments. Significantly, it was exactly the same pattern of inclusion and exclusion which was reproduced at a smaller scale within Mount Pleasant. Beaker sherds dominated in Site IV, Collared Urns and Food Vessels were found primarily in the outer ditch, yet with some representation at Site IV, Deverel-Rimbury ceramics were largely restricted to the outer ditch, and Wessex Biconical Urns excluded from the monument altogether (figure 7.17). We will consider this pattern and its significance in more detail below.

These phenomena indicate that while the character of the material order had changed from the later Neolithic into the Early Bronze Age, a degree of continuity existed in the role of Mount Pleasant as a location within which different traditions of artefacts could be evaluated in relation to each other. The cultural innovations of the Early Bronze Age had not emerged *ex nihilo*, but were the outcome in part of the very negotiation which took place within the henge. These changes were always based upon a reformulation of an existing order, in which particular elements of accepted local or general practice might continue to be utilised, according to the requirements of continuing social struggles. One such strand of continuity in local practice can be seen in the persistence of an association between large stones and the dead. The practice of placing inhumations beneath huge stones had by now been incorporated into round barrow burial, as for instance with the Wessex I interment in a barrow on Conygar Hill, or the burial with a knife-dagger in Bradford Peverell 7a (Warne 1866; Grinsell 1959). Similarly, a number of barrows on the Ridgeway contained burials in stone cists (as with Winterbourne St. Martin 5c: Sydenham 1844, 331), while in Winterbourne Came 18b, six primary burials and a cremation were covered by a cairn capped by a large stone engraved with three concentric circles. One barrow with a cist, Weymouth 8 (Drew and Piggott 1936, 20), may be dated by Beaker sherds attributed to the site in Dorchester Museum. This being the case, the introduction of large stones into round barrow practice in south Dorset may coincide with the construction of the

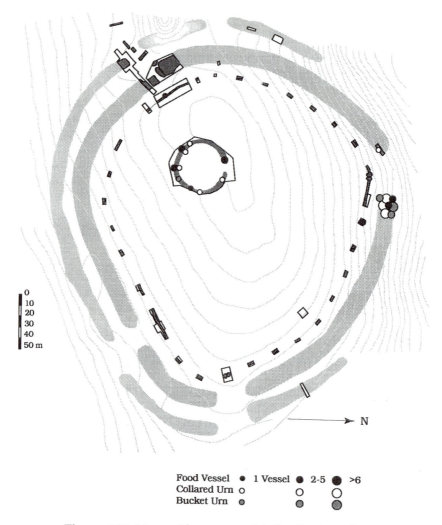

Food Vessel ● 1 Vessel ● 2-5 ● >6
Collared Urn ○ ○ ○
Bucket Urn ◉ ◉ ◉

Figure 7.17 Mount Pleasant: spatial distribution of Early
Bronze Age ceramics

local stone circles, and signal the elaboration of a set of associations linking
stone, boundaries and the dead, already discussed above. If this were so,
the construction of the cove at Mount Pleasant might represent another
way in which activities within the henge both mirrored and facilitated
developments in the surrounding landscape.

By the time that the full range of early Bronze Age ceramics was in
circulation, round barrows had begun to be constructed amongst the large

monuments which overlooked the Frome valley. Although Mount Pleasant was seemingly still in use for gatherings involving large numbers of people, the large round mound of the Conquer Barrow was constructed abutting the bank on the western side of the enclosure. Barrett (1994, 103) suggests that the barrow may have represented a platform, allowing a privileged group of people to view the interior of the monument from outside. Whatever the case, the Conquer Barrow formed one element in a linear barrow cemetery which had appropriated the earlier monumental alignment along the Alington ridge (Healy and Smith forthcoming). This also included a round mound built in the centre of the Flagstones enclosure, and another raised on one end of the Alington Avenue long mound. Finally, a complex multi-phase round barrow at Fordington Farm formed another part of the same cemetery (Bellamy 1991) (figure 7.18). Just as this configuration of the landscape established its legitimacy by referencing an earlier series of monuments, so the funerary practices within the Fordington barrow seem to quote themes of material deposition which extended back into the Neolithic. The primary burials, placed in two separate graves, were dated to 1765 ± 54 bc (*c.* 2131 BC) (UB-3304). Although rather late in date, the skeletons were disarticulated, a practice more common in the Neolithic, and each grave contained the body of at least one child as well as an adult (Bellamy 1991, 108). After a small mound had been raised over these graves, another burial was inserted into the barrow, probably associated with one of the phases of enlargement which eventually transformed it into a large bell barrow. This grave contained the remains of a young adult male, associated with a barbed and tanged arrowhead, which may have been the cause of death rather than a funerary gift. Also in the grave were four scapulae, a pelvis and two humeral fragments of cattle (Bellamy 1991, 114). The cattle bones, disarticulated bodies and child burials could all suggest a conscious anachronism: the use of this location for funerary practice was made legitimate by incorporating a series of references to much earlier depositional activities.

Mount Pleasant in the Bronze Age

The Early Bronze Age burials of the Dorchester area display an unusual richness and variety of material associations, including a large number of artefacts which suggest the existence of long-distance contacts. This density of material may or may not indicate that the area was one which enjoyed a position of particular influence and authority. What is clear is that the burials surrounding Mount Pleasant are evidence of a complex material order, in which a great variety of material symbols were deployed in episodic funerary events, which may only have been witnessed or fully comprehended by a minority of the population. While these rites involved the creation of relationships between categories of person and object in the

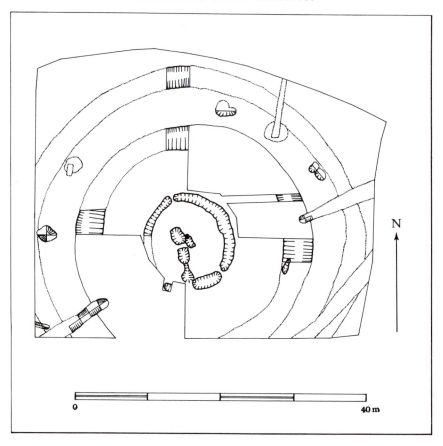

N

Figure 7.18 Plan of the Fordington Farm round barrow
(after Bellamy 1991)

present and earlier deposits and structures, this process was necessarily
piecemeal and incremental. By contrast, what may have been much larger
gatherings at Mount Pleasant provided a forum for the reproduction,
evaluation and even contestation of a whole system of material symbols.
The use and deposition of material items in this context was at once structured and structuring, its spatial ordering both reflecting and sanctioning
the symbolic division of the surrounding landscape. The deposition
of Bronze Age pottery at Mount Pleasant thus has a spatial distribution
as striking as that of later Neolithic ceramics (figure 7.17). At Site IV, as
already mentioned, layers 5 to 3 remain dominated by Beaker sherds (figure
7.13). Food Vessel and Collared Urn are both present in these layers, while
a single sherd of Bucket Urn is present in layer 3. Sherds of Food Vessel
are also present in the palisade trench, presumably having been deposited

alongside the Beaker material at the time of construction. In the outer henge ditch, Collared Urn sherds appear from layer 7 onwards in the northern entrance (where the great bulk of the Bronze Age ceramics were located), remaining the dominant style until layer 4. Bucket Urns are also present from layer 7 (dated to some time in the sixteenth century bc), and increase in their representation from this time onward. Woodward (1991, 150) dismisses this Deverel-Rimbury material as relating to settlement or domestic activity in the immediate vicinity, following the abandonment of the site. This does not satisfactorily explain the presence of Bucket Urn sherds through several successive stratigraphic horizons, consistently associated with other styles of pottery. Woodward similarly cites the absence of Wessex Biconical Urns as evidence for the 'political diminution' of the site, but this clearly rests upon a 'chest of drawers' notion of culture, in which the absence of a particular pottery style indicates a lack of activity in a given phase. Given the demonstrable contemporaneity of several traditions, some classificatory imperative must lie behind their relative distributions. Either the vessels themselves, or the practices in which they were employed, formed parts of a conceptual order governing deposition inside the henge and in other contexts.

Thus while the use of large monuments had ceased to be the norm over much of Britain, Mount Pleasant continued to hold a position of local significance, not simply as a centre for the gathering of a dispersed population, but also as a site for performances which articulated aspects of a complex material order. Material culture gives access to only a part of a means of communication which might equally be expected to be verbal, narrative and gestural. Moreover, the material order concerned should not be seen as a given, any more than should be the constituent elements of round barrow funerary practice. The rehearsing and re-creation of a culture necessarily involves its questioning, testing and transformation, and the adoption of contrasting (and antagonistic) positions by the people involved. The fate of Mount Pleasant in the later part of the second millennium bc may reflect the emergence of more firmly defined positions in relation to cultural/symbolic, economic and political resources. It was this period which saw a radical reorganisation of the landscape of southern Wessex, involving the laying out of field systems and enclosed settlements (Barrett *et al.* 1991, 143). This process is frequently associated with the use of Deverel-Rimbury ceramics (Barrett 1980). There is plentiful evidence for this development in the Dorchester area. Bronze Age enclosed settlements are known from Poundbury, Fordington Bottom and Winterbourne Steepleton amongst others (Woodward 1991; Green 1987), while a possible enclosure has been detected within the hillfort at Maiden Castle (Sharples 1991, 41). At Middle Farm, north of Maiden Castle, an enclosure and boundary system were excavated (Woodward and Smith 1987, 84), and at the Alington Avenue site an Early/Middle Bronze Age funerary enclosure was engulfed by a field system with droveways (Davies *et al.* 1985, 104). The precise dating of this activity may not be entirely coincident. A hut site with storage pits and boundaries at Rowden, Winterbourne Steepleton, appears to have dated to after 100 BC, for instance (Woodward 1991). One important element of the pattern which Davies, Stacey and Woodward (1985) point to is the deliberate destruction of large monuments, followed by their cultivation. Beside Mount Pleasant, this is the case with the Alington long mound and the Dorchester timber circle, where posts were burnt above ground level (Woodward *et al.* 1984, 101). At Maiden Castle, the date of cultivation over the causewayed enclosure and long mound is unclear. The disturbance is described as 'Beaker', and falls below the 'Bronze Age' turfline, but in the bank barrow ditch it occurs higher than material which produced a radiocarbon date of 1520 ± 70 bc (1748 BC) (Sharples 1991, 125). It is equally possible to argue for a Middle to Late Bronze Age cultivation and a final Bronze Age turf, given that the relationship between the round barrows on the hill and the turfline was not tested by excavation. Were this the case, the phenomenon of the removal of monuments from the landscape by agricultural activity would be a particularly widespread one in south Dorset.

We have already seen that the destruction of the Mount Pleasant palisade proceeded along lines dictated by the symbolic organisation of the enclosure. There are hints, too, that aspects of the new landscape were not purely functional: the three trussed burials in the ditch at Middle Farm, for instance. It seems unlikely that farming land was so much in demand that the considerable effort involved in the destruction of the monuments was a purely economic consideration. Instead, it is worth considering whether these areas were preferentially chosen for agricultural activity as a means of excising the influence of these structures from the land. Thus one symbolic order, based upon agricultural reproduction, replaces another in which landscape was symbolically appropriated through the construction of monuments. However, the break between the two was not total, and the new order was grounded on and germinated within the old. The landscape of the end of the second millennium was constructed through a transformation of existing resources.

CONCLUSIONS

In Chapter Six we argued that the complex interconnections between people, places, substances and artefacts in later Neolithic Britain formed a mobile economy which allowed a plurality of identities and practices to be sustained without declining into chaos. In such a world there could be no central places, since later Neolithic society was a web without a centre. The large henge monuments of Wessex and the huge gatherings of people which they would have facilitated allowed a particular form of authority to be generated, yet this may have been one element amongst many in a shifting pattern of power relations. Yet by the end of the Early Bronze Age, the henge at Mount Pleasant had become axial to a localised system of meaning. Although the material order of the period had become even more elaborate than that of the later Neolithic, the role of Mount Pleasant as an arena for the evaluation of material traditions turned it into an integral part of a system of meaning. This system of meaning would have been continually renewed and renegotiated, through performances carried out within the henge and in numerous other significant locations. While the later Neolithic material order had linked together a range of different contexts and practices, Mount Pleasant in the Early Bronze Age had become a conduit through which the entire local system of social and material relations flowed. Mount Pleasant was a microcosm of the social landscape of southern Dorset. Gradually, the internal world of the monument and the surrounding land came to reflect each other, as each became the context for the re-ordering of the other. Through this reciprocal relationship, material things like Beakers, Collared Urns, the bones of cattle, child burials and settings of large stones were drawn in to the henge, their existing connotations were drawn upon, and new associations were engineered. As the spatial configuration of Mount Pleasant was itself re-ordered, the conditions under which this engineering of cosmology might be witnessed were manipulated and restricted. Far more than in the Neolithic, Early Bronze Age Mount Pleasant was an *axis mundi*, a fulcrum for the exercise of power. The status of the site as one of the two surviving monumental foci in Early Bronze Age Wessex demonstrates the crucial role which it had come to hold in contemporary society. However, since this ordering of material things was based upon the spatial order of the monument, it is possible that its full elaboration would not have been known to all members of society.

AFTERWORD: ARCHAEOLOGY AND MEANING

——— •✦• ———

This book has sought to outline some principles which underpin a particular way of doing archaeology, by concentrating on the issues of time, culture and identity. The arguments which have been made concerning these questions have sometimes been similar in structure, and have often overlapped. In these last few pages, I should like to draw out some of the central themes which have been discussed, in order to clarify the main direction of the programme which has been proposed. One such strand, which has run throughout the book, has been the recognition that analytical science is only one way of gaining an understanding of the world. It represents at once a refined and an impoverished form of attunement, which is secondary to and derived from everyday modes of knowing. Human beings become aware of themselves and their surroundings in the context of everyday life: we find ourselves in the course of living. This means that whenever we choose to analyse some element of the world through science, we are always focusing upon something about which we have already formed an opinion. We are always already prejudiced in our understanding, because scientific knowing is always an elaboration upon everyday knowing: it does not begin with a blank slate. This emphasis upon the everyday has important consequences for the practice of archaeology. It is generally acknowledged that the day-to-day lives of people in the past represent a legitimate object of archaeological understanding, but I have suggested that one of the problems which we face in this enterprise lies in grasping this kind of life through an analytical investigation. Yet, at the same time, the particular way of thinking about material things as evidence which characterises archaeology is not entirely divorced from the ways in which most people conduct their lives. Like other forms of science, archaeological analysis involves a way of knowing which is derived from everyday forms of attunement to the world. What I take this to mean is that archaeology must be a fundamentally reflexive discipline. Whatever we learn about people's lives in the past should make us reflect upon the context within which we conduct archaeology in the present, and vice versa. Whatever analytical frameworks we use in order to understand the past should equally be turned onto the present.

This is no more than the form of enlightenment promised by the hermeneutic tradition (Johnson and Olsen 1992), in which an understanding of an alien horizon brings a reflection on the present. But at the same time, this perspective allows us to escape some of the negative connotations which Heidegger sometimes seems to attach to the everyday. In archaeology, one of our central concerns must surely involve finding a means to grasp habitual modes of human conduct, rather than overcoming them. Throughout this book, I have attempted to resist the reduction of time, culture and identity to any kind of essence. While I have suggested that these concepts are essential to understanding the human past, I have argued that each emerges from lived human experience. Time, culture and identity are aspects of a human engagement with the world, and yet in each case their character has been obscured by a modern way of thinking which is based upon opposed categories. This Cartesian logic begins by dividing the world into categories, which are held to exist as empirical objects, rather than to have been constructed in discourse. In turn, these concepts are then related to one another, and ordered hierarchically. Mind is opposed to body, nature to culture, natural science to human science. Implicit in this arrangement is a division between the primacy of the empirical world of substantial things, and the derived character of the world of the metaphysical, which is always held to be built on a more solid foundation. The 'facts' of nature are given and immutable, while cultural interpretations are insubstantial. Consequently, the economic base may be taken to have an absolute primacy over cultural superstructures, biological sex may be seen as a substrate of hard fact underlying the cultural attribution of gender, or geology and ecosystem dynamics may be seen as the ultimate truth which grounds cultural perceptions of landscape. Yet as I have hoped to show, categories like 'the economy', 'biological sex' and 'the ecosystem' are abstractions which are constructed in discourse. None of them precedes the human experience of the world from which they are abstracted, and their logical priority can only be maintained within a particular form of logic.

It is this same form of logic which has allowed human beings to conceive of themselves as objects: as biological organisms which have had a particular kind of consciousness added on as an afterthought. This notion of people as 'rational animals' permits some of the most pervasive Cartesian dualisms: the mind and the body are seen not simply as separate, but as being composed of entirely different kinds of substance, and culture is perceived as being bound up with the mental. In a sense, then, the continuing difficulties which archaeology has encountered in attempting to understand material culture can be traced back to a particular conception of what a human being represents. I have argued that this understanding has to be seen as historically located. While it may help to explain the ways in which people think about themselves in the contemporary west, it may none the less be wholly inappropriate to impose it on the non-western world, or European prehistory. Moreover, the modernist understanding of the world also involves a form of conceptual alienation of inanimate things, which again restricts our ability to interpret material culture. These problems are perhaps resolved when we reject the distinction between mind and body, and see culture not as something ethereal, opposed to nature and materiality, but as a means of human engagement in the world. Thus, cultural knowledge is best conceived as being composed of skills which allow people to cope with the world. These skills may have little significance in abstraction from the contexts in which they are routinely deployed. One aspect of culture as a means of worldly involvement is that it is inherently meaningful. However, rather than culture being composed of a set of codes which are imbued with abstract meaning, we might think of culture as a technology which allows the production of meaning through the concernful dealings which human beings have with their world. If we were to say that meaning is not a quality which is fixed in things, but is continually produced through the 'working' of the sets of relationships in which human beings find themselves enmeshed, it would then be meaning which is the defining quality of history.

History is a lived process in which the relationships between human beings and their world are continually transformed. This world itself, and the changes in the world which human beings incorporate into narratives, are distinguished by their significance. Yet ironically, while history is deeply implicated with temporality, historians like Braudel have often attempted to reduce time to an external calibration of events and processes. While accepting that historical processes may be meaningful, human and cultural, time is ultimately portrayed as being an attribute of nature, and thus a scientific phenomenon which serves as the substrate of history. Equally, although different communities around the world are recognised as having different understandings of time, these are seen as cultural interpretations which are secondary to the singular reality of sequential time. As I have hoped to show, time is the paradigm example of a phenomenon which the west presents as a scientifically verified external reality. But again, it is impossible to investigate time scientifically without first having the kind of experiential temporality which distinguishes human beings. Having at our disposal a series of possibilities which are drawn from the past is a distinctively human trait. This could easily be taken to suggest that human beings construct their own narratives of identity as entirely autonomous individuals. However, the practice of drawing on the past is both collective and cultural. Even our own personal histories are culturally mediated, interpreted in the context of culturally constructed tastes, predispositions and attunements.

Human beings are fundamentally temporal beings, in that they can recognise past, present and future as categorically separate. It is the ability to recall a personal past, to conceive of oneself as being alongside others in the present, and to plan for the future which renders us human. What we should not take this to mean, however, is that the collective social past, the past of the world, is separated from the present by a gulf or fracture. Past, present and future are categorically distinct as far as the human orientation toward the world is concerned, yet they are also inseparable, in that the future is continuously flowing into the past. There is no contradiction here, for while the time of the world is continuous, and not divided into distinct 'blocks', we can only distinguish its passing because we can separate past, present and future. Archaeology is made possible by the way in which we live amidst a materiality which is inherited from the past, and which is continually accruing and wasting away, as its significance is continually redefined and renegotiated.

I have suggested that temporality and the use of cultural knowledge are distinctively human characteristics. However, I should emphasise that neither of these should be seen as an attribute which is contained in the body or the mind of a single human being. What makes humans human is not something which is encapsulated in any one being. On the contrary, humans are human by virtue of their engagement in a world. Human beings are 'thrown' in that they always find themselves enmeshed in a web of relationships with people and other beings. This book has stressed that human beings are positioned: they are differentially connected to others, and they have differential access to events and knowledge. However, it is important to distinguish between an emphasis on positioning and a belief in 'the individual' as a transcendental subject who is context-free. Persons who are positioned are certainly different from each other, but they are different by virtue of their relational engagement in a world, not because of any qualities which they bring to that world. Human identity emerges out of this connectedness, rather than humans being born free and then choosing to enter into relationships with others. It is this point which distinguishes the perspective offered here from systems thinking, which first defines entities, and then explores the relationships between them. This illustrates the critical importance which the notion of relationality has had in this book. Human identities, material objects, and places all develop from a background of relationality. Certain social phenomena such as power, agency, care and concern are best considered as attributes of relational networks, rather than as things which issue out of individual isolated intelligences. It is for this reason that we can usefully consider artefacts as being social actors: they are imbedded in and articulate relations of care and power. Moreover, the relationships which constitute the world are constantly in motion. When we involve ourselves in the practice of interpretation, our intellectual labour 'works' the relationships in which a thing is embedded, in the production of meaning. It follows that any object, any thing, can represent a means of entry into the complex interconnectedness of the world.

This perspective enables us to return again to the issue of meaning, a question which has exercised archaeologists for some while (e.g. Hodder

1986; Barrett 1988a; Buchli 1995). It suggests that meaning is not a quality which is located in any one place or held in any one object, but that it is produced in the working of relationality. This in turn must affect the way in which archaeological evidence must be rendered meaningful in the present. As I attempted to demonstrate in Chapter One, most forms of archaeology are deeply modernist in outlook, believing meaning to be an attribute of the inner subjective consciousness of the individual. I suggest instead that a considerable part of the network of relationships through which meanings were created in the past is directly accessible to us in the present, in the form of archaeological evidence. That evidence is unavoidably recontextualised in the present, and in working the connections which spread out from ancient artefacts we produce an interpretation which is of and for the present (Shanks and Tilley 1987, 21). But it is an unhelpfully nostalgic position to hold that since past minds are unavailable to us, archaeological evidence is meaning*less*.

BIBLIOGRAPHY

———— •◆• ————

Abercromby, J. (1912) *A Study of the Bronze Age Pottery in Great Britain and Ireland.* Oxford: Clarendon.

Adkins, R. and Jackson, R. (1976) *Neolithic Axes from the River Thames.* London: British Museum.

Alderman, H. (1973) The work of art and other things. In: E. G. Ballard and C. E. Scott (eds) *Martin Heidegger: In Europe and America*, 157–69. The Hague: Martinus Nijhof.

Althusser, L. (1969) *For Marx.* London: Verso.

Althusser, L. and Balibar, E. (1970) *Reading Capital.* London: Verso.

Ammerman, A. J. and Cavalli-Sforza, L. L. (1971) Measuring the rate of spread of early farming in Europe. *Man* 6, 674–88.

Ammerman, A. J. and Cavalli-Sforza, L. L. (1973) A population model for the diffusion of farming into Europe. In: A. C. Renfrew (ed.) *The Explanation of Culture Change: Models in Prehistory*, 343–58. London: Duckworth.

Armor-Chelu, M. (1991) The faunal remains. In: N. Sharples, *Maiden Castle: Excavations and Field Survey 1985–6*, 139–51. London: English Heritage.

Ashbee, P. (1966) Fussell's Lodge long barrow excavations,1957. *Archaeologia* 100, 1–80.

Ashbee, P. , Smith, I. F. and Evans, J. G. (1979) Excavation of three long barrows near Avebury. *Proceedings of the Prehistoric Society* 45, 207–300.

Atkinson, R. J. C. (1956) *Stonehenge.* London: Hamish Hamilton.

Atkinson, R. J. C. , Brailsford, J. N. and Wakefield, H. G. (1951) A pond barrow at Winterbourne Steepleton, Dorset. *Archaeological Journal* 108, 1–24.

Avery, M. (1982) The Neolithic causewayed enclosure, Abingdon. In: H. J. Case and A. W. R. Whittle (eds) *Settlement Patterns in the Oxford Region*, 10–50.

Bachelard, G. (1964) *The Poetics of Space.* Boston: Beacon Press.

Bailey, A. M. (1985) The making of history: dialectics of temporality and structure in modern French social theory. *Critique of Anthropology* 5 (1), 7–31.

Bailey, G. (1981) Concepts, time-scales and explanations in economic prehistory. In: A. Sheridan and G. Bailey (eds) *Economic Archaeology*, 97–118. Oxford: British Archaeological Reports s96.

Bailey, G. (1983) Concepts of time in Quaternary prehistory. *Annual Review of Anthropology* 12, 165–92.

Bakels, C. C. (1982) The settlement system of the Dutch Linearbandkeramik. *Analecta Praehistorica Leidensia* 15, 31–43.

Bakels, C. C. (1987) On the adzes of the northwestern Linearbandkeramik. *Analecta Praehistorica Leidensia* 20, 53–85.

Barker, P. (1977) *Techniques of Archaeological Excavation.* London: Batsford.

Barrett, J. C. (1980) The evolution of later Bronze Age settlement. In: J. C. Barrett and R. J. Bradley (eds) *The British Later Bronze Age*, 77–100. Oxford: British Archaeological Reports.

Barrett, J. C. (1988a) Fields of discourse: reconstituting a social archaeology. *Critique of Anthropology* 7 (3), 5–16.

Barrett, J. C. (1988b) The living, the dead, and the ancestors: Neolithic and Early Bronze Age mortuary practices. In: J. C. Barrett and I. A. Kinnes (eds) *The Archaeology of Context in the Neolithic and Bronze Age,* 30–41. Sheffield: Department of Archaeology and Prehistory.

Barrett, J. C. (1991) Towards an archaeology of ritual. In: P. Garwood, D. Jennings, R. Skeates and J. Toms (eds) *Sacred and Profane.* Oxford: Oxford University Committee for Archaeology Monograph No. 32, 1–9.

Barrett, J. C. (1994) *Fragments From Antiquity.* Oxford: Blackwell.

Barrett, J. C., Bradley, R. J. and Green, M. (1991) *Landscape, Monuments and Society: The Prehistory of Cranborne Chase.* Cambridge: Cambridge University Press.

Barth, F. (1987) *Cosmologies in the Making: A Generative Approach to Cultural Variation in Inner New Guinea.* Cambridge: Cambridge University Press.

Barthes, R. (1981) Theory of the text. In: R. Young (ed.) *Untying the Text,* 31–47. London: Routledge & Kegan Paul.

Bassin, M. (1987a) Imperialism and the nation state in Friedrich Ratzel's political geography. *Progress in Human Geography* 11, 473–95.

Bassin, M. (1987b) Race contra space: the conflict between German *Geopolitik* and National Socialism. *Political Geography Quarterly* 6, 115–34.

Battaglia, D. (1990) *On the Bones of the Serpent: Person, Memory and Mortality in Sabarl Island Society.* Chicago: University of Chicago.

Behrens, H. (1981) The first 'Woodhenge' in central Europe. *Antiquity* 55, 172–8.

Bell, J. A. (1994) Interpretation and testability in theories about prehistoric thinking. In: C. Renfrew and E. Zubrow (eds) *The Ancient Mind: Elements of Cognitive Archaeology,* 15–21. Cambridge: Cambridge University Press.

Bellamy, P. S. (1991) The excavation of Fordington Farm round barrow. *Proceedings of the Dorset Natural History and Archaeological Society* 113, 107–32.

Bender, B. (1985) Prehistoric developments in the American midcontinent and in Brittany, northwest France. In: T. D. Proce and J. M. Brown (eds) *Prehistoric Hunter-Gatherers: The Emergence of Complexity,* 21–57. Orlando: Academic Press.

Bender, B. (1992) Theorising landscapes, and the prehistoric landscapes of Stonehenge. *Man* 27, 735–56.

Bender, B. (1993) Stonehenge – contested landscapes (medieval to present day). In: B. Bender (ed.) *Landscape – Politics and Perspectives.* London: Berg.

Berger, J. (1984) *And Our Faces, My Heart, Brief as Photos.* London: Readers and Writers.

Bertalanffy, L. von (1969) *General Systems Theory.* New York: Braziller.

Best, M. E. (1965) Excavation of three barrows on the Ridgeway, Bincombe. *Proceedings of the Dorset Natural History and Archaeological Society* 86, 102–3.

Bhabha, H. K. (1994) *The Location of Culture.* London: Routledge.

Bhaskar, R. (1989) *Reclaiming Reality: A Critical Introduction to Contemporary Philosophy.* London: Verso.

Binford, L. R. (1962) Archaeology as anthropology. *American Antiquity* 28, 217–25.

Binford, L. R. (1963) "Red ochre" caches from the Michigan area: a possible case of cultural drift. *Southwestern Journal of Anthropology* 19, 89–108.

Binford, L. R. (1965) Archaeological systematics and the study of culture process. *American Antiquity* 31, 203–10.

Binford, L. R. (1972a) Some comments on historical versus processual archaeology. In: L. R. Binford, *An Archaeological Perspective,* 114–21. New York: Seminar Press.

Binford, L. R. (1972b) Comments on evolution. In: L. R. Binford, *An Archaeological Perspective*, 105–113. New York: Seminar Press.

Binford, L. R. (1973) Interassemblage variability – the Mousterian and the 'functional' argument. In: A. C. Renfrew (ed.) *The Explanation of Culture Change*, 227–54. London: Duckworth.

Binford, L. R. (1981) Behavioral archaeology and the "Pompeii Premise". *Journal of Anthropological Research* 37, 195–208.

Binford, L. R. (1982a) Objectivity – explanation – archaeology 1981. In: C. Renfrew, M. Rowlands and B. Seagraves (eds) *Theory and Explanation in Archaeology*, 125–38. London: Academic Press.

Binford, L. R. (1982b) The archaeology of place. *Journal of Anthropological Archaeology* 1, 5–31.

Binford, L. R. (1983) *In Pursuit of the Past: Decoding the Archaeological Record*. London: Thames and Hudson.

Binford, L. R. (1987) Data, relativism and archaeological science. *Man* 22, 391–404.

Binford, L. R. (1989) The 'New Archaeology' then and now. In: C. C. Lamberg-Karlovsky (ed.) *Archaeological Thought in America*, 50–62. Cambridge: Cambridge University Press.

Bintliff, J. L. (ed.) (1991b) *The Annales School and Archaeology*. Leicester: Leicester University Press.

Bintliff, J. L. (1991a) Post-modernism, rhetoric and scholasticism at TAG: the current state of British archaeological theory. *Antiquity* 65, 274–8.

Blattner, W. D. (1992) Existential temporality in *Being and Time* (why Heidegger is not a pragmatist). In: H. Dreyfus and H. Hall (eds) *Heidegger: A Critical Reader*, 99–129. Oxford: Blackwell.

Bogucki, P. (1987) The establishment of agrarian communities on the North European plain. *Current Anthropology* 28, 1–24.

Bogucki, P. (1988) *Forest Farmers and Stockherders*. Cambridge: Cambridge University Press.

Bogucki, P. and Grygiel, P. (1981) Early Neolithic sites at Brześć Kujawski, Poland: preliminary report on the 1976–1979 excavations. *Journal of Field Archaeology* 8, 9–27.

Bogucki, P. and Grygiel, P. (1986) Early Neolithic sites at Brześć Kujawski, Poland: preliminary report on the 1980–1984 excavations. *Journal of Field Archaeology* 13, 121–37.

Bogucki, P. and Grygiel, P. (1993a) The first farmers of central Europe: a survey article. *Journal of Field Archaeology* 20, 399–426.

Bogucki, P. and Grygiel, P. (1993b) Neolithic sites in the Polish lowlands: research at Brześć Kujawski, 1933 to 1984. In: P. Bogucki (ed.) *Case-Studies in European Prehistory*, 147–180. Boca Raton: CRC Press.

Borofsky, R. (1987) *Making History: Pukapukan and Anthropological Constructions of Knowledge*. Cambridge: Cambridge University Press.

Boujot, C. and Cassen, S. (1992) Le developpement des premières architectures funeraires monumentales en France occidentale. In: C. T. Le Roux (ed.) *Paysans et Bâtisseurs: L'Emergence du Néolithique Atlantique et les Origines du Mégalithisme*, 195–211. Vannes: Revue Archéologique de l'Ouest, supplément 5.

Boujot, C. and Cassen, S. (1993) A pattern of evolution for the Neolithic funerary structures of the west of France. *Antiquity* 67, 477–91.

Bourdieu, P. (1970) The Berber house or the world reversed. *Social Science Information* 9, 151–70.

Bourdieu, P. (1977) *Outline of a Theory of Practice*. Cambridge: Cambridge University Press.

Bourdieu, P. (1990a) *The Political Ontology of Martin Heidegger.* Cambridge: Polity Press.

Bourdieu, P. (1990b) *The Logic of Practice.* Cambridge: Polity Press.

Boyd-Dawkins, W. (1902) On the cairn and sepulchral cave at Gop, near Prestatyn. *Archaeologia Cambrensis* 6th series, 2, 161–81.

Bradley, R. J. (1975) Maumbury Rings, Dorchester: the excavations of 1908–13. *Archaeologia* 105, 1–97.

Bradley, R. J. (1982) Position and possession: assemblage variation in the British Neolithic. *Oxford Journal of Archaeology* 1, 27–38.

Bradley, R. J. (1983) The bank barrows and related monuments of Dorset in the light of recent fieldwork. *Proceedings of the Dorset Natural History and Archaeological Society* 105, 15–20.

Bradley, R. J. (1984) *The Social Foundations of Prehistoric Britain.* London: Longmans.

Bradley, R. J. (1993) *Altering the Earth.* Edinburgh: Society of Antiquaries of Scotland.

Bradley, R. J. (1994) From the house of the dead. Paper presented at the conference of the Theoretical Archaeology Group, Bradford.

Bradley, R. J. and Chapman, R. (1986) The nature and development of long-distance relations in later Neolithic Britain and Ireland. In: C. Renfrew and J. F. Cherry (eds) *Peer-Polity Interaction and Socio-Political Change,* 127–36. Cambridge: Cambridge University Press.

Bradley, R. J. and Edmonds, M. R. (1993) *Interpreting the Axe Trade.* Cambridge: Cambridge University Press.

Bradley, R. J. and Thomas, J. S. (1984) Some new information on the henge monument at Maumbury Rings, Dorchester. *Proceedings of the Dorset Natural History and Archaeological Society* 106, 132–4.

Braidwood, R. J. and Willey, G. (1962) Conclusions and afterthoughts. In: R. J. Braidwood and G. Willey (eds) *Courses Toward Urban Life,* 330–59. Chicago: Aldine.

Braudel, F. (1972) *The Mediterranean and the Mediterranean World in the Age of Phillip II.* London: Collins.

Brewster, T. C. M. (1984) *The Excavation of Whitegrounds Barrow, Burythorpe.* Wintringham: John Gett.

Brodrick, H. (1924) Fox Holes, Clapdale – a rock shelter. *Yorkshire Rambler's Club Journal* 5, 112–16.

Buchli, V. (1995) Interpreting material culture: the trouble with text. In: I. Hodder, M. Shanks, A. Alessandri, V. Buchli, J. Carman, J. Last and G. Lucas (eds) *Interpreting Archaeology: Finding Meanings in the Past,* 181–93. London: Routledge.

Burgess, C. (1974) The Bronze Age. In: C. Renfrew (ed.) *British Prehistory: A New Outline,* 165–232. London: Duckworth.

Burgess, C. (1980) *The Age of Stonehenge.* London: Dent.

Burl, H. A. W. (1976) *Stone Circles of the British Isles.* Yale: Yale University Press.

Butler, J. (1990) *Gender Trouble: Feminism and the Subversion of Identity.* London: Routledge.

Butler, J. (1993) *Bodies That Matter.* London: Routledge.

Caillaud, R. and Lagnel, E. (1972) Le cairn et le crématoire néolithiques de la Hoguette à Fontenay-le-Marmion (Calvados) *Gallia Préhistoire* 15, 137–97.

Cambell, S. F. (1983) Attaining rank: a classification of shell valuables. In: J. Leach and E. Leach (eds) *The Kula: New Perspectives on Massim Exchange,* 229–48. Cambridge: Cambridge University Press.

Carlstein, T. (1982) *Time Resources, Society and Ecology. Vol. 1: Preindustrial Societies.* London: Allen & Unwin.

Case, H. J. (1969) Neolithic explanations. *Antiquity* 43, 176–86.

Case, H. J. (1977) The Beaker Culture in Britain and Ireland. In: R. Mercer (ed.) *Beakers in Britain and Europe,* 71–101. Oxford: British Archaeological Reports S26.

Cassen, S. (1993a) Le Néolithique le plus ancien de la façade atlantique de la France. *Munibe* 45, 119–29.

Cassen, S. (1993b) Material culture and chronology of the middle Neolithic of western France. *Oxford Journal of Archaeology* 12 (2), 197–208.

Chancerel, A. , Desloges, J. , Dron, J.-L. , and San Juan, G. (1992) Le debut du Néolithique en Basse-Normandie. In: C. T. Le Roux (ed.) *Paysans at Bâtisseurs: L'émergence du Néolithique Atlantique et les Origines du Mégalithisme,* 153–73. Rennes: Revue Archéologique de l'Ouest, Supplément No. 5.

Chappell, S. (1987) *Stone Axe Morphology and Distribution in Neolithic Britain.* Oxford: British Archaeological Reports 177.

Cherry, J. F. (1981) Pattern and process in the earliest colonisation of the Mediterranean islands. *Proceedings of the Prehistoric Society* 47, 41–68.

Childe, V. G. (1926) *The Dawn of European Civilisation.* London: Kegan Paul.

Childe, V. G. (1936) *Man Makes Himself.* London: Watts.

Childe, V. G. (1940) *Prehistoric Communities of the British Isles.* London: Chambers.

Childe, V. G. (1942) *What Happened in History.* Harmondsworth: Penguin.

Childe, V. G. (1950) *Prehistoric Migrations in Europe.* Oslo: Aschehaug.

Chippindale, C. (1990) The Stonehenge phenomenon. In: C. Chippindale *et al.* (eds) *Who Owns Stonehenge?* London: Batsford.

Clark, J. G. D. (1934) Derivative forms of the *petit tranchet* in Britain. *Archaeological Journal* 91, 32–58.

Clark, J. G. D. and Piggott, S. (1933) The age of the British flint mines. *Antiquity* 7, 166–83.

Clark, J. G. D. and Rankine, W. F. (1939) Excavations at Farnham, Surrey, 1937–8. *Proceedings of the Prehistoric Society* 5, 61–118.

Clark, S. (1985) The *Annales* historians. In: Q. Skinner (ed.) *The Rise of Grand Theory in the Human Sciences,* 177–98. Cambridge: Cambridge University Press.

Clark, S. H. (1990) *Paul Ricoeur.* London: Routledge.

Clarke, D. L. (1968) *Analytical Archaeology.* London: Methuen.

Clarke, D. L. (1970) *Beaker Pottery of Great Britain and Ireland.* Cambridge: Cambridge University Press.

Clarke, D. L. (1976) Spatial information in archaeology. In: D. L. Clarke (ed.) *Spatial Archaeology,* 1–32. Academic Press.

Clay, B. C. (1992) Other times, other places: agency and the big man in central New Ireland. *Man* 27, 719–33.

Cleal, R. (1991) The earlier prehistoric pottery. In: N. Sharples (ed.), *Maiden Castle: Excavations and Field Survey 1985–6,* 171–85. London: English Heritage.

Clifford, J. (1988) *The Predicament of Culture.* Cambridge, Massachusetts: Harvard University Press.

Constantin, C. and Demoule, J. P. (1982) Éléments non-Rubanés du Néolithique ancien entre les valées du Rhin Inférieur et de la Seine. VI – groupe de Villeneuve-Saint-Germain. *Helenium* 22, 254–71.

Coope, G. R. (1979) The influence of geology on the manufacture of Neolithic and Bronze Age stone implements in the British Isles. In: T. Clough and W. Cummins (eds) *Stone Axe Studies,* 98–101. London: Council for British Archaeology.

Cosgrove, D. E. (1984) *Social Formation and Symbolic Landscape.* London: Croom Helm.

Coudart, A. (1987) Spatial organisation, architectural style and relationships between domestic units in a small-scale sedentary egalitarian society. Paper presented at the conference of the Theoretical Archaeology Group, Bradford.

Coudart, A. (1991) Social structure and relationships in prehistoric small-scale societies: the Bandkeramik groups in Neolithic Europe. In: S. A. Gregg (ed.) *Between Bands and States*, 295–420. Carbondale: Southern Illinois University Press.

Craddock, P. , Cowell, M. , Leese, M. and Hughes, M. (1983) The trace element composition of polished flint axes as an indicator of source. *Archaeometry* 25, 135–63.

Cunnington, M. E. (1929) *Woodhenge.* Devizes: Simpson.

Cyrek, K. , Grygiel, R. and Nowak, K. (1986) The basis for distinguishing the ceramic Neolithic in the Polish lowlands. In: T. Malinowski (ed.) *Problems of the Stone Age in Pomerania*, 95–126. Warsaw: Warsaw University Press.

Davidson, J. L. and Henshall, A. S. (1991) *The Chambered Cairns of Orkney.* Edinburgh: Edinburgh University Press.

Davies, S. , Stacey, L. and Woodward, P. (1985) Excavations at Alington Avenue, Fordington, Dorchester 1984–5: Interim report. *Proceedings of the Dorset Natural History and Archaeological Society* 107, 101–10.

De Certeau, M. (1984) *The Practice of Everyday Life.* Berkeley: University of California Press.

de Grooth, M. E. Th. (1987) The organisation of flint tool manufacture in the Dutch Bandkeramik. *Annalecta Praehistorica Leidensia* 20, 26–51.

de Grooth, M. E. Th. (1991) Socio-economic aspects of Neolithic flint mining: a preliminary study. *Helinium* 31, 153–89.

de Roever, J. P. (1979) The pottery from Swifterbant – Dutch Ertebølle? *Helenium* 19, 13–36.

Deleuze, G. and Guattari, F. (1988) *Thousand Plateaux: Capitalism and Schizophrenia Volume 2.* London: Athlone.

Derrida, J. (1986) Différence. In: M. C. Taylor (ed.) *Deconstruction in Context: Literature and Philosophy*, 396–420. Chicago: University of Chicago.

Derrida, J. (1989) *Of Spirit: Heidegger and the Question.* Chicago: Chicago University Press.

Deutsche, R. (1991) Boy's town. *Society and Space* 9, 5–30.

Dews, P. (1987) *Logics of Disintegration.* London: Verso.

Dews, P. (1989) The return of the subject in late Foucault. *Radical Philosophy* 51, 37–41.

Dixon,P. (1988) The Neolithic settlements on Crickley Hill. In: C. Burgess, P. Topping, C. Mordant and M. Madison (eds) *Enclosures and Defences in the Neolithic of Western Europe*, 75–88. Oxford: British Archaeological Reports s403.

Domańska, L. (1989) Elements of a food-producing economy in the late Mesolithic of the Polish lowland. In: C. Bonsall (ed.) *The Mesolithic in Europe*, 447–55. Edinburgh: John Donald.

Douglas, M. (1966) *Purity and Danger.* London: Routledge and Kegan Paul.

Dovey, K. (1993) Putting geometry in its place: towards a phenomenology of the design process. In: D. Seamon (ed.) *Dwelling, Seeing and Designing*, 247–69. Albany: State University of New York Press.

Drew, C. D. and Piggott, S. (1936) Two Bronze Age barrows excavated by Mr Edward Cunnington. *Proceedings of the Dorset Natural History and Archaeological Society* 58, 18–25.

Dreyfus, H. (1991) *Being-in-the-World: A Commentary on Heidegger's 'Being and Time', Division 1.* Cambridge, Massachusetts: Massachusetts Institute of Technology Press.

Dreyfus, H. (1992) Heidegger's history of the Being of equipment. In: H. Dreyfus and H. Hall (eds) *Heidegger: A Critical Reader,* 173–85. Oxford: Blackwell.

Dreyfus, H. (1993) Heidegger on the connection between nihilism, art, technology and politics. In: C. B. Guignon (ed.) *The Cambridge Companion to Heidegger,* 289–316. Cambridge: Cambridge University Press.

Duncan, J. and Duncan, N. (1988) (Re)reading the landscape. *Society and Space* 6, 117–26.

Dupré, G. and Rey, P. P. (1978) Reflections on the relevance of a theory of the history of exchange. In: D. Seddon (ed.) *Relations of Production,* 171–208. London: Frank Cass.

Edmonds, M. R. (1993) Interpreting causewayed enclosures in the past and the present. In: C. Tilley (ed.) *Interpretative Archaeology,* 99–142. London: Berg.

Edmonds, M. R. and Thomas, J. S. (1987) The Archers: an everyday story of country folk. In: A. G. Brown and M. R. Edmonds (eds) *Lithic Analysis and Later British Prehistory,* 187–99. Oxford: British Archaeological Reports 162.

Edwardson, A. R. (1965) A spirally-decorated object from Garboldisham. *Antiquity* 39, 145.

Ekholm, K. (1972) *Power and Prestige: the Rise and Fall of the Kongo Kingdom.* Uppsala: Skriv Service AB.

Eogan, G. (1983) A flint macehead from Knowth, County Meath. *Antiquity* 57, 45–6.

Eogan, G. (1991) Prehistoric and early historic culture change at Brugh Na Boinne. *Proceedings of the Royal Irish Academy* 91C, 105–32.

Evans, J. G. , Rouse, A. J. and Sharples, N. M. (1988) The landscape setting of causewayed camps: some recent work on the Maiden Castle enclosure. In: J. C. Barrett and I. A. Kinnes (eds) *The Archaeology of Context in the Neolithic and Bronze Age: Recent Trends,* 73–84. Sheffield: J. Collis.

Farias, V. (1990) *Heidegger and Nazism.* Philadelphia: Temple University Press.

Fentress, J. and Wickham, C. (1992) *Social Memory.* Oxford: Blackwell.

Ferry, L. and Renaut, A. (1990) *Heidegger and Modernity.* Chicago: University of Chicago Press.

Fischer, A. (1982) Trade in Danubian shafthole axes and introduction of Neolithic economy in Denmark. *Journal of Danish Archaeology* 1, 7–12.

Flannery, K. V. (1972) Culture history versus culture process: a debate in American archaeology. In: M. P. Leone (ed.) *Contemporary Archaeology,* 102–7. Carbondale: Southern Illinois University Press.

Fleming, A. (1971) Territorial patterns in Bronze Age Wessex. *Proceedings of the Prehistoric Society* 37, 138–66.

Forde-Johnson, J. (1958) The excavation of two barrows at Frampton, Dorset. *Proceedings of the Dorset Natural History and Archaeological Society* 80, 111–32.

Foucault, M. (1970) *The Order of Things.* London: Tavistock.

Foucault, M. (1972) *The Archaeology of Knowledge.* London: Tavistock.

Foucault, M. (1977) Intellectuals and power. In: D. Bouchard (ed.) *Language, Counter-Memory, Practice,* 205–17. Oxford: Blackwell.

Foucault, M. (1980) Two lectures. In: C. Gordon (ed.) *Power/Knowledge,* 78–108. Brighton: Harvester.

Foucault, M. (1981) The order of discourse. In: R. Young (ed.) *Untying the Text,* 48–78. London: Routledge & Kegan Paul.

Foucault, M. (1984a) Space, knowledge, and power. In: P. Rabinow (ed.) *The Foucault Reader*, 239–56. Harmondsworth: Peregrine.

Foucault, M. (1984b) Nietzsche, genealogy, history. In: P. Rabinow (ed.) *The Foucault Reader*, 76–100. Harmondsworth: Peregrine.

Foucault, M. (1984c) What is enlightenment? In: P. Rabinow (ed.) *The Foucault Reader*, 32–50. Harmondsworth: Peregrine.

Foucault, M. (1985) *The Use of Pleasure.* Harmondsworth: Peregrine.

Foucault, M. (1988a) Technologies of the self. In: L. Martin, H. Gutman and P. Hutton (eds) *Technologies of the Self: A Seminar With Michel Foucault*, 16–49. London: Tavistock.

Foucault, M. (1988b) The ethic of care for the self as a practice of freedom. In: J. Bernauer and D. Rasmussen (eds) *The Final Foucault*, 1–20. Cambridge, Massachusetts: Massachusetts Institute of Technology Press.

Francis, E. L. , Francis, P. J. and Preston, J. (1988) The petrological identification of stone implements from Ireland. In: T. Clough and W. Cummins (eds) *Stone Axe Studies, Volume 2*, 137–40. London: Council for British Archaeology.

Friedman, J. (1976) Marxist theory and systems of total reproduction. Part 1: Negative. *Critique of Anthropology* 7 (2), 3–16.

Friedman, J. (1989) Culture, identity and world process. In: D. Miller, M. Rowlands and C. Tilley (eds) *Domination and Resistance*, 246–60. London: Unwin Hyman.

Friedman, J. and Rowlands, M. (1977). Notes towards an epigenetic model of the evolution of 'civilisation'. In: J. Friedman and M. Rowlands (eds), *The Evolution of Social Systems*, 201–76. London, Duckworth.

Fritz, J. (1978) Palaeopsychology today: ideational systems and human adaptation in prehistory. In: C. Redman *et al.* (eds) *Social Archaeology: Beyond Subsistence and Dating*, 37–60. London: Academic Press.

Garwood, P. (1991) Ritual tradition and the reconstitution of society. In P. Garwood, D. Jennings, R. Skeates and J. Toms (eds) *Sacred and Profane*, 10–32. Oxford: Oxford University Committee for Archaeology Monograph No. 32.

Gathercole, P. (1989) Childe's early Marxism. In: V. Pinsky and A. Wylie (eds) *Critical Traditions in Contemporary Archaeology*, 80–7. Cambridge: Cambridge University Press.

Geertz, C. (1973) Person, time and conduct in Bali. In: C. Geertz, *The Interpretation of Cultures*, 360–411. New York: Basic Books.

Gelven, M. (1989) *A Commentary on Heidegger's 'Being and Time'.* De Kalb: Northern Illinois University Press.

Gerloff, S. (1975) *The Early Bronze Age Daggers of Great Britain.* Munich: C. H. Beck/Praehistorische Bronzefunde.

Gibson, A. (1982) *Beaker Domestic Sites.* Oxford: British Archaeological Reports 107.

Gibson, W. J. (1944) Mace-heads of 'cushion' type in Britain. *Proceedings of the Society of Antiquaries of Scotland* 78, 16–25.

Giddens, A. (1981) *A Contemporary Critique of Historical Materialism, Volume 1.* London: Macmillan.

Giddens, A. (1984) *The Constitution of Society.* Cambridge: Polity Press.

Giddens, A. (1987) Time and social organisation. In: A. Giddens, *Social Theory and Modern Sociology*, 140–65. Cambridge: Polity Press.

Giddens, A. (1991) *Modernity and Self-Identity: Self and Society in the Late Modern Age.* Cambridge: Polity Press.

Gilks, J. A. (1973) The Neolithic and Early Bronze Age pottery from Elbolton Cave, Wharfdale. *Yorkshire Archaeological Journal* 45, 41–54.

Gilks, J. A. (1976) Excavations in a cave on Raven Scar, Ingleton, 1973–5. *Transactions of the British Cave Research Association* 3, 95–9.

Gilks, J. A. (1990) The prehistoric pottery from Fissure Cave and New Cave, Hartle Dale, near Bradwell, Derbyshire. *Derbyshire Archaeological Journal* 110, 6–23.

Gilks, J. A. and Lord, T. C. (1985) A late Neolithic crevice burial from Selside, Ribblesdale, North Yorkshire. *Yorkshire Archaeological Journal* 57, 1–5.

Goody, J. (1962) *Death, Property and the Ancestors*. London: Tavistock.

Gosden, C. (1989) Debt, production and prehistory. *Journal of Anthropological Archaeology* 8, 355–87.

Gosden, C. (1994) *Social Being and Time*. Oxford: Basil Blackwell.

Green, H. S. (1980) *The Flint Arrowheads of the British Isles*. Oxford: British Archaeological Reports 75.

Green, S. (1987) *Excavations at Poundbury. Volume 1: The Settlements*. Dorchester, Dorset Natural History and Archaeological Society Monograph 7.

Gregory, D. (1978) *Ideology, Science and Human Geography*. Hutchinson.

Gregory, D. (1989) Presences and absences: time–space relations and structuration theory. In: D. Held and J. Thompson (eds) *Social Theory of Modern Societies*, 185–214. Cambridge: Cambridge University Press.

Gregory, D. (1990) Chinatown, part three? Soja and the missing spaces of social theory. *Strategies* 3, 40–104.

Grinsell, L. V. (1959) *Dorset Barrows*. Dorchester: Dorset Natural History and Archaeological Society.

Gronenborn, D. (1990) Mesolithic-Neolithic interactions – the lithic industry of the earliest Bandkeramik site at Friedberg-Bruchenbrüken, Wetteraukreis (West Germany). In: P. M. Vermeersch and P. van Peer (eds) *Contributions to the Mesolithic in Europe*, 173–82. Leuven: Leuven University Press.

Grygiel, R. (1984) The household cluster as a fundamental social unit of the Brześć Kujawski Group of the Lengyel Culture in the Polish lowlands. *Prace I Materialy* 31, 43–270.

Haar, M. (1991) *The Song of the Earth: Heidegger and the Grounds of the History of Being*. Bloomington: Indiana University Press.

Habermas, J. (1993) Martin Heidegger: on the publication of the lectures of 1935. In: R. Wolin (ed.) *The Heidegger Controversy: A Critical Reader*, 186–97. Cambridge, Massachusetts: MIT Press.

Hacking, I. (1986) Self improvement. In: D. C. Hoy (ed.) *Foucault: A Critical Reader*, 235–40. Oxford: Blackwell.

Haraway, D. (1991) *Simians, Cyborgs and Women: The Reinvention of Nature*. London: Free Association Books.

Harding, P. (1988) The chalk plaque pit, Amesbury. *Proceedings of the Prehistoric Society* 54, 320–6.

Harries, K. (1993) Thoughts toward a non-arbitrary architecture. In: D. Seamon (ed.) *Dwelling, Seeing and Designing*, 41–60. Albany: State University of New York Press.

Harvey, D. (1973) *Social Justice and the City*. London: Edward Arnold.

Haugeland, J. (1992) Dasein's disclosedness. In: H. Dreyfus and H. Hall (eds) *Heidegger: A Critical Reader*, 27–44. Oxford: Blackwell.

Hawkes, C. F. C. (1940) *The Prehistoric Foundations of Europe*. London: Methuen.

Healy, F. and Smith, R. (forthcoming) Communal monuments and burials. In: *The Dorchester By-Pass: Excavations and Field Survey*. London: English Heritage.

Heidegger, M. (1959) *An Introduction to Metaphysics*. New Haven: Yale University Press.

Heidegger, M. (1962) *Being and Time*, translated by J. Macquarrie and E. Robinson. Oxford: Blackwell.

Heidegger, M. (1971a) The origin of the work of art. In: M. Heidegger, *Poetry, Language, Thought*, 15–88. New York: Harper & Row.

Heidegger, M. (1971b) The thing. In: M. Heidegger, *Poetry, Language, Thought*, 163–86. New York: Harper & Row.

Heidegger, M. (1971c) '... Poetically man dwells ...' In: M. Heidegger, *Poetry, Language, Thought*, 211–29. New York: Harper & Row.

Heidegger, M. (1977a) The question concerning technology. In: M. Heidegger, *The Question Concerning Technology and Other Essays*, 3–35. New York: Harper & Row.

Heidegger, M. (1977b) Building dwelling thinking. In: D. F. Krell (ed.) *Martin Heidegger: Basic Writings*, 319–40. London: Routledge & Kegan Paul.

Heidegger, M. (1993a) "Only a god can save us": *Der Spiegel's* interview with Martin Heidegger. In: R. Wolin (ed.) *The Heidegger Controversy: A Critical Reader*, 91–116. Cambridge, Massachusetts: MIT Press.

Heidegger, M. (1993b) The self-assertion of the German university. In: R. Wolin (ed.) *The Heidegger Controversy: A Critical Reader*, 29–39. Cambridge, Massachusetts: MIT Press.

Heidegger, M. (1993c) Modern science, metaphysics and mathematics. In: D. F. Krell (ed.) *Martin Heidegger: Basic Writings* (Second Edition), 267–305. London: Routledge.

Heidegger, M. (1993d) Overcoming metaphysics. In: R. Wolin (ed.) *The Heidegger Controversy: A Critical Reader*, 67–90. Cambridge, Massachusetts: MIT Press.

Heidegger, M. (1993e) Letter on humanism. In: D. F. Krell (ed.) *Martin Heidegger: Basic Writings* (Second Edition), 213–65. London: Routledge.

Heidegger, M. (1993f) What is metaphysics?. In: D. F. Krell (ed.) *Martin Heidegger: Basic Writings* (Second Edition), 89–109. London: Routledge.

Helms, M. (1979) *Ancient Panama: Chiefs in Search of Power*. Austin: University of Texas.

Herne, A. (1988) A time and a place for the Grimston bowl. In: J. C. Barrett and I. A. Kinnes (eds) *The Archaeology of Context in the Neolithic and Bronze Age: Recent Trends*, 2–29. Sheffield: Department of Archaeology and Prehistory.

Hibbs, J. (1983) The Neolithic of Brittany and Normandy. In: C. Scarre (ed.) *Ancient France*, 271–323. Edinburgh: Edinburgh University Press.

Hodder, I. R. (1974) Regression analysis of some trade and marketing patterns. *World Archaeology* 6, 172–89.

Hodder, I. R. (1982) Theoretical archaeology: a reactionary view. In: I. Hodder (ed.) *Symbolic and Structural Archaeology*, 1–16. Cambridge: Cambridge University Press.

Hodder, I. R. (1984) Burials, houses, women and men in the European Neolithic. In: D. Miller and C. Tilley (eds) *Ideology, Power and Prehistory*, 51–68. Cambridge: Cambridge University Press.

Hodder, I. R. (1985) Post-processual archaeology. In: M. B. Schiffer (ed.) *Advances in Archaeological Method and Theory*, Vol. 8, 1–26. London: Academic Press.

Hodder, I. R. (1986) *Reading the Past: Current Approaches to Interpretation in Archaeology*. Cambridge: Cambridge University Press.

Hodder, I. R. (1988) Material culture texts and social change: a theoretical discussion and some archaeological examples. *Proceedings of the Prehistoric Society* 54, 67–76.

Hodder, I. R. (1989) This is not an article about material culture as text. *Journal of Anthropological Archaeology* 8, 250–69.

Hodder, I. R. (1990) *The Domestication of Europe*. Oxford: Blackwell.

Hodder, I. R. and Orton, C. (1976) *Spatial Analysis in Archaeology*. Cambridge University Press.

Hodgson, J. (1988) Neolithic enclosures in the Isar Valley, Bavaria. In: C. Burgess, P. Topping, C. Mordant and M. Maddison (eds) *Enclosures and Defenses in the Neolithic of Western Europe*, 363–90. Oxford: British Archaeological Reports s403.

Houlder, C. (1968) The henge monuments at Llandegai. *Antiquity* 42, 216–31.

Hugh-Jones, C. (1979) *From the Milk River*. Cambridge: Cambridge University Press.

Illet, M. (1983) The early Neolithic of north-east France. In: C. Scarre (ed.) *Ancient France*, 6–33. Edinburgh: Edinburgh University Press.

Ilett, M. , Constantin, C. , Coudart, A. and Demoule, J. P. (1982) The late Bandkeramik of the Aisne valley: environmental and spatial organisation. *Analecta Praehistorica Leidensia* 15, 45–61.

Ingold, T. (1984) Time, social relations and the exploitation of animals: anthropological reflections on prehistory. In: J. Clutton-Brock and C. Grigson (eds) *Animals in Archaeology Vol. 3: Early Herders and their Flocks*, 3–12. Oxford: British Archaeological Reports s202.

Ingold, T. (1986a) *Evolution and Social Life*. Cambridge: Cambridge University Press.

Ingold, T. (1986b) *The Appropriation of Nature: Essays on Human Ecology and Social Relations*. Manchester: Manchester University Press.

Ingold, T. (1993) The temporality of the landscape. *World Archaeology* 25, 152–74.

Ingold, T. (forthcoming). 'People like us': the concept of the anatomically modern human. Paper presented at the Pithecanthropus Centennial Congress, Leiden 1993.

Jager, B. (1985) Body, house and city: the intertwinings of embodiment, inhabitation and civilisation. In: D. Seamon and R. Mugerauer (eds) *Dwelling, Place and Environment*, 215–25. New York: Columbia University.

Jay, M. (1984) *Marxism and Totality: the Adventures of a Concept from Lukács to Habermas*. Cambridge: Polity.

Johnson, H. and Olsen, B. (1992) Hermeneutics and archaeology: on the philosophy of contextual archaeology. *American Antiquity* 57 (3), 419–36.

Jones, S. (forthcoming). Discourses of identity in the interpretation of the past. In: Gamble, C. , Graves, P. and Jones, S. (eds) *European Communities: Archaeology and the Construction of National Identity*. London: Routledge.

Jordanova, L. (1989) *Sexual Visions: Images of Gender in Science and Medicine Between the Eighteenth and Twentieth Centuries*. London: Harvester Wheatsheaf.

Josephides, L. (1991) Metaphors, metathemes, and the construction of sociality: a critique of the new Melanesian ethnography. *Man* 26, 145–61.

Kant, I. (1901) Transcendental aesthetic. In: J. Watson (ed.) *The Philosophy of Kant*, 22–39. Glasgow: J. Maclehose and Sons.

Kaye, H. J. (1984) *The English Marxist Historians*. Cambridge: Polity Press.

Keeley, L. H. (1992) The introduction of agriculture to the western north European plain. In: A. B. Gebauer and T. D. Price (eds) *Transitions to Agriculture in Prehistory*, 81–95. Madison: Prehistory Press.

Keeley, L. H. and Cahen, D. (1989) Early Neolithic forts and villages in N. E. Belgium: a preliminary report. *Journal of Field Archaeology* 16, 157–76.

Keiller, A. , Piggott, S. and Wallis, F. S. (1941) First report of the sub-committee on the petrological identification of stone axes. *Proceedings of the Prehistoric Society* 7, 50–72.

Kenworthy, J. B. (1977) A reconsideration of the 'Ardiffery' finds, Cruden, Aberdeenshire. *Proceedings of the Society of Antiquaries of Scotland* 108, 80–93.

Kenworthy, J. B. (1981) The flint axe-blade and its cultural context. *Proceedings of the Society of Antiquaries of Scotland* 111, 189–92.

Kinnes, I. A. (1982) Les Fouaillages and megalithic origins. *Antiquity* 56, 24–30.

Kinnes, I. A. (1984) Microliths and megaliths: monumental origins on the Atlantic fringe. In: G. Burrenhult (ed.) *The Archaeology of Carrowmore*, 367–70. Stockholm: University of Stockholm.

Kinnes, I. A. (1985) Circumstance not context: the Neolithic of Scotland as seen from outside. *Proceedings of the Society of Antiquaries of Scotland* 115, 115–57.

Kinnes, I. A. (1988) The cattleship Potempkin: the first Neolithic in Britain. In: J. Barrett and I. Kinnes (eds) *The Archaeology of Context in the Neolithic and Bronze Age*, 2–8. Sheffield.

Kinnes, I. A. (1992) *Non-Megalithic Long Barrows and Allied Structures in the British Neolithic.* London: British Museum.

Kinnes, I. A., Gibson, A. and Needham, S. (1983) A dating programme for British Beakers. *Antiquity* 57, 218–19.

Kinnes, I. A., Gibson, A., Ambers, J., Bowman, S., Leese, M. and Boast, R. (1991) Radiocarbon dating and British Beakers: the British Museum programme. *Scottish Archaeological Review* 8, 35–68.

Kinnes, I. A., Schadla-Hall, T., Chadwick, P. and Dean, P. (1983) Duggleby Howe reconsidered. *Archaeological Journal* 140, 83–108.

Kirk, T. (1991) Structure, agency and power relations *'chez les derniers chasseurs-cueilleurs'* of northwest France. In: R. W. Preucel (ed.) *Processual and Post-processual Archaeologies*, 108–25. Carbondale: Southern Illinois University Press.

Kirk, T. (1993) Space, subjectivity, power and hegemony: megaliths and long mounds in the earlier Neolithic of Brittany. In: C. Tilley (ed.) *Interpretative Archaeology*, 181–24. London: Berg.

Kirk, T. (1995) Constructions of death in the early Neolithic of the Paris Basin. In: M. Edmonds and C. Richards (eds) *Understanding the Neolithic of North-Western Europe.* Glasgow: Cruithne Press.

Kopytoff, I. (1986) The cultural biography of things: commodification as process. In: A. Appadurai (ed.) *The Social Life of Things*, 64–91. Cambridge: Cambridge University Press.

Kozlowski, J. K. (1989) The lithic industry of the eastern Linear Pottery Culture in Slovakia. *Slovenska Archaeologia* 37, 377–98.

Kreutz, A. M. (1990) Die ersten bauern Mitteleuropas. *Annalecta Praehistorica Leidensia* 23, 1–251.

Kristeva, J. (1986a) Women's time. In: T. Moi (ed.) *The Kristeva Reader*, 187–213. Oxford: Blackwell.

Kristeva, J. (1986b) Word, dialogue and novel. In: T. Moi (ed.) *The Kristeva Reader*, 34–61. Oxford: Blackwell.

Kukzycka-Leciejewiczawa, A. (1983) The oldest Linear Pottery communities and their contribution to the neolithization of Polish territories. *Archaeologia Polona* 21/22, 47–61.

Lacan, J. (1977) The mirror stage as formative of the function of the I. In: J. Lacan, *Écrits: A Selection*, 1–7. London: Tavistock.

Laclau, E. and Mouffe, C. (1985) *Hegemony and Socialist Strategy: Towards a Radical Democratic Politics.* London: Verso.

Laclau, E. and Mouffe, C. (1987) Post-Marxism without apologies. *New Left Review* 166, 79–106.

Lacoue-Labarthe, P. (1990) *Heidegger, Art and Politics.* Oxford: Blackwell.

LaFontaine, J. S. (1978) Introduction. In: J. S. LaFontaine (ed.) *Sex and Age as Principles of Social Differentiation*, 1–20. London: Academic Press.

Lang, R. (1985) The dwelling door: towards a phenomenology of transition. In: D. Seamon and R. Mugerauer (eds) *Dwelling, Place and Environment*, 201–14. New York: Columbia University.

Lanting, J. N. and Van der Waals, J. D. (1972) British Beakers as seen from the continent. *Helenium* 12, 20–46.

Larsson, L. (1988) A construction for ceremonial activities from the late Mesolithic. *Meddelanden Från Lunds Universitets Historiska Museum* 7, 5–18.

Larsson, L. (1990) The Mesolithic of southern Scandinavia. *Journal of World Prehistory* 4, 257–309.

Latour, B. (1993) *We Have Never Been Modern.* London: Harvester Wheatsheaf.

Le Rouzic, Z. , Péquart, M. and Péquart, S. J. (1923) *Carnac: Fouilles Faites dans la Région, Campagne 1922: Tumulus de Cruncy, Tertre du Manio, Tertre du Castellic.* Nancy.

Leakey, L. S. B. (1951) *Preliminary excavations of a Mesolithic site at Abinger Common, Surrey.* Surrey Archaeological Society Research Paper 3.

Lemert, C. G. and Gillan, G. (1982) *Michel Foucault: Social Theory as Transgression.* New York: Columbia University.

Lévi-Strauss, C. (1966) *The Savage Mind.* London: Weidenfield and Nicholson.

Lewis, G. (1980) *Day of Shining Red: An Essay on Understanding Ritual.* Cambridge: Cambridge University Press.

Lewthwaite, J. (1981) Ambiguous first impressions: a survey of recent work on the early Neolithic of the west Mediterranean. *Journal of Mediterranean Anthropology and Archaeology* 1, 292–307.

Lindstrom, L. (1990) *Knowledge and Power in a South Pacific Society.* Washington: Smithsonian Institution Press.

Longworth, I. (1979) The pottery. In: G. J. Wainwright, *Mount Pleasant, Dorset; Excavations 1970–71.* London: Society of Antiquaries.

Longworth, I. and Kinnes, I. A. (1985) *Catalogue of the Excavated Prehistoric and Romano–British Material in the Greenwell Collection.* London: British Museum Pubications.

Louwe-Kooijmans, L. P. (1976) Local developments within a borderland. *Oudheidkundige Mededelingen* 57, 226–97.

Louwe-Kooijmans, L. P. (1980) De midden-neolitische vondelsgroep van Het Vormer bij Wijchen en het cultuurpatroon rond de Zuidelijke Noordzee circa 3000 v. Chr. *Oudheidkundige Mededelingen* 61, 116–208.

Louwe-Kooijmans, L. P. (1987) Neolithic settlement and subsistence in the wetlands of the Rhine/Meuse delta of the Netherlands. In: J. Coles and A. Lawson (eds) *European Wetlands in Prehistory*, 227–51. Oxford: Clarendon.

Louwe-Kooijmans, L. P. (1993) The Mesolithic/Neolithic transformation in the lower Rhine basin. In: P. Bugucki (ed.) *Case Studies in European Prehistory*, 95–145. Boca Raton: CRC Press.

Lüning, J. (1982a) Research into the Bandkeramik settlement of the Aldenhovener Platte in the Rhineland. *Analecta Praehistorica Leidensia* 15, 1–29.

Lüning, J. (1982b) Siedlung und siedlungslandschaft in Bandkeramischer und Rössener ziet. *Offa* 1982, 9–33.

Lüning, J., Kloos, V. and Albert, S. (1989) Westliche nachbarn der Bandkeramischen Kultur: La Hoguette und Limburg. *Germania* 67, 355–420.

Lynch, F. (1969) The contents of excavated tombs in north Wales. In: T. G. E. Powell, J. W. X. P. Corcoran, F. Lynch and J. G. Scott (eds) *Megalithic Enquiries in the West of Britain*, 149–76. Liverpool: Liverpool University Press.

Lynch, F. (1976) Towards a chronology of megalithic tombs in Wales. In: G. C. Boon and J. M. Lewis (eds) *Welsh Antiquity*, 63–79. Cardiff: National Museum of Wales.

McInnes, I. (1968) Jet sliders in late Neolithic Britain. In: J. Coles and D. D. A. Simpson (eds) *Studies in Ancient Europe*, 137–44. Leicester: Leicester University Press.

MacKie, E. (1977) *Science and Society in Prehistoric Britain*. London: Elek.

MacSween, A. (1992) Orcadian Grooved Ware. In: N. Sharples and A. Sheridan (eds) *Vessels for the Ancestors: Essays on the Neolithic of Britain and Ireland*, 259–71. Edinburgh: Edinburgh University Press.

Madsen, T. (1979) Earthen long barrows and timber structures: aspects of the early Neolithic mortuary practice in Denmark. *Proceedings of the Prehistoric Society* 45, 301–20.

Maltby, J. M. (1979) *Faunal Studies on Urban Sites: the Animal Bones from Exeter 1971–1975*. Sheffield: Department of Prehistory and Archaeology.

Manby, T. G. (1974) *Grooved Ware Sites in Yorkshire and the North of England*. Oxford: British Archaeological Reports 9.

Manby, T. G. (1979) Typology, materials, and distribution of flint and stone axes in Yorkshire. In: T. Clough and W. Cummins (eds) *Stone Axe Studies*, 65–81. London: CBA.

Mansell-Playdell, J. C. (1892) An ancient interment on the Verne, Portland. *Proceedings of the Dorset Natural History and Archaeological Society* 13, 232–8.

Marcus, G. E. and Fisher, M. J. (1986) *Anthropology as Cultural Critique: An Experimental Moment in the Human Sciences*. Chicago: Chicago University Press.

Marshall, D. N. (1977) Carved stone balls. *Proceedings of the Society of Antiquaries of Scotland* 108, 40–72.

Mercer, R. J. (1980) *Hambledon Hill: a Neolithic Landscape*. Edinburgh: Edinburgh University Press.

Metcalf, P. (1981) Meaning and materialism: the ritual economy of death. *Man* 16, 563–78.

Midgley, M. S. (1985) *The Origin and Function of the Earthen Long Barrows of Northern Europe*. Oxford: British Archaeological Reports s259.

Midgley, M. S. (1992) *T. R. B. Culture: The First Farmers of the North European Plain*. Edinburgh: Edinburgh University Press.

Midgley, M. S., Pavlů, I., Rulf, J. and Zápotocká, M. (1993) Fortified settlements or ceremonial sites: new evidence from Bylany, Czechoslovakia. *Antiquity* 67, 91–6.

Milisauskas, S. (1972) An analysis of Linear Culture longhouses at Olszanica B1, Poland. *World Archaeology* 4, 57–74.

Milisauskas, S. (1973) Investigation of an early Neolithic community in Poland. *Current Anthropology* 14, 287–90.

Milisauskas, S. and Kruk, J. (1989) Neolithic economy in central Europe. *Journal of World Prehistory* 3, 403–46.

Milisauskas, S. and Kruk, J. (1993) Archaeological investigations on Neolithic and Bronze Age sites in southeastern Poland. In: P. Bogucki (ed.) *Case Studies in European Prehistory*, 63–94. Boca Raton: CRC Press.

Miller, D. (1982) Structures and strategies: an aspect of the relationship between social hierarchy and cultural change. In: I. Hodder (ed.) *Symbolic and Structural Archaeology*, 89–98. Cambridge: Cambridge University Press.

Mizoguchi, K. (1995) The 'materiality' of Wessex Beakers. *Scottish Archaeological Review* 9, 175–85.

Modderman, P. J. R. (1975) Elsloo, a Neolithic farming community in the Netherlands. In: R. Bruce-Mitford (ed.) *Recent Archaeological Excavations in Europe*, 260–80. London: Routledge & Kegan Paul

Modderman, P. J. R. (1988) The Linear Pottery Culture: diversity in uniformity. *Berichten Van de Rijksdienst voor het Oudheidkundig Bodermonderzoek* 38, 63–139.

Moore, H. (1986) *Space, Text and Gender.* Cambridge: Cambridge University Press.

Morphy, H. (1991) *Ancestral Connections.* Chicago: Chicago University Press.

Mugerauer, R. (1985) Language and the emergence of the environment. In: D. Seamon and R. Mugerauer (eds) *Dwelling, Place and Environment,* 51–70. New York: Columbia University Press.

Mugerauer, R. (1993) Towards an architectural vocabulary: the porch as a between. In: D. Seamon (ed.) *Dwelling, Seeing and Designing,* 103–28. Albany: State University of New York Press.

Murray, M. (1970) *Modern Philosophy of History: Its Origin and Destination.* The Hague: Martinus Nijhof.

Nielsen, P. O. (1986) The beginning of the Neolithic – assimilation or complex change? *Journal of Danish Archaeology* 5, 240–3.

O'Connor, T. (1991) Science, evidential archaeology and the new scholasticism. *Scottish Archaeological Review* 8, 1–8.

O'Kelly, M. and Shell, C. (1979) Stone objects and a bronze axe from Newgrange, Co. Meath. In: M. Ryan (ed.) *The Origins of Metallurgy in Atlantic Europe,* 127–44. Dublin: The Stationery Office.

Oakley, K. P. (1965) Folklore of fossils, part two. *Antiquity* 39, 117–25.

Ollman, B. (1971) *Alienation: Marx's Conception of Man in Capitalist Society.* Cambridge: Cambridge University Press.

Olafson, F. A. (1993) The unity of Heidegger's thought. In: C. Guignon (ed.) *The Cambridge Companion to Heidegger,* 97–121. Cambridge: Cambridge University Press.

Olsen, B. (1990) Roland Barthes: from sign to text. In: C. Tilley (ed.) *Reading Material Culture,* 163–205. Oxford: Blackwell.

Parry, J. (1982) Sacrificial death and the necrophagous ascetic. In: M. Bloch and J. Parry (eds) *Death and the Regeneration of Life,* 74–110. Cambridge: Cambridge University Press.

Patrik, L. (1985) Is there an archaeological record? In: M. B. Schiffer (ed.) *Advances in Archaeological Method and Theory, Volume 3,* 27–62. London: Academic Press.

Patton, M. (1994) Neolithisation and megalithic origins in north-western France: a regional interaction model. *Oxford Journal of Archaeology* 13 (3), 279–93.

Peebles, C. and Kus, S. (1977) Some archaeological correlates of ranked societies. *American Antiquity* 42, 421–48.

Peers, R. N. R. and Clarke, D. L. (1967) A Bronze Age beaker burial and Roman site at Broadmayne. *Proceedings of the Dorset Natural History and Archaeological Society* 88, 103–5.

Péquart, M. and Péquart, S. J. (1954) *Höedic, Deuxième Station Nécropole du Mésolithique Côtier Armoricain.* Anvers: De Sikkel.

Peterson, G. (1993) Kanengamah and Pohnpei's politics of concealment. *American Anthropologist* 95, 334–52.

Pfaffenberger, B. (1988) Fetishised objects and humanised nature: towards an anthropology of technology. *Man* 23, 236–52.

Phillips, P. (1982) *The Middle Neolithic in Southern France.* Oxford: British Archaeological Reports s142.

Pierpoint, S. (1980) *Social Patterns in Yorkshire Prehistory, 3500–750 BC.* Oxford: British Archaeological Reports 74.

Piggott, S. (1938) The Early Bronze Age in Wessex. *Proceedings of the Prehistoric Society* 4, 52–106.

Piggott, S. (1946) The chambered cairn of 'the Grey Mare and Colts'. *Proceedings of the Dorset Natural History and Archaeological Society* 67, 30–3.

Piggott, S. (1953) Secondary Neolithic burials at Church Dale, near Monyash, Derbyshire, 1937–9. *Proceedings of the Prehistoric Society* 19, 228–30.

Piggott, S. (1954) *The Neolithic Cultures of the British Isles.* Cambridge: Cambridge University Press.

Piggott, S. (1963) Abercromby and after: the Beaker cultures of Britain reconsidered. In: I. Ll. Foster and L. Alcock (eds) *Culture and Environmnent,* 53–91. London: Routledge & Kegan Paul.

Pitts, M. (1982) On the road to Stonehenge: report on the investigations beside the A344. *Proceedings of the Prehistoric Society* 48, 75–132.

Pöggeler, O. (1993) Heidegger's political self-understanding. In: R. Wolin (ed.) *The Heidegger Controversy: A Critical Reader,* 198–244. Cambridge, Massachusetts: MIT Press.

Pollard, J. (1992) The Sanctuary, Overton Hill, Wiltshire: a reassessment. *Proceedings of the Prehistoric Society* 58, 213–26.

Powell, T. G. E. (1973) Excavation of the chambered cairn at Dyffryn Ardudwy, Merioneth, Wales. *Archaeologia* 54, 44–6.

Pred, A. (1977) The choreography of existence: comments on Hagerstrand's Time-Geography and its usefulness. *Economic Geography* 53, 207–21.

Radley, J. (1968) The York hoard of flint tools. *Yorkshire Archaeological Journal* 42, 131–2.

Raistrick, A. (1936) Excavations at Sewell's Cave, Settle, West Yorkshire. *Proceedings of the University of Durham Philosophical Society* 9, 191–204.

Ratzel, F. (1884) *A History of Ancient Times.* London: Macmillan.

Ray, K. W. (1987) Material metaphor, social interaction and historical interpretations: exploring patterns of association and symbolism in the Igbo-Ukwu corpus. In: I. R. Hodder (ed.) *The Archaeology of Contextual Meanings,* 66–77. Cambridge: Cambridge University Press.

Relph, E. (1993) Modernity and the reclamation of place. In: D. Seamon (ed.) *Dwelling, Seeing and Designing,* 25–40. Albany: State University of New York Press.

Renfrew, C. (1973) Monuments, mobilisation and social organisation in Neolithic Wessex. In: C. Renfrew (ed.) *The Explanation of Culture Change,* 539–58. London: Duckworth.

Renfrew, C. (1975) Trade as action at a distance: questions of integration and communication. In: J. A. Sabloff and C. C. Lamberg-Karlovsky (eds) *Ancient Civilisation and Trade,* 3–59. Albuquerque: University of New Mexico Press.

Renfrew, C. (1976) Megaliths, territories and population. In: S. de Laet (ed.) *Acculturation and Continuity in Atlantic Europe,* 198–220. Bruges: De Tempel.

Renfrew, C. (1979) *Investigations in Orkney.* London: Society of Antiquaries.

Renfrew, C. (1986) Introduction: peer-polity interaction and socio-political change. In: C. Renfrew and J. F. Cherry (eds) *Peer-Polity Interaction and Socio-Political Change,* 1–18. Cambridge: Cambridge University Press.

Richards, C. C. (1988) Altered images: a re-examination of Neolithic mortuary practices in Orkney. In: J. C. Barrett and I. A. Kinnes (eds) *The Archaeology of Context in the Neolithic and Bronze Age: Recent Trends,* 42–56 Sheffield, University Press.

Richards, C. C. (1993) Monumental choreography: architecture and spatial representation in late Neolithic Orkney. In: C. Tilley (ed.) *Interpretative Archaeology,* 143–78. London: Berg.

Richards, C. C. and Thomas, J. S. (1984) Ritual activity and structured deposition in later Neolithic Wessex. In: R. Bradley and J. Gardiner (eds) *Neolithic Studies*, 189–218. Oxford: BAR.

Ricoeur, P. (1981) The model of the text: meaningful action considered as a text. In: P. Ricoeur, *Hermeneutics and the Human Sciences*, 197–221. Cambridge: Cambridge University Press.

Ricoeur, P. (1984) *The Reality of the Historical Past*. Milwaukee: Marquette University Press.

Ricoeur, P. (1988) *Time and Narrative, Volume 3*. Chicago: Chicago University Press.

Ricoeur, P. (1991) Narrative identity. In: D. Wood (ed.) *On Paul Ricoeur: Narrative and Interpretation*, 188–99. London: Routledge.

Ritchie, R. (1992) Stone axeheads and cushion maceheads from Orkney and Shetland: some similarities and contrasts. In: N. Sharples and A. Sheridan (eds) *Vessels for the Ancestors*, 213–20. Edinburgh: Edinburgh University Press.

Roe, F. E. S. (1968) Stone maceheads and the latest Neolithic cultures of the British Isles. In: J. Coles and D. D. A. Simpson (eds) *Studies in Ancient Europe*, 145–72. Leicester: Leicester University Press.

Rose, G. (1993) *Feminism and Geography: The Limits of Geographical Knowledge*. Oxford: Polity Press.

Rowley-Conwy, P. (1983) Sedentary hunters: the Ertebølle example. In: G. Bailey (ed.) *Hunter-Gatherer Economy in Prehistory*, 111–26. Cambridge: Cambridge University Press.

Royal Commission on Historic Monuments (RCHM) (1970) *An Inventory of Historical Monuments in the County of Dorset. Volume 2, South-East, Part Three*. London: Her Majesty's Stationery Office.

Rubin, D. C. (1986) Introduction. In: D. C. Rubin (ed.) *Autobiographical Memory*, 3–16. Cambridge: Cambridge University Press.

Sahlins, M. (1974) *Stone Age Economics*. London: Tavistock.

Sakellaridis, M. (1979) *The Mesolithic and Neolithic of the Swiss Area*. Oxford: British Archaeological Reports s67.

Scarre, C. (1983) The Neolithic of west-central France. In: C. Scarre (ed.) *Ancient France*, 223–70. Edinburgh: Edinburgh University Press.

Scarre, C. (1992) The early Neolithic of western France and megalithic origins in Atlantic Europe. *Oxford Journal of Archaeology* 11, 121–54.

Schiffer, M. B. (1972) Archaeological context and systemic context. *American Antiquity* 37, 156–65.

Schiffer, M. B. (1987) *Formation Processes of the Archaeological Record*. Albuquerque: New Mexico University Press.

Schneider, J. and Weiner, A. B. (1989) Introduction. In: A. B. Weiner and J. Schneider (eds) *Cloth and Human Experience*, 1–29. Washington: Smithsonian Institution Press.

Schollar, I. (1959) Regional groups in the Michelsberg culture. *Proceedings of the Prehistoric Society* 25, 52–134.

Shanks, M. (1992) *Experiencing the Past*. London: Routledge.

Shanks, M. (1994) The life of an artefact. Manuscript.

Shanks, M. and Tilley, C. (1987) *Social Theory and Archaeology*. Cambridge: Polity.

Shanks, M. and Tilley, C. (1989) Archaeology into the 1990s. *Norwegian Archaeological Review* 22, 1–54.

Sharples, N. M. (1984) Excavations at Pierowall Quarry, Westray, Orkney. *Proceedings of the Society of Antiquaries of Scotland* 114, 75–125.

Sharples, N. M. (1985) Individual and community: the changing role of megaliths in the Orcadian Neolithic. *Proceedings of the Prehistoric Society* 51, 59–74.

Sharples, N. M. (1991) *Maiden Castle: Excavations and Field Survey 1985–6.* London: English Heritage.

Shee Twohig, E. (1981) *The Megalithic Art of Western Europe.* Oxford: Clarendon.

Shennan, S. J. (1982) Ideology, change and the European Early Bronze Age. In: I. Hodder (ed.) *Symbolic and Structural Archaeology,* 155–61. Cambridge: Cambridge University Press.

Sheppard, T. (1926) Hoard of Neolithic axes from East Yorkshire. *The Naturalist* 1926, 262–4.

Sheridan, A. (1992) Scottish stone axeheads: some new work and recent discoveries. In: N. Sharples and A. Sheridan (eds) *Vessels for the Ancestors,* 194–212. Edinburgh: Edinburgh University Press.

Sherratt, A. (1990) The genesis of megaliths: monumentality, ethnicity and social complexity in Neolithic north-west Europe. *World Archaeology* 22 (2), 147–67.

Sherratt, A. (1993) The relativity of theory. In: N. Yoffee and A. Sherratt (eds) *Archaeological Theory: Who Sets the Agenda?,* 119–30. Cambridge: Cambridge University Press.

Simpson, D. D. A. (1968) Food Vessels: associations and chronology. In: J. Coles and D. D. A. Simpson (eds) *Studies in Ancient Europe,* 197–209. Leicester: Leicester University Press.

Simpson, D. D. A. and Ransom, R. (1992) Maceheads and the Orcadian Neolithic. In: N. Sharples and A. Sheridan (eds) *Vessels for the Ancestors,* 221–43. Edinburgh: Edinburgh University Press.

Simpson, D. D. A. and Thawley, J. E. (1972) Single grave art in Britain. *Scottish Archaeological Forum* 4, 81–104.

Skinner, Q. (1985) (ed.) *The Return of Gand Theory in the Human Sciences.* Cambridge: Cambridge University Press.

Smart, B. (1986) The politics of truth and the problem of hegemony. In: D. C. Hoy (ed.) *Foucault: A Critical Reader,* 157–74. Oxford: Blackwell.

Smith, I. F. (1956) *The Decorative Art of Neolithic Ceramics in S. E. England and its Relations.* Unpublished Ph.D. thesis, University of London.

Smith, J. A. (1876) Notes on small ornamented balls found in different parts of Scotland. *Proceedings of the Society of Antiquaries of Scotland* 11, 29–62.

Smith, R. A. (1921) Hoards of flint celts. *Archaeologia* 21, 113–24.

Smith, R. A. (1932) Flint implements found near Wakefield. *Antiquaries Journal* 12, 449–51.

Soudský, B. (1962) The Neolithic site of Bylany. *Antiquity* 36, 190–200.

Spanos, W. V. (1993) *Heidegger and Criticism: Retrieving the Cultural Politics of Destruction.* Minneapolis: Minnesota University Press.

Starling, N. (1985) Colonisation and succession: the earlier Neolithic of central Europe. *Proceedings of the Prehistoric Society* 51, 41–58.

Startin, D. W. A. (1978) Linear Pottery Culture houses: reconstruction and manpower. *Proceedings of the Prehistoric Society* 44, 143–59.

Stevenson, R. B. K. (1947) 'Lop-sided' arrowheads. *Proceedings of the Society of Antiquaries of Scotland* 51, 179–82.

Stopes, M. C., Oakley, K. P. , and Wells, L. H. (1952) A discovery of human skulls, with stone artefacts and animal bones, in a fissure at Portland. *Proceedings of the Dorset Natural History and Archaeological Society* 74, 39–47.

Strathern, M. (1980) No nature, no culture: the Hagen case. In: C. P. MacCormack and M. Strathern (eds) *Nature, Culture and Gender,* 174–222. Cambridge: Cambridge University Press.

Strathern, M. (1988) *The Gender of the Gift.* Berkeley: University of California Press.

Strathern, M. (1990) Presentation for the motion (1). In: T. Ingold (ed.) *The Concept of Society is Theoretically Obsolete*, 4–11. Manchester: Group for Debates in Anthropological Theory.

Strum, S. and Latour, B. (1987) The meaning of social: from baboons to humans. *Social Science Information* 26, 783–802.

Stuiver, M. and Becker, B. (1993) High-precision calibration of the radiocarbon time scale AD 1950–6000 BC. *Radiocarbon* 35, 35–65.

Stuiver, M. and Pearson, G. W. (1993) High-precision bidecadal calibration of the radiocarbon time scale, AD 1950–500 BC and 2500–6000 BC. *Radiocarbon* 35, 1–23.

Sydenham, J. (1944) An account of the opening of some barrows in south Dorsetshire. *Archaeologia* 30, 327–38.

Taçon, P. S. (1991) The power of stone: symbolic aspects of stone use and tool development in western Arnhem Land, Australia. *Antiquity* 65, 192–207.

Taylor, C. (1992) Heidegger, language, and ecology. In: H. Dreyfus and H. Hall (eds) *Heidegger: A Critical Reader*, 247–69. Oxford: Blackwell.

Taylor, J. (1980) *Bronze Age Goldwork of the British Isles.* Cambridge: Cambridge University Press.

Thomas, J. S. (1988a) Neolithic explanations revisited: the Mesolithic–Neolithic transition in Britain and south Scandinavia. *Proceedings of the Prehistoric Society* 54, 59–66.

Thomas, J. S. (1988b) The social significance of Cotswold-Severn burial rites. *Man* 23, 540–59.

Thomas, J. S. (1991a) *Rethinking the Neolithic.* Cambridge: Cambridge University Press.

Thomas, J. S. (1991b) Reading the Body: Beaker funerary practice in Britain. In: P. Garwood, D. Jennings, R. Skeates and J. Toms (eds) *Sacred and Profane*, 33–42. Oxford: Oxford University Committee for Archaeology Monograph 32.

Thomas, J. S. (1992) Monuments, movement, and the context of Megalithic art. In: A. Sheridan and N. Sharples (eds) *Vessels for the Ancestors*, 143–55. Edinburgh: Edinburgh University Press.

Thomas, J. S. (1993) The politics of vision and the archaeologies of landscape. In: B. Bender (ed.) *Landscape: Politics and Perspectives*, 19–48. London: Berg.

Thomas, J. S. (1995) Where are we now? Archaeological theory in the 1990s. In: P. J. Ucko (ed.) *Archaeological Theory: A World Perspective*, 343–62. London: Routledge.

Thomas, J. S. and Tilley, C. Y. (1993) The axe and the torso: symbolic structures in Neolithic Brittany. In: C. Tilley (ed.) *Interpretative Archaeology*, 225–326. London: Berg.

Thomas, N. (1991) *Entangled Objects: Exchange, Material Culture and Colonialism in the Pacific.* Cambridge, Mass.: Harvard University Press.

Thompson, E. P. (1963) *The Making of the English Working Class.* Harmondsworth: Penguin.

Thompson, E. P. (1978) *The Poverty of Theory.* London: Merlin.

Thompson, M. W. and Ashbee, P. (1957) Excavation of a barrow near the Hardy Monument, Black Down, Portesham, Dorset. *Proceedings of the Dorset Natural History and Archaeological Society* 23, 124–36.

Thorpe, I. J. (1984) Ritual, power and ideology: a reconsideration of earlier Neolithic rituals in Wessex. In: R. J. Bradley and J. Gardiner (eds) *Neolithic Studies*, 41–60. Oxford: British Archaeological Reports 133.

Thorpe, I. J. and Richards, C. C. (1984) The decline of ritual authority and the introduction of Beakers into Britain. In: R. J. Bradley and J. Gardiner (eds)

Neolithic Studies: A Review of Some Current Research, 67–84. Oxford: British Archaeological Reports 133.

Thrift, N. (1991) For a new regional geography 2. *Progress in Human Geography* 15, 456–65.

Tilley, C. Y. (1989) Interpreting material culture. In: I. Hodder (ed.) *The Meanings of Things*, 185–94. London: Unwin Hyman.

Tilley, C. Y. (1990) (ed.) *Reading Material Culture*. Oxford: Blackwell.

Trigger, B. G. (1980) *Gordon Childe: Revolutions in Archaeology*. London: Thames & Hudson.

Trigger, B. G. (1989) *A History of Archaeological Thought*. Cambridge: Cambridge University Press.

Tringham, R. E. (1991) Households with faces: the challenge of gender in architectural remains. In: J. Gero and M. Conkey (eds) *Engendering Archaeology: Women and Prehistory*, 93–131. Oxford: Basil Blackwell.

Tschumi, B. (1994) *Architecture and Disjunction*. Cambridge, Massachusetts: MIT Press.

Ucko, P. J. (1995) Archaeological interpretation in a world context. In: P. J. Ucko (ed.) *Theory in Archaeology: A World Perspective*, 1–27. London: Routledge.

van der Velde, P. (1979) On Bandkeramik social structure. *Analecta Praehistorica Leidensia* 12, 1–242.

van der Velde, P. (1990) Bandkeramik social inequality – a case study. *Germania* 68, 19–38.

Veit, U. (1989) Ethnic concepts in prehistory: a case study on the relationship between cultural identity and archaeological objectivity. In: S. J. Shennan (ed.) *Archaeological Approaches to Cultural Identity*, 33–56. London: Unwin Hyman.

Vico, G. (1968) *The New Science*. Ithaca: Cornell University Press.

Vycinas, V. (1961) *Earth and Gods: An Introduction to the Philosophy of Martin Heidegger*. The Hague: Martinus Nijhof.

Vyner, B. (1988) The Street House Wossit: the excavation of a Late Neolithic and Early Bronze Age palisaded ritual monument from Street House, Loftus, Cleveland. *Proceedings of the Prehistoric Society* 54, 173–202.

Wainwright, G. J. (1967) The excavation of Hampton stone circle, Portesham. *Proceedings of the Dorset Natural History and Archaeological Society* 88, 103–5.

Wainwright, G. J. (1971) The excavation of a late Neolithic enclosure at Marden, Wiltshire. *Antiquaries Journal* 51, 177–239.

Wainwright, G. J. (1979) *Mount Pleasant, Dorset; Excavations 1970–71*. London: Society of Antiquaries.

Wainwright, G. J. (1989) *The Henge Monuments*. London: Thames & Hudson.

Wainwright, G. J. and Longworth, I. (1971) *Durrington Walls: Excavations 1966–1968*. London: Society of Antiquaries.

Wansleben, M and Verhart, L. B. M. (1990) Meuse valley project: the transition from the Mesolithic to the Neolithic in the Dutch Meuse valley. In: P. M. Vermeersch and P. van Peer (eds) *Contributions to the Mesolithic in Europe*, 389–42. Leuven: Leuven University Press.

Warne, C. (1866) *Ancient Dorset*. Bournemouth: Sydenham.

Weiner, A. (1992) *Inalienable Possessions: the Paradox of Keeping-While-Giving*. Berkeley: University of California Press.

Weiner, A. B. (1989) Why cloth? Wealth, gender and power in Oceania. In: A. B. Weiner and J. Schneider (eds) *Cloth and Human Experience*, 33–72. Washington: Smithsonian Institution Press.

Wheeler, R. E. M. (1943) *Maiden Castle, Dorset*. London: Society of Antiquaries.

Whittle, A. W. R. (1977) Earlier Neolithic enclosures in north-west Europe. *Proceedings of the Prehistoric Society* 43, 329–48.

Whittle, A. W. R. (1985) *Neolithic Europe: A Survey.* Cambridge: Cambridge University Press.

Whittle, A. W. R. (1991) A late Neolithic complex at West Kennet, Wiltshire, England. *Antiquity* 65, 256–62.

Whittle, A. W. R. (1995) *Europe in the Neolithic: The Making of New Worlds.* Cambridge: Cambridge University Press.

Wolin, R. (1990) *The Politics of Being: The Political Thought of Martin Heidegger.* New York: Columbia University Press.

Wood, D. (1993) Reiterating the temporal: toward a rethinking of Heidegger on time. In: J. Sallis (ed.) *Reading Heidegger: Commemorations,* 136–59. Bloomington: Indiana University Press.

Woodward, P. J. (1988) Pictures from the Neolithic: discoveries from the Flagstones House excavations, Dorchester, Dorset. *Antiquity* 62, 266–74.

Woodward, P. J. (1991) *The South Dorset Ridgeway: Survey and Excavations 1977–84.* Dorchester: Dorset Natural History and Archaeological Society.

Woodward, P. J. and Smith, R. J. (1987) Survey and exavation along the route of the southern Dorchester by-pass, 1986–7: an interim note. *Proceedings of the Dorset Natural History and Archaeological Society* 109, 79–89.

Woodward, P. J. , Davies, S. , and Graham, A. H. (1984) Excavations on the Greyhound Yard car park, Dorchester, 1984. *Proceedings of the Dorset Natural History and Archaeological Society* 106, 99–106.

Wylie, A. (1982) Epistemological problems raised by a structuralist archaeology. In: I. Hodder (ed.) *Symbolic and Structural Archaeology.* Cambridge: Cambridge University Press.

Zimmerman, M. E. (1990) *Heidegger's Confrontation With Modernity.* Bloomington: Indiana University Press.

Zimmerman, M. E. (1993) Heidegger, Buddhism and deep ecology. In: C. Guignon (ed.) *The Cambridge Companion to Heidegger,* 240–69. Cambridge: Cambridge University Press.

Zvelebil, M. and Rowley-Conwy, P. (1984) Transition to farming in northern Europe: a gatherer-hunter perspective. *Norwegian Archaeological Review* 17, 104–27.

Zvelebil, M. and Rowley-Conwy, P. (1986) Foragers and farmers in Atlantic Europe. In: M. Zvelebil (ed.) *Hunters in Transition,* 67–93. Cambridge: Cambridge University Press.

INDEX